Michael Crowder

Sometime Professor of History at Ahmadu Bello University
and currently Visiting Professor
at the University of Lagos

West Africa

An Introduction to its History

Longman

Longman Group UK Limited,
Longman House, Burnt Mill, Harlow,
Essex CM20 2JE, England
and Associated Companies throughout the world

First published 1977
Third impression 1990

Produced by Longman Group (FE) Ltd
Printed in Hong Kong

ISBN 0 582 60003 0

Contents

Preface

This volume is especially designed as an introduction to the history of West Africa for students reading for the West African School Certificate, the East African Certificate of Education and the General Certificate of Education. It is hoped that it will serve as a useful background study to more advanced histories such as Basil Davidson and F. K. Buah: *A History of West Africa, 1000–1800* and J. B. Webster and Adu Boahen: *The Revolutionary Years: West Africa Since 1800*. It is also hoped that it may serve the needs of the general reader interested in an outline of the history of West Africa from the earliest times to the present day.

This history owes a considerable debt to a number of historians both for their published work and for advice they have given me from time to time. I owe a particular debt to the contributors to the Longman *History of West Africa*, which I co-edited with Professor J. F. Ade Ajayi. I would also like to acknowledge my debt to the work or advice of the following colleagues: Professor J. F. Ade Ajayi, Dr I. A. Asiwaju, Professor Adu Boahen, Mr Basil Davidson, Professor J. D. Fage, Professor Robin Horton, Mr J. E. Lavers, Professor Roland Oliver,

Professor Thurstan Shaw, Mr R. S. Smith, Professor Lalage Bown, and the contributors to the volume on *West African Resistance* which I edited in 1971.

It is not the custom to footnote or list sources on the pages of a volume such as this. If any of the above recognise their work on these pages I crave their indulgence and thank them for their inspiration.

I should like to express especial gratitude to Mr Paul Thatcher who went through this manuscript with a view to its suitability for the audience for which it is intended and revised and expanded the chapters relating to the colonial period.

Finally I should like to express particular thanks to Mr David Royle, Miss Anne Walmsley and Mr Tim Horsler of Longman for the encouragement they have given me over the years in which this manuscript was in preparation. I owe a very special debt to Miss Jenny Lee for her patience in seeing this book through the press, and to Miss Sue Cawson who designed it.

MICHAEL CROWDER
Lagos 1976

Acknowledgements

The publishers are grateful to the following for permission to reproduce photographs:

Aerofilms: page 2; Afrique Photo: page 27 (top); Agricultural Information Section, Enugu; Nigeria: page 20 (top); Dr I. A. Asiwaju: page 154 (top); Paul Bohannan: page 20 (bottom); British Library: page 74; British Museum, London: pages 41, 43 (top); Camera Press: pages 30 (left) John C. Shepard, 124 R. Harrington, 155, 177, 183, 184, 185 (left), 185 (right), 189 (left), 189 (right) United Nations, 193; J. Charpy: page 66; Church Missionary Society: pages 75 (top left), 75 (top right), 75 (bottom), 88 (left), 89, 115, 117, 130; Clarendon Press Ltd: page 171; Bruce Coleman Ltd: pages 12 (left) George Schaller, 12 (top right) S. C. Bisserot, 12 (bottom right) Helmut Albrecht; Documentation Française: page 178; Edinburgh University Gazette: page 109; Establissement Cinématographique et Photographique des Armées: page 15 (right); Mary Evans: pages 16, 69 (bottom), 80 (right), 81, 112 (left), 112 (right), 113, 119, 128; William Fagg: page 39; Werner Forman Archive: pages 3 (left), 3 (right), 18, 48, 49, 56 (bottom), 59, 104, 121, 154 (bottom); Fotomas Index: page 54; Ghana Film Industry Corporation: page 29; Ghana Information Services: page 172; John Hillelson Agency Ltd: pages 186 (left) Thomas Hopker, 187; Historical Pictures Service, Chicago: pages 27 (bottom), 52, 169 (right); Alan Hutchison Library: pages 23, 51; Keystone: page 151 (left); Sylvia Maclean: page 107; Mansell Collection: pages 90, 114; Museum Voor Land-en Volkenkunde, Rotterdam: page 57 (left);

National Portrait Gallery, London: page 101 (bottom); Popperfoto: pages 21, 57 (right), 70 (right), 150, 157, 161, 163 (top left), 163 (right), 166, 167, 173, 181, 194 (top), 194 (bottom); Public Record Office, London: page 9; Radio Times Hulton Picture Library: pages 30 (right), 31, 69 (top), 125 (right), 140, 142, 147, 169 (left); Rapho, France: page 17; Jean Ribière: page 186 (right); Royal Commonwealth Society: page 80 (left); Thurstan Shaw: page 10 (left), 10 (right); Piere Verger: page 56 (top).

The photographs appearing on pages 8, 70 (left) and 139 were taken from: 'Power & Diplomacy in Northern Nigeria' by R. A. Adeleye.

The publishers regret that they have been unable to trace the copyright owners of the following photographs, and would like to apologise for any infringement of copyright caused: pages 22, 38, 43 (left), 43 (bottom right), 63, 76, 84, 91, 99 (left), 99 (right), 125 (left).

The publishers are also grateful to the West African Examinations Council for permission to reproduce sixteen past examination questions which appear between pages 200 and 202. The diagram on page 20 is based on a diagram in *Tribes Without Rulers*, edited by J. Middleton and D. Tait, published by Routledge and Kegan Paul.

In the colour section:
British Museum: page 4 C,D,E, and F; Commonwealth Institute: page 3 C; Werner Forman Archive: page 1, 2 A,B,C, 3 A,D,G, 4 A and B, 5 B; Alan Hutchison Library: pages 2 D,E,F,G, 3 B,E,F,H, 4 G,H, 5 A.

List of maps

I The lands and peoples of West Africa

1 West Africa defined

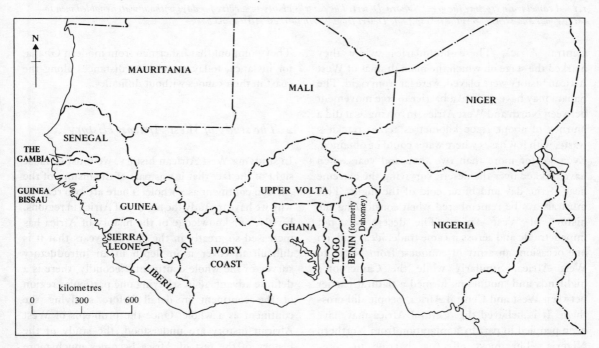

Map 1.1 Political map of West Africa.

West Africa is the term used today to describe that part of the great African continent which consists of the independent English-speaking states of Nigeria, Ghana, Sierra Leone and the Gambia; the independent French-speaking states of Mauritania, Senegal, Mali, Niger, Guinea, Upper Volta, Ivory Coast, Togo and Benin (formerly Dahomey); Guinea-Bissau and Liberia. It forms a natural geographical region, as it is bounded to the north by the Sahara Desert, to the west and south by the Atlantic Ocean, and to the east by the Cameroon's mountains and highlands, which form a barrier between West and

1.1   *A camel train crossing the great Sahara Desert. The camel's ability to survive for days without water enabled men to carry goods and ideas across the inhospitable Desert from North to West Africa and back.*

Central Africa. These boundaries, while they marked the stage on which the main dramas of West African history were played, were far from rigid. The Sahara may have seemed a barrier to free movement between North and West Africa, involving as it did a journey of about 1,500 kilometres across trackless waste, with few oases where water could be obtained. Even so, for more than two thousand years, men have trekked over the desert, surviving the extreme heat of the day and bitter cold of the night. This must always be remembered when considering the history of West Africa. The desert was not impenetrable and across it came trade, ideas and, on one occasion, an army of conquest from North to West Africa. Similarly while the Cameroon's highlands and mountains formed a natural barrier between West and Central Africa, people did cross them. It is believed that Central Africa may have been peopled in part by a migration from Northern Nigeria. The most effective barrier to communication with other peoples appears to have been the Atlantic Ocean, since boats suitable for sailing long distances were not developed by the coastal fishermen. Even when the Europeans arrived in such boats at the end of the fifteenth century, they did not teach Africans how to make them. Furthermore, some historians believe that there is evidence of long distance trade along the west coast as far as Angola.

They point out that fishermen from modern Ghana, for instance, today travel long distances along the coast in their canoes without difficulty.

2 The study of West African History

In studying West African history, we must not lose sight of the fact that it was part of the history of the African continent as a whole. There are two reasons why we have to study the history of Africa in regions. Firstly, our knowledge of the history of Africa has increased so greatly in the past ten years that it is difficult to cover it in depth in an introductory survey of the whole continent. Secondly, there is a definite advantage in studying one particular region of the continent in detail before studying the continent as a whole. Once the problems of West African history are understood, the study of the history of the rest of Africa becomes much more easy, for it shares some of these same problems.

3 The geographical features of West Africa

Within West Africa, which is nearly as large as the United States and measures about 3,000 kilometres from west to east, there are great geographical

1.2 *A typical stretch of cultivated savannah near Kano in Northern Nigeria showing the dry bed of the River Hadeija which only flows with water in the rainy season.*

1.3 *Mangrove forest in the Niger Delta.*

variations. However, we can divide it broadly into two major regions which will be important for our understanding of its history: the savannah and the forest. In the savannah, with its open woodlands and grasslands, movement is more easy than in the dense forest. Also, crops which grow in the savannah are different from those which grow in the forest. The tsetse fly, which kills cattle and horses, makes it almost impossible to keep them in the forest zone. However, large areas of the northern savannah are free from the tsetse fly. Rainfall is heavier in the forest than in the savannah, and the rainy season lasts much longer.

Over and above this broad distinction between the savannah and the forest, we must take into account the series of mountains and highlands that spread across West Africa, for example the Jos Plateau and the highlands of Futa Djallon. These mountains and highlands were very important in the history of West Africa for many peoples were able to take refuge there and defend themselves successfully from their enemies. In some cases, such mountain people remained largely isolated from the main currents of West African history.

A very important feature of the geography of West Africa is its many major rivers, the most important of which are the Niger, Benue, Senegal,

Gambia and Volta. These were navigable for long stretches by canoe and made travel between very distant areas easy, where it would have been difficult by land.

The maps on pages 4 and 5 show the principal features of the geography of West Africa: the southern fringe of the Sahara Desert; the Cameroon's highlands and mountains (Montane vegetation); the savannah zone and the forest belt; the mountains and highlands that are strung out like a chain from west to east across the savannah; and finally the major rivers.

4 The changing map of West Africa

In looking at the map of the savannah and forest of West Africa we must remember that it is based on the distribution of vegetation today. Two thousand years ago the vegetation would have been somewhat different.

The Sahara has extended its frontiers southwards in historical times, that is during the past two thousand or so years. This has been the result, not of further adverse changes in climate, but of the activities of man. Excessive cultivation and grazing of animals on the Sahara fringe removed grass cover and made the land desert. Similarly clearing of the

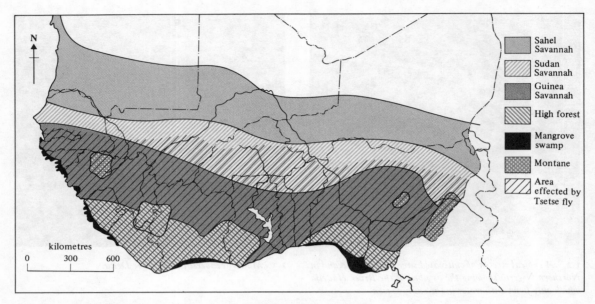

Map 1.2   Vegetation belts and areas affected by the tsetse fly in West Africa.

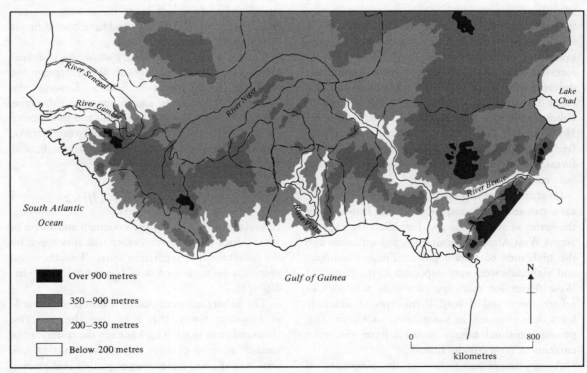

Map 1.3   West Africa: relief.

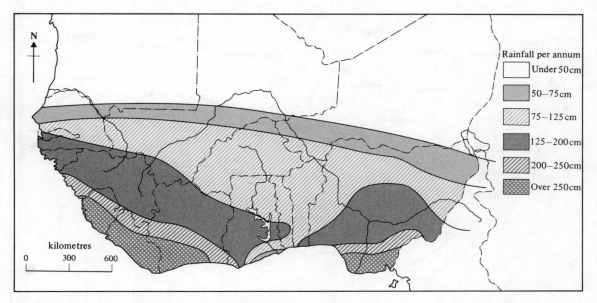

Map 1.4   Rainfall in West Africa.

forest and annual bush-firing has pushed the forest fringe southwards. In more recent years, the extensive cultivation of groundnuts and cotton in the savannah has removed tree-cover, while the cultivation of cocoa, coffee, rubber and palm-trees has thinned the forest. In many areas felling of trees for timber without replanting them has turned vast stretches of forest into savannah. Finally in the past fifty years, largely because of improved medical services and better food supplies, the population of West Africa has doubled putting increased pressure on the land. Nevertheless, large areas of the forest belt still remain sparsely populated as do great stretches of the savannah. Today the population of West Africa is well over 100 million. We may suppose that, at the beginning of historical times in West Africa, that is some two thousand years ago, the population did not exceed 10 million, and may have been even less.

5 The importance of geography for history

When in a later chapter we come to consider what were the factors behind the rise of the great states of

West Africa like Ghana, Mali, Songhai, Oyo, Benin and Asante we must keep the geography of Africa clearly in mind. We must also be clear exactly what we mean by 'forest'. It is often thought that the West African forest in ancient times was like the impenetrable jungles of South-East Asia. This was not so: movement through the forest was relatively easy by way of cleared footpaths. The tall trees, with wide cover, did not allow dense undergrowth to grow below them because of lack of light. A second point we must remember is how close to the coast the savannah came. Between Accra and Cotonou it actually reached the coast. (See Map 1.2.) It was because of this that the great Yoruba Kingdom of Oyo, standing on the edge of the savannah and the forest, and relatively free of tsetse fly, was able to use its cavalry to dominate that stretch of coast.

6 The inhabitants of West Africa

Most of the inhabitants of West Africa are normally described as being of Negro stock, though on the desert fringe there are Berber, Tuareg and Moors who are of Caucasoid stock. Over the centuries there

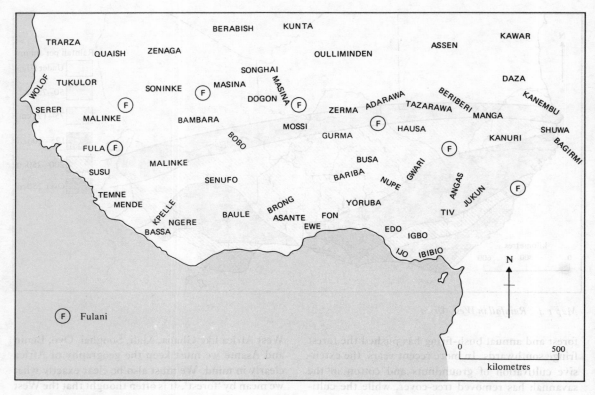

Map 1.5   Major ethnic groups in West Africa.

has been a great deal of intermingling between these two major groups. One product of this intermingling has been the light-skinned Fulani, who have Caucasoid features, but speak a language from the group of languages spoken by the majority of Negro inhabitants of West Africa. By contrast, the dark-skinned, Negroid Hausa speak a language from the group of languages spoken by the Caucasoids. It is therefore very difficult to classify people by their facial or physical appearance. For every rule, we can find a hundred exceptions. Paul Bohannan, the well-known anthropologist, has written that the most we can say is that 'if one stands at Suez and looks south and southwest, people tend to get darker the farther one goes'.

Variety is perhaps the chief characteristic of the peoples of West Africa. They comprise many different ethnic groups, speaking many different languages, practising many different religions, which in pre-colonial times were organised in communities that ranged from small hamlets of a hundred people to big cities of many thousands that were centres of states with a population of several million inhabitants.

The peoples of West Africa do, however, have many features in common. Those inhabiting the savannah today cultivate, for their own personal use, sorghum, millet, maize, citrus fruits, groundnuts, cassava and rice. Those parts of the northern savannah that are free from the tsetse fly support the herds of cattle of the Fulani nomads. The people of the forest cultivate cassava, yams, both the imported and indigenous varieties, bananas, plantains, rice and palm-produce, citrus fruits and kola-nuts.

While initially all the inhabitants of West Africa practised their indigenous religions, since the tenth century A.D. Islam, which was brought across the desert, has gained many converts in the savannah. In more recent times it has gained converts in the forest belt too. Today over fifty percent of the population of West Africa is Muslim. Christianity, which only started active conversion of West Africans in the nineteenth century, has gained the majority of its converts in the forest belt, but probably less than ten percent of West Africans are Christians today.

Most West African societies are patrilineal: that is the relationships between members of the same family are determined through the male line. How-ever, in Ghana, Sierra Leone and Senegal there are groups which are matrilineal: that is relationships in the family are determined through the female line. We shall concern ourselves with the importance of family relationships later when we come to consider how people governed themselves. Before that we must discuss the means by which we are able to discover the history of the people of West Africa.

2 The sources of West African history

1 Documents

The most obvious source of information for the historian is the document: newspapers, official government papers, private letters and books written during the period being studied. For the greater part of the period of West African history we are studying, few documents are available. For the period that more documents are available the majority come from Europeans who wrote about Africa as outsiders, whether they came as traders, missionaries or administrators. There are, however, a fair number of documents written by Arabs who visited the savannah states as travellers or traders. While the European slave-traders rarely bothered to convert the West Coast Africans with whom they did business to Christianity, let alone teach them reading and writing, the Arab traders not only converted people of the savannah to Islam, but taught a fair number how to write. We are fortunate, therefore, in having quite a large number of historical documents written by scholars of the savannah states. The problem is that the documents

2.1 & 2 *One of the main sources of West African history is the document. Here are two documents relating to nineteenth century West African history. The one on the left is in Arabic and is the treaty made in 1853 between the Caliph Aliyu Baba of Sokoto and Dr Heinrich Barth, the great German explorer, signing on behalf of Queen Victoria of England. The one on the right is the written confirmation of a treaty made between Abu Bukari, King of Mossi and his chiefs on the one hand and George Ekim Ferguson representing the Gold Coast Government.*

relating to the history of West Africa are widely scattered: in private homes; in libraries; in the archives of Arab and European countries. A historian of pre-colonial Benin has, for instance, to work in the archives of Portugal, Holland, Italy and Britain.

2 Oral tradition

The second major source of evidence for the historian of pre-colonial West Africa, particularly in the non-Muslim areas, is oral tradition. Most

African peoples have traditions concerning their origin and their early history; praise poems about kings and heroes, and stories about battles they fought against their neighbours. Sometimes even the title of a king will give a clue to the past. Disputes brought before judges can be particularly valuable. The contesting parties will bring evidence about custom to support their cases. Genealogies, that is family trees tracing family ancestors, or lists of kings are particularly useful to the historian. Some African states actually appointed official historians whose task it was to recall the past history of the state and record present history.

The use of oral tradition is very difficult because since it is handed down from generation to generation it can easily get changed. Peoples' memories can be faulty. Sometimes people will deliberately change oral tradition to support their own purposes. For instance, in Yorubaland each major kingdom will have a different version as to which were the original crowned heads of Yorubaland, invariably including their own *oba* or ruler in the original list. On the other hand evidence from documents can be just as faulty. The writer of the document may be prejudiced. You only have to read the daily newspapers in which they all report the same event to see how four different journalists will write four very different accounts about the same event. Whether the historian is using documents or oral tradition he must always be very careful how he uses them. And it is very important for the new student of history to understand what kind of evidence history is based on. It is equally important that he realise that history, because of the nature of its evidence, is constantly being rewritten. This is particularly true of African history. In five years time this book may have to be re-written, as new evidence is discovered, or as existing evidence is revised. We should not be discouraged by this. The excitement of history is that we are constantly re-writing it and gaining new understanding in the light of fresh evidence.

3 Archaeology

A third major source of evidence for the historian of Africa is the work of archaeologists. We have learnt a

2.3 & 4 *Right : archaeology is one of the main sources for our knowledge of the pre-history of West Africa. Here Professor Thurstan Shaw, leading an excavation team from the University of Ibadan, measures up a trench in the Iwo Eleru rock shelter where a 10,000 year old skeleton of a man was found – the oldest yet discovered in West Africa.*
Above: one of the main tasks of the archaeologist in the field is the careful sorting of the artifacts he digs up for subsequent analysis in the laboratory. Here Professor Shaw and his assistants sort findings from the Iwo Eleru rock shelter. On the extreme right is Dr Fred Anozie, who first became interested in archaeology when as a school boy he saw Professor Shaw excavating in his home town of Igbo Ukwu. Today he is lecturer in Archaeology at the University of Nigeria at Nsukka.

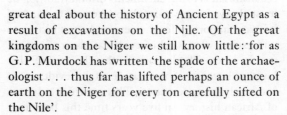

great deal about the history of Ancient Egypt as a result of excavations on the Nile. Of the great kingdoms on the Niger we still know little : for as G. P. Murdock has written 'the spade of the archaeologist . . . thus far has lifted perhaps an ounce of earth on the Niger for every ton carefully sifted on the Nile'.

Through archaeologists we have come to know about the Nok Culture of northern Nigeria, the cultures of Ife and Igbo Ukwu. The trouble with the findings of the archaeologists is that so far they do not give an even picture of the development of the peoples of Africa in the earliest times. The material of the archaeologists lies hidden under the earth. Few archaeologists are working in West Africa, and naturally they dig only those sites that seem *likely* to reveal material. They do not know beforehand what they will find or whether they would have got better

results by digging elsewhere. Moreover archaeological work is expensive and the findings are difficult to interpret.

The Nok Culture, with its superb terra-cottas, was discovered by accident : the first of the terra-cottas was found by a tin-miner on the Jos Plateau while digging his mine. The Igbo-Ukwu culture was discovered as a result of a man digging in his backyard for mud to build a new house. What we need urgently, therefore, is a large number of archaeologists working in the field if we are to obtain a balanced picture of the early past.

4 Other sources of evidence

Another source of evidence for the historian is the study of languages. Linguists can tell by comparing the languages of the peoples of West Africa which groups are closely related to each other. They can also tell roughly how long ago two peoples who once shared the same language began to develop their own separate languages.

Surviving customs and traditions also often give assistance to historians.

Botanists can also help us in the study of history by examining the distribution of plants. They can tell us which plants are indigenous, that is belonged originally to Africa, and which plants were introduced from overseas, that is from Asia, the Americas and Europe.

Now that we have the setting and the sources for West African history, let us examine its beginnings.

3 Early Man in West Africa *

1 The origin of Man

Present evidence from fossil remains suggests that Man had his origin in the savannah of eastern and southern Africa. It seems probable that it was there that the ancestors of Man took a different path of development from the ancestors of the apes, such as the gorilla, the chimpanzee and the orang-outang.

3.1, 2 & 3 *Man achieved his dominance over animals that were more powerful than him, such as the lion and the elephant (top right and above), and over cleverer animals such as the chimpanzee (right) with which he shares a common ancestor, as a result of the development of his skills of speech and tool-making.*

* The author is indebted to Professor Thurstan Shaw for his advice and considerable assistance in drafting this chapter.

Man and the apes are descended from a common ancestor. Man, however, is distinguished from the apes in many ways, two of which are most important for our understanding of how he came to dominate the animals. The first difference was that while apes can make very crude tools, Man developed the ability to make more efficient ones and to go on improving them. The second difference is that while apes can communicate with each other by means of gestures or signs, as well as by a limited range of sounds, Man developed the use of sounds for communication into what we call speech.

Man began to make tools to a set pattern about two million years ago. We do not know just how or when Man developed speech. Early Man became better and better adapted to the world he lived in and gained more control over it. For example, although early men could not run as fast as a lion or a leopard, and did not have their powerful teeth or claws, they had tools and weapons. What is more, they were able to cooperate with each other, using speech and, above all, their superior cunning and intelligence. Thus, although they were physically weak, they were able to hunt stronger animals in a way in which the apes could not.

In the long history of life, different kinds of animals survived because their bodies became well adapted to the environment in which they lived. For instance some animals, like the lion, developed powerful teeth and claws with which to kill other animals for meat. Others, like the gazelle, with weak teeth and no claws, developed great speed so that they could escape from the lion or the leopard. The chameleon developed the ability to change its colour to match its surroundings so that it could not be seen by animals hunting it. Animals did not develop in this way on purpose. They did not realise what was taking place. What was happening was that those lions with weak teeth and small claws were killed more easily than those with powerful teeth and strong claws. This meant that it was mainly strong lions that mated, and produced stronger young. From recent history we can see how animals adapt to the circumstances around them. In the 1950s Australia was plagued by rabbits which were eating much of the farmers' crops. A disease called myxomatosis, which was deadly to rabbits, was disco-vered. Rabbits were deliberately infected with this disease, and let out among the uninfected rabbits. Soon nearly all the rabbits in Australia were dead. A few, however, survived the disease and developed immunity to it. They did not do this deliberately. They were just lucky. Those rabbits that survived mated with each other to produce young to whom they passed on their immunity to myxomatosis. Australia is again facing a problem from rabbits.

2 *Man dominates the animals*

The case of Man was slightly different. Unlike the gorilla and chimpanzee, which use both arms and legs for moving about on the ground and in the trees, Man adopted a way of life on the ground in which he learnt to walk upright, leaving his hands free for holding tools and weapons. This meant that his jaw did not have to stick out so much for grasping and carrying things, and this enabled his brain-case to grow larger. His brain developed in such a way that he could make tools and develop speech. This gave him an advantage over other animals. When his environment changed, he could solve the problem of how to live in it. For example the polar bear, which lives in the freezing cold of the North Pole, developed a thick furry coat to protect itself. It would find it difficult to survive in the forests of West Africa because its coat would make it too hot. Man in the North Pole region did not develop a thick furry coat like the polar bear, but he killed polar bears and used their skins as a coat. The men of the North Pole, the Eskimos, would not die if they were brought to West Africa. All they would have to do would be to change their polar bear furs for cotton clothes.

Man did not change his body to deal with changed environments; he used his brain to solve the problem of survival. Thus instead of developing sharp fangs like the lion or the leopard in order to kill his prey, he made a substitute, in the form of a spear. In fact, fangs can be a disadvantage when meat is scarce and you have to rely on wild fruit, roots and berries. Man developed teeth which were equally as good for eating meat as for eating fruit and veg-etables. Just as with the animals such changes took place unconsciously. Those men with teeth adapted for eating both fruit and meat were more likely to survive than those with large fangs.

Man eventually became the most adaptable of animals because his brain developed more and more so that he could make better and better tools and communicate with his fellows more easily as he increased the number of words in his speech. Although the most impressive developments of man have taken place in the last two thousand years, we must not forget that it was those developments that took place over two million years ago that established his dominant position over the animal kingdom.

Another important distinction between Man and animals lies in the nature of their societies. Many kinds of animals cooperate for a common purpose such as hunting and killing of other animals for food. The human family is however different from any animal family because it is so organised that the young can grow up and stay with their mothers and fathers until the latter die. This makes it easier to pass on knowledge and skills learnt by one generation to the next. Man is a 'learning' animal. While some animals like dogs are able to learn certain things, they do not have speech to pass the knowledge on to their offspring. Man's education thus began thousands of years ago as his speech developed.

Two or three hundred thousand years ago man learnt to use fire. This gave him another advantage over the animals since he could use it to protect himself against them. Furthermore, he could use fire to cook and to increase the variety of food he ate.

3 The Stone Age in West Africa

The period from the time when Man began to dominate the animals and before he discovered how to smelt iron is known as the Stone Age, because his weapons and tools were mainly made from stone. In Africa the Stone Age has been divided by archaeologists into three periods:

Early Stone Age =
roughly 2 million B.C. to 35,000 B.C.
Middle Stone Age =

roughly 35,000 B.C. to 15,000 B.C.
Late Stone Age =
roughly 15,000 B.C. to 5,000 B.C.

Unfortunately we have much less evidence on all periods of the Stone Age in West Africa than we do for the rest of the continent. Much more work will have to be done by archaeologists before we can obtain a clearer picture of the development of Man during the Stone Age in West Africa.

However we do have a considerable amount of evidence for men of the Early Stone Age living on the Jos Plateau and some for other parts of West Africa, namely the Futa Djallon highlands, the area north of the upper reaches of the River Senegal and in particular present-day Mauritania where many sites have been found. There is also evidence for his presence in the Togo-Atacora Mountains.

With changes to a drier climate early Stone Age Man seems to have moved southwards into woodland areas, particularly along the banks of all-season rivers which could assure him of a regular supply of water.

While early Stone Age Man had not developed into *homo sapiens*, that is men similar to ourselves, Man of the Middle Stone Age seems to have developed into something very near to him.

We do not have much more evidence for Middle Stone Age Man in West Africa than we do for Early Stone Age Man. Material indicating his presence has been found in the Jos Plateau and the Lirue Hills to the north of it, in Ghana, Ivory Coast, and Dakar. Middle Stone Age Man is characterised by the greater specialisation of his tools, and by variations in the type of tools he made from one region to another.

Late Stone Age Man is characterised by his development of ground-stone axes and small stone tools such as arrow-heads and harpoon heads. These are known as *microliths*: *micro* = small; *lith* = stone. Microlithic industries have been found in a number of sites in West Africa, sometimes associated with potsherds, or fragments of pottery, and hoe-like tools, indicating that the producers of these tools practised agriculture. Not all the men inhabiting West Africa in the period from about 15,000 to about 5,000 B.C. developed in the same

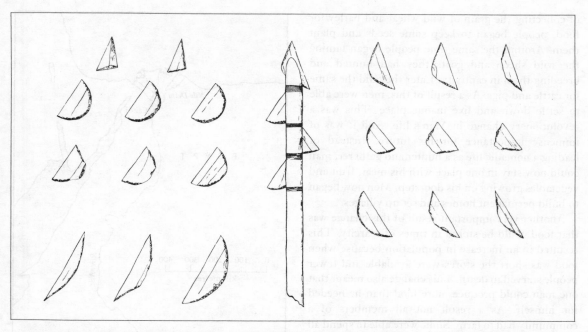

3.4 *Late Stone Age microliths found in West Africa showing the probable way in which they were fixed to sticks of wood to make arrows. (By permission of Professor Thurstan Shaw.)*

way at the same time. Some continued to make tools characteristic of the Middle Stone Age, some developed the art of pottery, while some began to practise a rudimentary form of agriculture. Professor Thurstan Shaw, the leading authority on the archaeology of West Africa, has suggested that the Late Stone Age in West Africa can be divided into two main phases. The first began not later than 10,000 B.C. and took two forms. One had microlithic industries and was associated with hunting in the savannah. The other did not develop these industries and is associated with the forest mainly in the south-western part of West Africa. The second phase began soon after 3,000 B.C. and took four main forms. The first predominated in the savannah and in addition to making microliths the people associated with it knew how to make pottery and ground-stone axes. The second, characteristic of the sahel, the area between the desert and the savannah, had few microliths, but its people made harpoons and fish-hooks from bone indicating a fishing economy. The third was characteristic of the coast

where the people exploited the resources of the lagoons and estuaries. The last was characteristic of the forest where people developed pottery and ground-stone axes but not microliths.

It was during the latter half of the Late Stone Age that men in West Africa began to practise agriculture.

4 *The beginning of farming*

About thirty thousand years ago the changes that had taken place in Man's body over the thousands of years before were complete. Man's body by this time was similar to that of all the races of mankind today. The men of those days were clever at making tools, at hunting and collecting food that grew wild. They travelled widely hunting game and looking for fruits and berries.

About ten thousand years ago, there began in south-west Asia a slow change from hunting and gathering to the practice of producing food. Instead of collecting the grain of wild wheat and barley for food, people began to keep some seeds and plant them. Around the same time people began taming the wild sheep and goats they had hunted and breeding them in captivity. Later they did the same for cattle and pigs. As a result of this, men were able to settle down and live in one place. This was a revolutionary change in Man's life. And it was of immense importance for his future. Instead of leading a nomadic life as a hunter and gatherer, man could now stay in one place with his meat, fruit and vegetables growing on his doorstep. Men now began to build permanent homes and set up villages.

Another very important result of this change was that food could be stored in times of scarcity. This resulted in an increase in population because when food was short the stores were available and fewer people starved to death. This change also meant that one man could produce more food than he needed for himself. As a result not all members of a community had to farm. Some were able to spend all their time on other jobs, such as making tools, weapons, baskets, pots, or weaving cloth or building boats or houses. Others were able to become priests and rulers, while others travelled long distances in search of the materials needed for various crafts and this was the beginning of trade. Such people exchanged their products or services for the food produced by those who devoted their time to

3.5 *In Africa agriculture first developed on the Nile where the annual flooding made intensive farming possible. The shadoof has been in use as a method of irrigation since early times.*

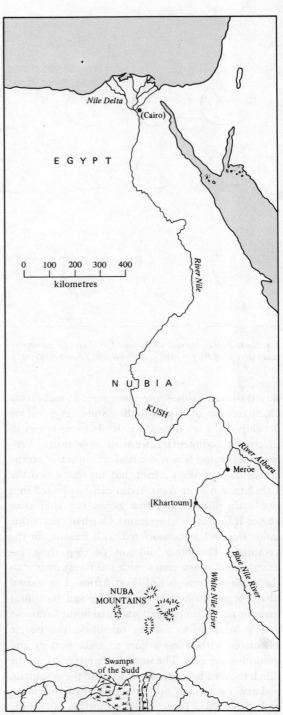

Map 3.1   The Ancient Nile.

farming. As a result the community as a whole became wealthier and divided into different classes.

In Africa, agriculture began about seven thousand years ago in the north-east point of the continent. In the valley of the River Nile in Egypt, wheat and barley were grown on the fertile silt irrigated by the river. The resulting agricultural wealth was the basis of ancient Egyptian civilisation, which began about five thousand years ago.

5 *The beginning of farming in West Africa*

When agriculture was beginning in the Nile Valley, the Sahara Desert was much smaller than it is at present. Its highland areas in particular supported grass and trees. Thus about the same time as agriculture was beginning in Egypt, it was possible for the same thing to be happening in parts of what is now the Sahara Desert. Paintings and engravings on rocks in these areas show wild animals, such as elephants, hippopotami, and giraffes which could not possibly live there now. Later drawings show domesticated animals such as cattle. The paintings also show men, many of whom are Negroes.

When these more fertile parts of the Sahara became too dry for agriculture and there was no longer enough grass for the cattle, people moved southwards into the moister savannah areas, bringing their cattle with them.

In these savannah areas south of the Sahara it is difficult to grow wheat and barley, and the people had to domesticate suitable tropical grasses. They had been collecting the seeds of these grasses for food for a very long time. The most important were guinea corn, bulrush millet, finger millet and African rice. On the forest margins people had used African yams and palm-nuts as a source of food for a long time. As time went on some of them moved deeper into the forest taking the yams and palm trees with them. These grew well there once men had cleared space in the thick forest. What we do not know for certain is whether Man in West Africa invented agriculture and learnt to domesticate animals without outside influences, or whether he was taught these skills by men moving into his lands from the Sahara. Some experts believe that agricul-

3.6 *Frescoes of cattle found at Tassili in the heart of the Sahara Desert not only show that it was once fertile but that its inhabitants kept domesticated animals.*

ture was invented independently on the Niger bend near Timbuktu, and others believe that men in the forest areas had also learnt how to plant and harvest some root crops without outside help.

6 *The coming of iron*

Clearing the forest for planting yams and palm trees was made much easier when iron became available for making tools and weapons. Before that, agricultural implements had been made of stone and wood.

About three and a half thousand years ago some people in the Hittite Empire of Asia Minor discovered how to smelt iron. They already knew how to smelt another metal, copper, by heating the rock containing it to such a temperature that the metal separated itself from the rock. Later they mixed copper with tin to make bronze, which makes harder and tougher weapons and tools than copper. Iron is even harder, and the rocks which contain it are commoner than those which contain copper or tin. The ancient Egyptians used copper and bronze, but a knowledge of these metals did not spread into the rest of Africa because of the drying up of the Sahara and because the natural route southwards up the Nile is blocked by the vast swamps of the southern Sudan and the 'Sudd'. The Egyptians did not use iron until after 600 B.C. partly because they had been able to develop a very efficient civilisation using tools of copper and bronze.

By this time the ancient Kingdom of Kush was established along a stretch of the Nile which is now in the Republic of the Sudan. At one time Kush controlled the Kingdom of Egypt. Later, the capital was moved further south to a place called Meröe, north of modern Khartoum. Here, great iron-smelting activity took place. Kush probably supplied Egypt with much of its iron, and it is likely that from Meröe the knowledge of iron-smelting spread into eastern Africa. It may also have spread from here into West Africa. It seems more likely, however, that West Africa derived its knowledge of iron from ancient Carthage, which is today a suburb of modern Tunis, where iron tools and weapons were made earlier than in Egypt. This would have been as a result of trade across the Sahara Desert.

Iron-smelting furnaces have been found in Nigeria dating before 300 B.C. associated with what archaeologists call 'the Nok Culture'. This culture was named after the little village of Nok in central Nigeria, west of the Jos Plateau, and is remarkable for its beautiful sculptures made in baked clay, called terra-cotta. The knowledge of iron-working spread slowly throughout West Africa but we will have to await further research before we can obtain a clearer picture as to how it did so. We do know from excavations of occupation mounds in the valley of the Niger that men there knew how to smelt iron as early as the second century B.C. By contrast, in northern Sierra Leone evidence indicates that people there did not learn the art until the eighth century A.D.

It is unlikely that iron-working was an inde-

3·7   *The famous Jema'a head, one of the finest terra-cottas from the Nok Culture so far found.*

pendent invention in West Africa, as it would be very difficult to discover how to do this without a previous knowledge of how to smelt copper. The importance of iron to West Africa was immense. With iron tools agriculture became more efficient and food became more abundant. Fewer people died of starvation. As in ancient Egypt, the surplus of food made it possible for people to become specialists such as craftsmen, traders, priests and rulers. In this way, by the end of the first millennium A.D., the foundations had been laid for the political, cultural and economic developments which took place in West Africa at about this time.

4 Non-centralised societies *

1 The origins of West African societies

Much of the history of West Africa is concerned with peoples who lived in large states such as those of Mali, Benin and Asante. But a large number of Africans did not live in states and they are usually left out of the history books. Some historians have tended to dismiss peoples who lived in non-centralised societies as somehow inferior to those who lived in states. But one society is not necessarily better than another because it is organised on a larger scale. The United States of America is not necessarily better than a small state like Denmark. Though the USA is much richer than Denmark, a much larger proportion of its inhabitants live in poverty, the streets of many of its major cities are unsafe, and it is deeply troubled by drug-taking. The farmer living in a state like Gobir in northern Nigeria was not necessarily better off than the farmer living in a non-centralised society like that of the Tiv who also live in northern Nigeria. Indeed, his standard of living may even have been lower because of the heavy taxes he had to pay. Usman dan Fodio, the leader of the Holy War against the King of Gobir, was to complain of this in the early nineteenth century. Nor should we make the mistake of thinking that people in non-centralised societies have no history. It is just that it is much more difficult to find out than that of states, which had written records or employed professional historians.

* The author is indebted to Professor Robin Horton for advice on the drafting of this chapter.

What do we mean when we describe people as living in non-centralised societies? We mean that such people had no generally acknowledged ruler or rulers. That is no one man or group of men ruled them.

2 The bond of lineage

The first type of non-centralised society which we will consider is that which was held together by the bond of lineage. The basis of such societies was the extended family or lineage, and members of such societies owed their primary loyalty to their lineage. Typical of such societies were the Tiv and the central Igbo. Such a lineage based society might number many hundreds of thousands of people. Its lack of rulers did not mean that the people were without any law. Rather they simply maintained law and order by means other than those involving centralised government. We shall see later how they did this.

People who lived in such societies were mainly farmers, though the nomadic Fulani live in lineage based societies too.

In these societies the family worked together to produce the things it needed. But certain farming operations needed more than just the family, so close neighbours gave assistance to each other. Families produced most of what they needed themselves and when they did need to buy goods from other people they did so by barter rather than

4.1   *Communal clearing of the land by Igbo farmers in south-eastern Nigeria.*

money. Since money was not commonly used, a young man could not buy land for himself. Instead, he worked on his father's land, which one day he would inherit. Or, in some societies, where inheritance was through the maternal side, he would settle with his wife's family. Even where a young man went to settle on new land he would try and do so near to his family land. For, not only did he want to live near the land he would one day inherit, but also he liked to have his relatives nearby so that when he needed help with clearing land he could call on

them. It is easier to ask relations for help than strangers. In such societies, your relationship with another man becomes all important. The principle of obligation to your relations has a very strong influence on you. Indeed, among the Tiv, people reckoned their obligation to other people by the closeness of their relationship. And everyone knew in what way, however distantly, he was related to fellow members of society.

In societies like the Tiv, where people did not live in villages, but in small compounds each containing a family group, closely related people lived near to each other. Distantly related people lived far from each other. If you take a photograph of Tivland from the air you will see hundreds of small compounds surrounded by farmland, all about the same distance from each other. Such a pattern of settlement was possible if the population did not grow too fast and if there was no lack of new land. When overcrowding did take place in one area, some of its inhabitants would migrate to a new area. There, these people might find themselves settling close to people who were only very distantly related to them. So that the principle of close cooperation with close relatives could continue to work, the newcomers and the people already settled there would invent a close relationship. That is they would be adopted as close

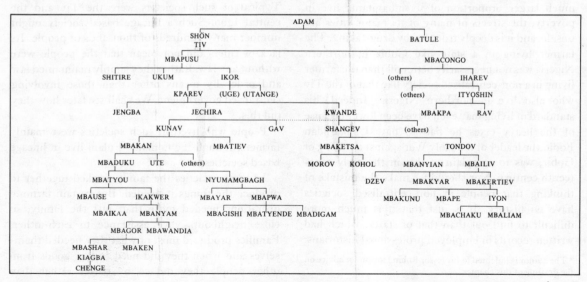

4.2   *The geneaology of the Tiv showing how every Tiv can trace his descent from Tiv himself and work out his relationship with every other Tiv.*

cousins even though they were really very distant ones.

Of course in such societies there had to be law and order. What happened if there was a dispute? If a dispute arose between two persons, it was settled by the relatives of the two men quarrelling, according to customary rules handed down from generation to generation. If your brother was quarrelling with your second cousin, you automatically supported your brother, even if you thought your brother was in the wrong. Similarly, your second cousin's brothers would support him rather than your brother. In any dispute, people would side with the man most closely related to them. If, however, a man's close relatives saw that he was a constant trouble-maker who picked quarrels with no just cause, they could deter him by swearing an oath that they would no longer protect him from outsiders. To settle the dispute, each group would choose a leader, and the two leaders would argue it out. Once the dispute was settled, the man chosen as leader would resume his ordinary place in society. For, as we have seen, in non-centralised societies people did not recognise anybody as having permanent authority over them. However, if people were attacked by outsiders, they would choose someone to lead them, but only until the attack had finished. Leadership was thus only temporary.

There was of course some idea of permanent authority in non-centralised societies. In each compound, there was a head of the family, who organised farming activities and settled disputes within the compound.

3 Pastoralists

Cattle-herders, or pastoralists, like the Fulani who are found across the savannah of West Africa, also live in lineage based societies. At first there would seem to be little in common between these cattle nomads and sedentary farmers like the Tiv. But in fact with regard to their social organisation there are striking similarities. In the first place, like the Tiv, the basic unit of production is the family consisting of the man, his wives and children. During the dry season when in search of fresh pastures for their

4.3 *Nomadic Fulani herding their cattle.*

cattle, the Fulani operate as a family unit. But during much of the year several closely related families – that is from the same lineage – will group together and, like the Tiv, help each other on tasks that one family cannot undertake with its own members alone. Furthermore, the young Fulani man, like the young Tiv, will live and work with those from whom he expects to inherit – in this case cattle and not farmland. Thus, though their ways of life differ considerably, both groups are essentially lineage-based.

4 The bond of the land

What happened when a society such as we have described above grew so large that there was no more land available to it? Perhaps further settlement of land was blocked by a range of mountains, or unfertile swamps. In such cases people would have to migrate to other areas and ask for land from people who had plenty to spare. If this was agreed to, you now had a society with two distinct groups in it. You had the original land-owning lineage and the new-comers. You thus had a society made up of two distinct groups whose common bond was the land they now shared. Society could no longer be looked on as one large family. In such societies the head of the land-owning lineage became the overall head of the community, as well as retaining his Priesthood of the Earth. This meant it was he who sanctioned the laws by which the original inhabitants and the new-comers agreed to live. Typical of such societies are the Sisala and Lodaaga of northern Ghana.

Where, however, the new-comers outnumbered the land-owners a rather different balance was struck in the community. The new-comers became the 'owners of the people' and their leader became the overall head. The head of the land-owning lineage, however, retained his Earth Priesthood, for the new-comers were always reluctant to offend the spirits of the earth by removing the Earth Priest for fear of failure of crops. Typical of such societies are the Konkomba of northern Ghana.

In both these types of societies we begin to see the idea of permanent authorities emerging either in the position of the Earth Priest as overall head of the community or in the leader of the new-comers as overall head. We also see people beginning to think of themselves as living on a particular area of land. Rather than thinking of themselves in terms of family (or lineage) relationship, they began to think

of themselves in terms of living on the same land or territory. The bond of land became more important than the bond of lineage. Most important of all people looked up to the leader of owner of the people or the leader of the owner of the land as fixed authorities whose decisions they must respect.

5 Village-bonded societies

What happened if people living in either of the two societies described above were subjected to frequent attacks by outsiders? Now, if you are a farmer, to have your compound in the middle of the land you farm is ideal. You only have a short distance to walk to your fields. When harvest time comes you only have short distances over which to carry your yams or your grain for storing. But if you are attacked by outsiders, it is difficult to defend yourself, because your neighbours are scattered in small compounds

4.4 *An African village surrounded by a stockade for defensive purposes.*

like your own, and you only have your immediate male relations to help you. The village with a wall or stockade around it, where four or five hundred people are grouped together, is much better for defence. The adult males have a much better chance of organising themselves for the defence. But the fields cultivated by a village of this size are scattered over a great area of land and long distances have to be travelled to the farm. Whatever the disadvantages of the village to the farmer, when people were under constant threat of attack by outsiders they would prefer to live in the comparative safety of the village.

Now in villages, people would find themselves living close to their near relatives as well as their distant relatives, or if they came from land-bonded societies, to people who were not related to them at all. While people still continued to feel closer to their near relatives, they also felt very close to even unrelated people, who lived near them, and shared in their daily lives. If the village was attacked, people depended for their safety as much on their distant relatives and unrelated people as their close relatives. Indeed, in the village, people came to have loyalty not only to their close relatives but to the village as a whole, for the village represented security to them. To maintain unity in the village, institutions that cut across family ties began to emerge. In many villages the men were organised into age grade associations. Thus your eldest brother might be in one age grade association while you were in another. If the two associations came into conflict, you would support the fellow members of your own association rather than your brother's association. The Ijo villages of the eastern Delta of the Niger provide good examples of such villages.

The head of the family which owned the land on which the village was built became recognised as head of the village. He would be Priest of the Earth Cult which sanctioned the laws of the whole community. Because a large group of people living together needs to be governed, certain administrators had to be appointed. In cases of war, a war-leader was needed. Someone had to organise the building and repair of the village wall, so a 'Director of Public Works' would be chosen. Such positions were usually distributed among the different families making up the village.

Most important in a large community is the enforcement of law and order. Now if a man commits a crime which is punishable by death, someone has to condemn him, and someone has to execute him. Now in a small community, this means that the criminal may be condemned and executed by members from a family other than his own. This of course can make the family of the condemned man very bitter against the family of the man who executed their relative. To make justice as impersonal as possible, many villages developed what are called secret societies. Such societies would be open to all adults no matter what their family. Young men would be initiated into these societies in such a way that they would change their loyalty away from their family towards the community as a whole. A young man would go through a ceremony in which his old life would *die* and he would be re-born into a new life in which his loyalty was to the secret society. Typical of such societies are the Ekoi of the Cross-River with

4.5 *Part of the ceremony of the Bondo secret society in Sierra Leone.*

their Ekpe secret society and many of the village societies of Liberia and Sierra Leone with their Poro secret society.

When a man committed a crime, the secret society would sit in judgement. If it decided to condemn the man to death, the decision was announced as the decision of *all* the members. Even if some members were opposed to the judgement, once the majority had decided, all had to accept the decision. Since all members were sworn to secrecy, no-one outside the society would ever know who had been for, or who had been against. For the penalty of breaking the secret was death. This meant that no-one outside the society could ever know which families were for the verdict and which were against.

Even the identity of the man who executed the criminal was kept a secret. The executioner would wear a mask so that no-one could know who he was, or from which family he came.

Thus we see in the village an attempt to break down loyalty to the family and replace it with loyalty to the community.

6 The origins of states

It used to be believed that all states in West Africa owed their rise to cattle herding nomads. These nomads, having learnt to herd cattle, herded men. This theory was put forward because racially prejudiced Europeans were not prepared to believe that black people could organise states by themselves. But we have seen that the cattle Fulani, far from living in states, lived in a non-centralised society where the small family group herded the cattle. Other racially prejudiced Europeans believed that small bands of light-skinned invaders imposed themselves on black African farmers and organised them into states. Yet other historians have tried to suggest that the widespread existence of states ruled by divine kings was the result of the spread of the idea from Egypt.

All these theories seek a single outside explanation for the rise of states in West Africa. But, even though there is no, or very little, evidence for these theories, we must ask ourselves, how did Black Africans organise states by themselves? Now there is nothing

in the first type of society we examined – such as that of the Tiv – to indicate that a state could emerge from it, nor indeed is there in that of the Fulani nomads. But if we look at the societies where the original land-owners and the new-comers lived together, and if we look at the village society, we can begin to see the possibilities of a state emerging.

In both of these societies certain essential features of the state emerged. The first essential of a state is to have an authority at the head whom all members of the state recognise. When pressure of land forced people to migrate onto the land of other people, we see either of two situations emerge: the head of the land-owning lineage becomes head of the entire community or, where the new-comers outnumbered the land-owners, the emergence of a dual headship with the leader of the new-comers as overall head. In the village, the authority of the head of the land-owning family became acknowledged by all. Further, the authority of the secret society as the giver and enforcer of laws was recognised by all.

A second very important element in the state is that its members should consider loyalty to the state as being more important than loyalty to the groups of which it is made up. Thus, while in the lineage-bonded society loyalty was above all to one's relations, in the land-bonded society, loyalty may have been first to the leader of the group to which you belonged; but ultimately, both land-owners and new-comers owed allegiance to the total community which they jointly made up. In the village, strong emphasis was placed on the idea of loyalty to the community as a whole through age grade associations and secret societies.

The third most important feature of the state is the concept of its existing in a certain territory. Now while there is no shortage of land, farmers in the lineage-bonded society had no idea of boundaries or frontiers to their land. But when people were forced by over-population to migrate on to other people's land, they became aware of the idea of a definite tract of land belonging to a group of people. In the land-bonded society, the owners of the people recognised that a certain tract of land in which they were allowed to settle belonged to a group whom they identified as the owners of the land.

In the village, a wall indicated the limit of the area

inhabited by its people, and the boundaries of their farms marked the limits of their territory.

The various types of leaders who emerged in land-bonded and village-bonded societies were revered by their people because of the spiritual backing they enjoyed either as Priest of the Earth Cult or the ancestral cults. The decisions they made were not those of ordinary men but of persons in special communication with either the forces of the earth or with the ancestors. In this we can see the seeds of divine kingship, that is of rulers whose authority is based as much on their special relationship with spiritual forces as on force.

So even in some societies which are often called *stateless*, we can see elements of the state. What sort of factors contributed to the growth of the state in West Africa? One of the most important was clearly trade. It is significant that the great states of West Africa were all situated on important trade routes while the non-centralised societies were situated far from them. Trade made the growth of larger communities possible. Furthermore such communities had to control the trade routes through their land and make them safe. Another major factor in the development of states was threat of attack by outsiders. If several villages were under constant threat from outside, they might combine into a larger village or town to defend themselves better.

5 Early savannah states to 1450

1 Ghana, Mali and Kanem-Borno

In the savannah of West Africa, on the fringes of the Sahara Desert, there developed three great states before 1450: Ghana, Mali and Kanem-Borno. Many other smaller states developed alongside them, such as the Hausa states in what is now Northern Nigeria. Here we shall be concerned mainly with the rise of the three major states – Ghana, Mali and Kanem-

Borno. Each of them at the height of its power could be considered an empire. That is, their rulers held sway not only over their own kingdoms but also over other kingdoms whose rulers paid tribute to them.

The origins of Ghana, situated in the far western savannah on the very fringes of the desert, are obscure. It may have existed as early as the fifth century A.D. or even before. Certainly by the eighth century A.D. it had become important enough for its

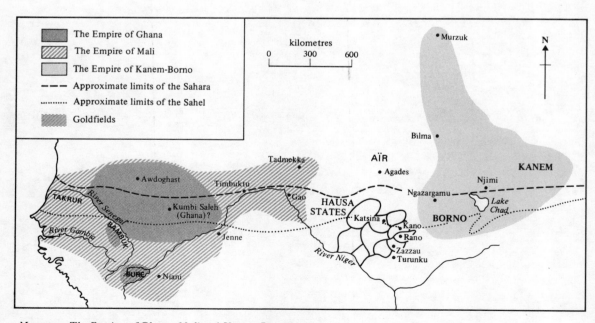

Map 5.1 The Empires of Ghana, Mali and Kanem-Borno.

5.1 *A train of camels loaded with goods arrives in the Sahel from the Sahara.*

fame as 'the land of gold' to reach Baghdad. There, in the court of the Caliph, the most important of the rulers of the Muslim world at the time, news of Ghana was recorded by the great geographer Al-Fazari. At first Mali was a tributary Kingdom of Ghana and its origins are also obscure. It became an independent state only in the thirteenth century, and did not develop into a major savannah power until the following century. Kanem was founded in the ninth or tenth century A.D. and was at first situated to the north-east of Lake Chad, strictly outside West Africa as we have defined it. However, by the late fifteenth century its centre of power had shifted to Borno, south-west of Lake Chad. It is for this reason that as a state it is often referred to as Kanem-Borno.

2 *The importance of trans-Saharan trade*

The growth of this series of states along the fringe of the Sahara can best be explained by the special trade opportunities that such a situation offered. We have seen that trade had been carried across the Sahara for many hundreds of years before the Christian era. Carthage imported ivory and gold from West Africa. Shortly after A.D. 100, the camel was introduced to Africa, increasing the possibilities for trans-Saharan trade. The camel, as distinct from the horse and donkey, which up until now had been the main means of transport for Saharan traders, can travel many days without needing to stop for water. Moreover, it is a much larger animal and can carry a

greater load of goods.

When the Arabs conquered North Africa in the seventh century A.D. they found that the Berbers, the original inhabitants of that area, traded across the desert to West Africa. One of the main items of their trade was gold. This was to be of particular importance to the Arabs, since gold was the basis of their monetary system. West Africa, with its great reserves of gold, was to become the major source of its supply to the Arab world, and from there to Europe and Asia.

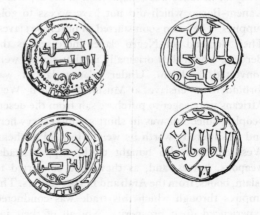

5.2 *Examples of Arab Gold coins of the twelfth and thirteenth centuries. Much of the gold coinage of the Arab world was made with gold imported from West Africa.*

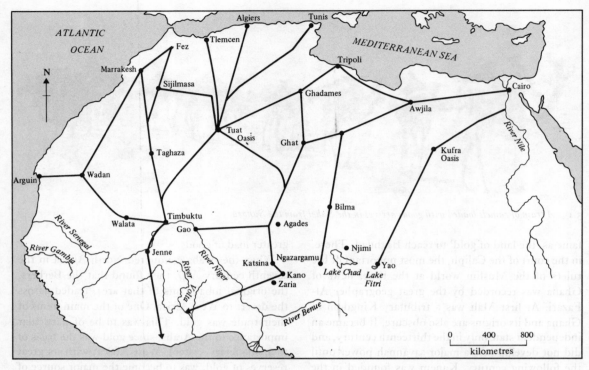

Map 5.2   Trans-Saharan trade routes.

The Arabs were not only interested in gold but also in ivory, as well as ostrich feathers and leather. Ivory for instance was a major item in the exports of Kanem-Borno which did not have access to gold supplies. They also soon started to purchase slaves. Their demand for Negro slaves increased as the Berbers, whom they originally used as slaves, were converted to Islam. Under Islamic law it was forbidden to enslave a Muslim. In turn West Africans were eager to purchase salt from the desert peoples, since salt was in short supply everywhere and was literally worth its weight in gold to them. West Africans also bought cloth, copper beads, weapons, horses, and, as they were converted to Islam, books, from the Arab and Berber traders. The empires through which this trade was conducted experienced great prosperity. Not all of their inhabitants had to farm: with money gained from trade food-stuffs could be imported and some citizens could be released to specialise full-time in such occupations as traders, builders, smiths, crafts-men and even entertainers. The taxes levied on goods passing through their kingdoms enabled rulers to employ full-time administrators and support large armies and even equip them with imported weapons. These armies enabled them to secure trade routes, crush rebellions against their rule, protect their citizens from outside attack, and conquer neighbouring peoples. Indeed some peoples voluntarily joined these empires for the protection and security they could provide for them.

3 *Extent and composition of the savannah states*

All three empires at their height covered large areas of land, much larger than the majority of states in Europe in the eleventh century A.D. Perhaps the most interesting feature of these states was that they were multi-ethnic, that is they included within their frontiers peoples from many different ethnic groups.

To these people they offered not only the security their superior military power could provide, but also the opportunity to participate in the trans-Saharan trade.

Sometimes subject peoples would continue to be ruled by their own kings, who acknowledged the authority of the imperial ruler by paying him tribute. And sometimes they would be directly administered by imperial governors, who were either members of the royal family or royal slaves.

4 Islam

Another common feature of these empires was the increasingly important role Islam was to play in them. The North African traders who crossed the desert were mostly Muslim. On their visits they converted some of their West African colleagues; others were converted by example. Some Arabs settled for considerable lengths of time in the imperial capitals, building mosques and encouraging the local people to attend them. Islam does not have priests in the Christian sense, and it is an obligation for every Muslim to spread his faith. Because many Muslims learnt how to read and write, they became particularly useful to the imperial rulers, who to begin with continued to follow their own religions. They helped with tax collection and other aspects of government where it was necessary to keep records. This is similar to the role played by clerics in the courts of European kings during the Middle Ages.

West African merchants found conversion to Islam very useful, not only because it gave them the opportunity to learn how to read and write, but also because it made them members of the larger Muslim world. Whatever their native language, they could communicate in Arabic with West Africans as well as with Arabs. They had no problems in trading in North Africa itself.

One of the most significant results of conversion to Islam was that West Africans had a new and wider loyalty to a world religion that cut across tribal and national loyalties.

5 Ghana

The ruling group of Ghana were the Soninke. They called their kingdom Wagadu. The reason why Arabs knew it as Ghana is that *ghana*, meaning war-leader, was one of the titles used for the kings of Wagadu. Their capital was almost certainly at Kumbi Saleh, which was recently excavated. Our information about early Ghana is very slight except for references to its connections with the gold trade. The largest extent of Ghana is difficult to determine, but it seems to have been limited to the west by the Senegal River where the smaller state of Takrur

5.3 *Part of the excavated ruined city of Kumbi Saleh, probable capital of Ancient Ghana.*

flourished. To the south it exercised some form of control over Bambuk where it obtained its gold supplies. To the east it extended its rule to the Niger. To the north it was bounded by the Sahara, but it did control the Berber town of Audoghast which was the southern terminus of the trans-Sahara caravan route to Sijilmasa.

The ruler of Ghana clearly followed his own religion, despite the fact that he used Muslim officials and a separate Muslim city grew up outside his capital. The king of Ghana, like that of Kanem-Borno, was considered to be divine by his subjects, that is he was a god on earth and was worshipped as such by them. One of the main functions of the king, apart from his role as chief priest of the state, was to control trade. Succession to the office of the king appears to have been matrilineal, since Al-Bakri, the Spanish Arab traveller, wrote in the eleventh century that 'it is their custom that a king is succeeded only by his sister's son'.

Al-Bakri, who visited the court of Tunku Menin, the reigning King of Ghana in 1065 A.D., noted that the King, while wielding great power, was praise-worthy in his conduct, being a lover of justice. He possessed a huge army which Al-Bakri estimated at 200,000 of whom 40,000 were bowmen. There was also a large cavalry unit. He levied taxes on imported salt and gold to pay for the administration of the Empire. For instance the King levied a tax of one dinar of gold on each donkey-load of salt that came into Ghana. His people were only allowed to sell gold-dust, all nuggets (large pieces of gold) remain-

5.4 *Fort Knox in the United States of America where the country's gold reserves are stored.*

ing under his control, 'otherwise gold would be so abundant that its value would depreciate'. Today the Americans do a similar thing. Their paper currency is backed by gold. They therefore buy up large quantities of gold from modern Ghana and South Africa and horde it in Fort Knox. If they did not buy up this gold, then the market would be flooded with it and the value would go down. This would mean the value of their currency would also fall. Like the kings of Ghana they try to keep the value of gold high by not allowing too much on the market at one time.

6 The Almoravids and the fall of Ghana

To maintain their control of the trans-Saharan trade the kings of Ghana had allied with Berbers of the Zenata group, who lived under Ghanaian rule in Audoghast, but ruled Sijilmasa independently. The great rivals of the Zenata were the Sanhaja who were also Berbers. During the eleventh century they were swept by a puritanical movement demanding the return of its members to a pure form of Islam. This became known as the Almoravid movement, from the Arabic *al-Murabitun*. This name was derived either from the fact that the movement began from a *ribat* (or fortified religious settlement) or from the manner in which they fought. Because of internal rivalries the movement split into two. One group, under Ibn Tashufi, continued the conquest of Morocco where he established the Almoravid dynasty. Later they crossed into Spain to help those emirs who were fighting against the Christians and Muslims who had compromised with the enemies of Islam. They also founded the great city of Marrakesh in Morocco which became their capital, and from which Morocco took its name. After taking control of Sijilmasa, the Almoravids conquered Audoghast in 1055.

The other group, led by Abubakar b.Umar, allied with Ghana's western neighbour, Takrur, which had already accepted Islam, and invaded Ghana whose rulers still followed their traditional religion. In about 1076/7 the Almoravids finally conquered Ghana, and began converting its inhabitants to Islam. It is not clear whether the Almoravids

5.5 *A view of the city of Marrakesh, capital of the Almoravid dynasty of Morocco, drawn in 1846.*

deposed the ruler of Ghana or imposed a ruler of their own choice.

Almoravid rule did not last long and by the beginning of the twelfth century A.D. Ghana had regained its independence. It continued to flourish and as late as 1153/4 Al-Idrisi still considered Ghana the greatest kingdom in the western savannah. But thereafter the power of Ghana declined. It had been weakened by the Almoravid conquest. Later on it lost its position as the principal terminus of the trans-Saharan caravan trade to Walata. Some of its tributary kingdoms asserted their independence so that by the thirteenth century it had become much smaller and weaker.

Ghana was succeeded as the most important state in the area by its former subject state, Sosso, which in turn was replaced by Mali.

7 Mali

According to tradition the Sosso gained their independence from Ghana as a result of the Almoravid invasion. In 1180 a Soninke soldier, called Diara Kante, overthrew the ruling Soninke dynasty of Sosso, and one of his successors, Sumanguru Kante, later conquered Ghana. Shortly afterwards he conquered the small state of Mali which had been a tributary of Ghana. Tradition records that Sumanguru put to death all the royal family of Mali except a crippled prince, Sundiata Keita. Sundiata is the subject of a great epic still sung to this day by the *griots* or professional praise-singers of modern Mali. Various versions of his life exist. Despite being a cripple he is remembered as a great hunter and warrior. He is also remembered, like Sumanguru Kante, as a powerful magician.

Sundiata had gone into exile because of jealousies between his mother and the reigning queen who had attempted to murder him. After the slaughter of the royal family by Sumanguru Kante, he was the only prince left alive. His people sent for him to come and rid them of the tyrannical rule of Sumanguru. He led a successful rising of Malinke chiefdoms against the Sosso and his defeat of Sumanguru is remembered as a trial of strength between two great magicians of

5.6 *A map of West Africa drawn in 1558.*

whom Sundiata proved the more powerful.

Sundiata was the founder of the great independent state of Mali which at its height extended westwards to the Gambia and eastwards along the Niger to Gao, capital of the small Songhai state which became tributary to Mali. To the north Mali controlled the caravan termini of the southern Sahara; to the south the new gold-fields of Bure as well as those of Bambuk, on the Upper Niger. Most significant of all, Mali's central area was the savannah itself, whereas that of Ghana had been the less fertile Sahara fringe.

Sundiata's son, Mansa (or King) Uli, went on a pilgrimage to Mecca during the reign of the Mameluk Sultan of Egypt, Babyars (1260–77), showing that Islam had now become the state religion of Mali. By the reign of Mansa Musa (1312–1337), it had become firmly established among the ruling classes. It was Mansa Musa's pilgrimage to Mecca in 1324 that literally put Mali on the map. During his stay in Egypt on his way to Mecca he spent and gave away so much gold that there was a devaluation of currency. As a result of this his fame spread as far as Europe where in 1339 Angelino Dulcert included 'Rex Melly' or King of Mali on his map of Africa. The Catalan map of Abraham Cresques of about 1375 shows 'Mussa Melli' seated on a gold throne, wearing a gold crown and describes him as 'the richest and most noble King in all the land'.

8 The importance of trade to Mali

Gold continued to be the most important export of the area and was the basis of Mali's wealth. The King of Mali, like his predecessors in Ghana, maintained a monopoly of trade in this item. So powerful did Mali become in the fourteenth century, as a result of the gold trade, that it expanded east along the Niger, conquering Jenne and Timbuktu, which both owed their growth into important trade centres to this period.

Ibn Battuta, the most famous traveller of his time, who had been as far afield as China, visited Niani, capital of Mali, in 1353. He was greatly impressed by the way in which the Mansa of the day ruled, writing:

> The negros possess some admirable qualities. They are seldom unjust and have a greater abhorrence of injustice than any other people. Their Sultan shows no mercy to anyone who is guilty of the least act of it. Neither traveller nor inhabitant in it has anything to fear from robbers or men or violence. They do not confiscate the property of any white man (Arab) who dies in their country, even if it be uncounted wealth.

This was perhaps the greatest achievement of the savannah states: to maintain peace and justice over vast areas in which trade could be freely carried on.

Ibn Battuta, however, noted the tensions that existed at court. These were to be among the causes of Mali's decline, and its eventual conquest by its subject state of Songhai.

As Mali expanded eastwards its main axis became the River Niger and its most important trading towns became Timbuktu and Jenne. It began to tap the gold resources of the Akan forest as well as those of Bure. Its wealth gave rise to a class of scholars, based principally at Timbuktu and Jenne. In Timbuktu the Sankore mosque became a renowned centre of scholarship, equivalent to the medieval universities of Europe.

9 The decline of Mali

We can trace Mali's decline from the beginning of the fifteenth century. Mali suffered from numerous internal weaknesses especially succession disputes and civil wars. Moreover the Mossi from the south raided as far as Timbuktu. Macina and Songhai, which were tributary states of Mali, became restive under its rule. Tuaregs, who had been the original owners of Timbuktu, raided its north-east frontiers. In the second half of the fifteenth century, the Songhai, under their brilliant leader, Si Ali, or Sonni Ali the Great, conquered Jenne and Timbuktu and replaced Mali by Songhai as the most important power in the western savannah.

10 The achievement of Mali

At its height Mali was one of the largest empires in the contemporary world. It controlled a complex net-work of trade routes from the desert to the forest. Along these, Muslim traders from Wangara, known as Dyula, moved freely, establishing trading posts. Through their close cooperation with each other, based on their common faith in Islam, these Dyula traders helped bring the Empire great prosperity. Through credit, which they introduced into the commercial system of West Africa long before the Europeans started it on the coast, they linked Sahara, savannah and forest.

Mali was recognised by important North African powers like Morocco and Egypt with whom ambassadors were exchanged. Perhaps most important of all it was in Mali that Muslim scholarship first flourished on a large scale in the savannah. It was to begin a tradition that lasted down the centuries.

11 Kanem-Borno

The Empire of Kanem-Borno developed independently of Ghana and Mali. This is not surprising when you look at its position on the map. It lay far away from both Ghana and Mali, situated to the north-east of Lake Chad. The original home-land of Kanem was separated from the lands to the south by Lake Chad and those to the west by a great tract of barren land and desert.

Tradition records that Kanem was founded by the great Arab hero Sayf b. Dhi Yazan who gained control of a group of Negro nomads called the Magumi. He founded a dynasty which ruled Kanem-Borno until 1846 and which was certainly one of the longest lived dynasties in world history. The dynasty was known as the Sefawa dynasty after his first name. The kings were known as *mais* and their kingdom appears to have been founded in the ninth or tenth century A.D.

The early state appears to have been nomadic: not the result of the conquest of sedentary peoples by nomads but the grouping together of various nomad groups in the area. To begin with these nomads had no fixed capital nor did they live in towns. It was more like a confederation of nomads under an acknowledged ruling group. The first mention of fixed towns is not made until the twelfth century when Al-Idrisi records the towns of Manan and Njimi. Later Njimi, whose site has not been fixed, became the capital of Kanem.

We know very little indeed about early Kanem. It is however clear that it was the terminus of the caravan route to Tunis and Tripoli through Bilma and Zawila in the Fezzan. No doubt it was along this route that Islam reached Kanem, in much the same way that it did Ghana.

Islam had certainly become important in Kanem by the eleventh century for Mai Hume is recorded as the thirteenth ruler but the first to make the pilgrimage. By the late twelfth century or early thirteenth century we can suppose that Islam had become the state religion. One Mai, Dunama Dib-alemmi, at this time made the pilgrimage three times during his reign. In the 1240s a hostel was founded in Cairo specially for students from Kanem.

Kanem was initially composed of a series of different nomadic groups but under skilful rulers, who followed a careful policy of inter-marriage with their subjects' leading families, they merged into a single group speaking a single language, Kanuri. By the thirteenth century the Kanuri had become so powerful that they began to expand their control over non-Kanuri peoples. They also took over control of the Fezzan, with an outpost there some 1,300 kilometres from Njimi. To the south, however, their expansion met with fierce resistance from local peoples collectively known as the So.

During the fourteenth century Kanem came under great pressure from a powerful group of nomads called the Bulala. At the same time there were quarrels within the royal family as to who should succeed to the throne. Indeed the history of the fourteenth century sometimes seems to be just a series of succession disputes and wars with the Bulala. Finally the Bulala drove the strife-torn Sefawa leaders out of their homeland forcing them to settle in Borno.

Not until Mai Ali Gaji came to the throne at the end of the fifteenth century, did the Sefawa begin to see an end to their troubles. First of all he put an end to their succession disputes; second he founded a

new capital at Ngazargamu; and third he began to gain ground against the Bulala. Indeed, so great was his achievement in restoring the fortunes of the Sefawa that his successor was able to drive the Bulala out of Njimi.

12 Government, trade and Islam

Unfortunately we do not have any contemporary accounts of Kanem-Borno for this period written in the detail with which Ibn Battuta described Mali. But we can say a little about the organisation of the state in this early period. Clearly, as Map 5.2 shows, Kanem-Borno was principally a trading state, built up along a trans-Saharan trade route. It exchanged the goods of North Africa with those of the savannah and forest to its south. Ivory, kola and slaves were its most important exports.

Islam became the state religion from the twelfth century onwards, though the kings, while practising Muslims, maintained their divine status, a fact which is stressed in early Arab accounts of Kanem.

To begin with the Kingdom was governed through royal princes. But since these princes often used their provinces as a basis to contest the king-ship, they were replaced by royal slaves and kept at home.

The forced movement of the state southwards, and its consequent incursion into Borno, extended the rule of these original nomads over Negro agriculturists. We know very little about these farmers except that they were skilled potters and many of them lived in small walled villages. Some of these have been excavated, and have revealed interesting figurines similar to, but not as beautiful as, those of the Nok Culture.

13 Hausa states

As the Sefawa moved south, they also came into contact with the Hausa people to their immediate west. The Hausa had already established a number of small states, some of which like Kano, Katsina and Zazzau (Zaria) were already quite powerful at the time of the arrival of the Sefawa.

We know very little about the early history of the Hausa. They were clearly the indigenous inhabitants of the area and had begun to live in large villages and towns surrounded by defensive walls. Within the walls were lands for cultivation in times of siege. During times of peace they farmed the surrounding countryside. These walled towns were known in Hausa as *birane* (sing. *birni*). Some of these towns, especially those on very fertile land or situated in good positions for trade became very rich. They expanded their territory either by peaceful arrangement or by conquest. The latter seems the more likely method, in view of how common defensive walls were in their towns and villages.

Tradition records that there were seven major states in Hausaland based on *birane* or walled towns. These are said to have been founded by sons of an immigrant conqueror called Bayajidda. One son founded Biram, another son founded Daura, Katsina, Kano, Rano, Zazzau (Zaria) and Gobir. There were certainly many other small states at the time, but these were probably the most important then. The most powerful among them by the fifteenth century were Kano, Katsina and Zazzau. Kano and Katsina were clearly well situated as southern termini of the trans-Saharan trade while Zazzau, lying on the southern borders of Hausaland, had access to the products of the southern savannah and forest. Significantly Zaria, the capital of Zazzau, is said to have been important as a slavemarket. Gobir does not seem to have risen to importance until after the fifteenth century. It lay to the north, on the fringes of the Sahara area.

Islam appears not to have gained a significant hold in the area until the second half of the fifteenth century when the kings of Kano, Katsina and Zazzau not only accepted Islam personally, but also adopted it as the state religion. Muslim ideas on administration were introduced into these states, mosques were built and Muslim law to some extent replaced traditional law.

Before that it would seem that the Hausa kings ruled according to the traditional forms of Hausa government, even when they were Muslims themselves. It is clear that these Hausa, or Bayajidda rulers, had established their authority over indigenous rulers. *The Kano Chronicle* describes an existing group of priest-kings who after the Bayajidda conquest continued in authority for some time. It is not until after the fifteenth century that we begin to have detailed and more reliable information about the Hausa states.

14 Small savannah states

Across the savannah of West Africa there were numerous small states like Kano, whose history is as yet very vague before the fifteenth century. Only brief mentions can be made of the more important ones. We have already talked of Takrur, the oldest Muslim state of West Africa according to the records. For periods it was subject to Ghana and Mali. With the collapse of Mali it gained its independence under a new ruling dynasty of Fulani. South of Takrur lay the small kingdom of Wollof, which by the end of the fifteenth century had gained control of much of modern Senegal. Wollof was described by the Venetian explorer, Cadamosto, who visited it in 1445. The ruler of the Wollof was known as the Burba, and his office was elective. The Wollof state was to grow powerful on the basis of both the Saharan and Atlantic trades. By the mid-sixteenth century the Portuguese recorded that the Bourba Djollof had an army of 10,000 cavalry and 100,000 soldiers.

Another important savannah state at this time was Mossi. This kingdom was placed strategically between Mali and the rich gold-producing areas of the Akan Forest. Mossi was divided into states, Yatenga, Fada N'Gurma and Wagadugu, which was to become the senior of the three. Little is known about them in this period, except that they were able to raid into Mali territory and even attacked Timbuktu in 1338 and penetrated 500 kilometres into the Sahara to Walata.

We should have to spend much space listing what little we know about all the savannah states of West Africa in this period. What is important here is that as you begin the study of West African history in depth, you should not think that the only important developments in the West African savannah were Ghana, Mali and Kanem-Borno. It is only that we know much more about them at present.

6 States of the forest before 1500

1 Ife, Benin and Oyo

Despite the difficulties of communication in the forest, states emerged there not long after the rise of the savannah states. It is very difficult to be sure when the three most important of these states, Ife, Benin and Oyo were founded, but they were clearly in existence well before the end of the fifteenth century when Portuguese sailors first visited the Kingdom of Benin.

Ife, Benin and Oyo share a common myth of origin: both the ruling dynasties of Oyo and Benin acknowledge Ife as their original home. Ife and Benin have become world famous for their strikingly beautiful bronzes. Oyo, while it never achieved the same stature as the other two states in the field of art, was by the early eighteenth century probably the most powerful state of its day in the whole of West Africa.

2 The Ife myth of creation

According to the Yoruba myth of creation, Ife was the original home of Man. Olorun, the supreme god of the Yoruba, let his son, Oduduwa, down from heaven on a chain carrying a five-toed cockerel, a palm-nut and a handful of earth. The earth was scattered by Oduduwa over the water. It was then scratched by the five-toed cockerel and became dry land in which the palm-nut germinated to become a palm-tree. This palm-tree had sixteen fronds which represented the sixteen crown rulers of Yorubaland. This is only one version of a myth which, with many variations, was accepted throughout Yorubaland as the explanation of how man was created. For the Yoruba it was the equivalent of Genesis for the early Jews.

While in each version the original number of crowned heads may vary, as indeed does the list of those who were the original crowned heads, nearly all Yoruba agree that Ife was their original home. Thus, although Ife had become a very small state by the eighteenth century, it has always retained its prestige as the original home of the Yoruba and its ruler, the *Oni*, is highly respected as the keeper of the ancient shrines of the Yoruba.

3 The growth of Ife

Whilst the Ife myth of creation asserts that its ruling dynasty is descended directly from Oduduwa as the son of God, other myths describe Oduduwa as a prince who arrived from the east. This has led to a great deal of discussion as to how the Ife dynasty really established itself. Ife traditions tell of an indigenous group of inhabitants, 'the Igbo', against whom the Ife had to fight many battles. One such tradition is that of Moremi, an Ife woman, who promised the *orişa* (god) of a local stream that if she could learn the secret of the Igbo's power, she would make any sacrifice demanded of her. She then allowed herself to be captured by the Igbo on one of

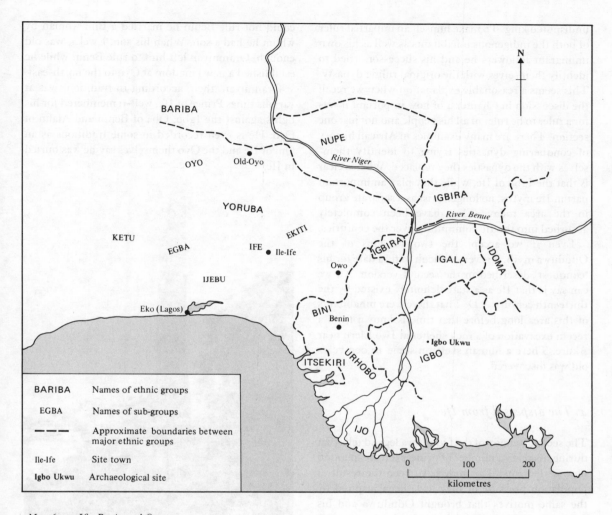

Map 6.1   Ife, Benin and Oyo.

their attacks on Ife, in which, as usual they were
dressed in terrifying masks and raffia costumes. The
King of the Igbo made Moremi his wife and during
her stay Moremi learnt that the Igbo attackers were
really only humans dressed in raffia. She escaped
back to Ife and taught the people to defend
themselves by setting light to the raffia costumes of
the Igbo with torches. The Ife no longer feared the
Igbo, but Moremi, when she was called on to make
her sacrifice, found to her horror that her only son
was alone acceptable to the *orisa*. She sacrificed him
to the stream in which he had to be drowned. In Ife
today she is still revered as a national heroine and

each year the Edi Festival is held in her honour.

Now what are we to make of the two myths about
Oduduwa? One says he is the first man on earth. The
other says he came from the east to Ife, and support
for the idea that the Ife were not the original
inhabitants of Ife is given by the Moremi story. It
would appear that the most satisfactory explanation
is one that says there were in fact two different
Oduduwas. The first Oduduwa of the Ife myth of
creation was the first ruler of the original inhabitants
of Ife. The second Oduduwa was leader of a people
'from the east' who conquered the original inhabitants and after many struggles became their

undisputed king. To make himself an impartial ruler of both the indigenous inhabitants as well as his own immigrant followers he and his successors tried to identify themselves with the original ruling dynasty. This seems a reasonable explanation when we recall the discussion in Chapter 4 of how important it was for a ruler to be ruler of all his people and not just one section. There are many examples in African history of conquering dynasties trying to identify themselves with the dynasties they replaced. What is clear is that the Igbo of Ife, while they play an important part in Ife myths, no longer exist as a separate group in the area today. They have been completely absorbed into the Ife community over the centuries.

Even if we accept the two versions of the Oduduwa myth, it is very difficult to fix a date for his 'conquest' described in the second version. All we can say is that Ife as a state definitely existed by the thirteenth century A.D. That there were inhabitants of this area long before that time is known from a recent excavation of a rock shelter at Iwo Eleru near Akure. There a human skeleton some 10,000 years old was discovered.

4 The dispersal from Ife

The second version of the Oduduwa legend tells that during his reign a number of princes left Ife to found new settlements. This may have been the result of population pressure or may have been inspired by the same motives that brought Oduduwa and his followers to Ife in the first place. Anyhow, in Ife today the place from which the princes dispersed is still remembered as Itajero, the place of conference, and is situated just outside the Oni's palace. Tradition has it that a number of princes were given crowns and told to found new kingdoms. The *number* of princes and the *names* of the kingdoms which they founded varies from kingdom to kingdom in Yorubaland. As with the original creation myth, each Yoruba kingdom would like to assert that it is one of the original foundations.

One of the princes to leave Ife was Oranmiyan, who is variously described as son or grandson of Oduduwa. He first left for Benin where he founded the present dynasty. Convinced that a non-Bini

could not rule Benin he married a Bini woman by whom he had a son. When his son, Eweka, was old enough, Oranmiyan left him to rule Benin while he established a new kingdom at Oyo to the north-east.

Oranmiyan, then, according to tradition, was at various times Prince of Ife, well-remembered for his fights against the Igbo, Oba of Benin and Alafin of Oyo. He is even recorded in some traditions as an Oni of Ife and the Oyo themselves say he was buried in Ife.

6.1 *Oranmiyan's staff, a huge granite monolith with which, tradition has it, Oranmiyan drove off the enemies of Ife.*

5 *Ife as a state*

We know very little about Ife as a state. Even the character of its ruling dynasty is in dispute. The Ife version holds that the present ruling dynasty is descended directly from Oduduwa. At Oyo, it is insisted that Oranmiyan, when he left Ife, placed a slave, Adimu, in charge of the royal shrines and that the present Ife dynasty is descended from Adimu.

6.2 *A bronze figure of an Oni of Ife showing the sort of regalia that the early rulers of Ife used to wear.*

We have only the slenderest documentary evidence for Ife before the nineteenth century. Duarte Pacheco Pereira, a Portuguese visitor to Benin at the end of the fifteenth century, seems to be describing the Oni of Ife when he talks of a great ruler who 'is considered among the Negroes as the Pope is among us'. He says that the Oba of Benin acknowledged this ruler as his superior. Pereira, however, placed him as living to the *east*, not west, of Benin. Again de Barros, another Portuguese visitor, also described a king to the *east* of Benin 'held in great veneration as are the supreme Pontiffs among us' and who was placed behind 'silk curtains . . . like some sacred object'.

These references have been used to suggest that the myth of an Ife origin for Benin may not represent actual facts. However, to this day Benin kings acknowledge Ife as their original home. In Ife itself there is a site called 'The Heaven of the Kings of Benin' where it appears they were given a token burial on their death. Once again, the importance of being very careful with both oral tradition and documentary evidence must be emphasised.

Of Ife itself we know only what archaeological evidence can give us. The famous Ife bronzes and terra-cottas are of a very high order of artistic and technological skill. They depict a ruling class which wore elaborate clothes and regalia. While none of the buildings of ancient Ife have survived we do find pavements made from carefully laid pieces of broken pots (potsherds).

A recent survey of the walls of Ife show them to have been extremely complex, fanning out like a spider's web from the Afin (the palace), the original centre of the town.

Ife must have been an important centre of trade since the bronze heads, of which twenty are known, are actually *brass* and contain little tin. Some are actually made of pure copper. Now no copper is found in Nigeria or in its western and eastern neighbours. This means that the copper must have been imported from the Sahara, since these heads pre-dated the arrival of the Europeans on the coast at the end of the fifteenth century. In Benin, which the Portuguese visited in 1486, bronzes, whose method of casting, tradition says, was imported from Ife, were already in existence. Frank Willett, the leading expert on the art of Ife, believes that Ife reached the height of its artistic achievements around the thirteenth or fourteenth centuries. Recent carbon dates would confirm this pre-European origin.

What were these superb heads used for? The most likely explanation is that they are death masks of Onis of Ife or other important people. In nearby Owo, to this day, when an important person dies, a death mask is carved as realistically as possible for his funeral.

6 Benin

Our knowledge of early Benin is as obscure as that of Ife. Before the arrival of Oranmiyan, the state had undergone upheaval with the attempt by its leading

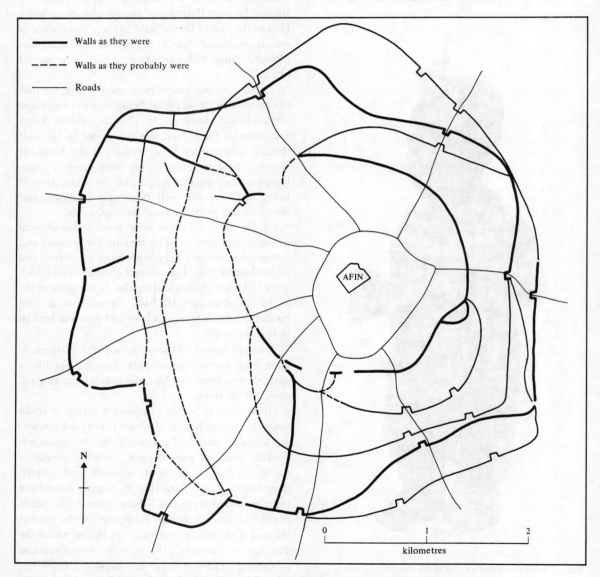

Map 6.2   A map of the development of the Ife walls based on the tracings of Paul Ozanne, the archaeologist.

chiefs to change the form of government by which it was ruled. They tried to replace the existing system of hereditary succession to the position of *Ogiso*, as the rulers of Benin were known, by one of election. This would give the leading chiefs greater say in government. However the first Ogiso under this new system attempted to have his son recognised as his successor. The upheavals that followed led to the 'invitation' of Oranmiyan, an outsider, to be King of Benin. This of course may be a cover-up for the conquest of Benin by Oranmiyan and his party. Oranmiyan's successors may have wished to 'legitimise' their rule by asserting that they were not 'unpopular conquerors' but came by 'invitation'. On the other hand, there are a number of examples of African peoples in times of internal troubles inviting an outsider to rule over them.

The state Oranmiyan took over appears to have been very small. The conquests which were to make Benin the substantial Empire it was when the Europeans arrived took place under one of Oranmiyan's successors. The small state was based on the Edo-speaking peoples of the immediate Benin area. We do not know why Benin developed into a town, for the Edo normally live in villages. Either for reasons of defence or trade, several villages fused into a large town that dominated the surrounding villages. The town itself was in fact a series of villages grouped together. This is clear from a study of Benin's highly complex wall system, where walls surrounded not only the city but its individual village-sections.

The Ogiso was effectively Paramount Chief of Benin. Under him were the *Uzama* who probably represented the various villages of which Benin was composed.

7 Ewedo, Oguola and Ewuare the Great

Even though Oranmiyan was acknowledged as King by the Uzama, it is clear that they carefully limited his power and that of his immediate successors. Tradition has it that the fourth ruler of Oranmiyan's dynasty, Ewedo, was the first to restrict the powers of the Uzama, by making them stand in his presence and forbidding them to carry symbolic royal swords.

6.3 *A bronze head of the Queen Mother of Benin. One of the finest works of art to come out of Benin where, legend has it, the art of bronze casting was learnt from Ife. This bronze was probably made in the sixteenth century.*

More important, he established himself in a new palace with a new group of chiefs who were dependent on him and could rival the Uzama. He divided this new group of chiefs into three sections. A clever oba could play one section off against the other. He also renamed Edo, Ubini, pronounced Benin by the Europeans.

Oguola, successor to Ewedo, is reputed to have introduced brass-casting from Ife. The Oranmiyan dynasty is also said to have introduced new types of weapons and the use of horses.

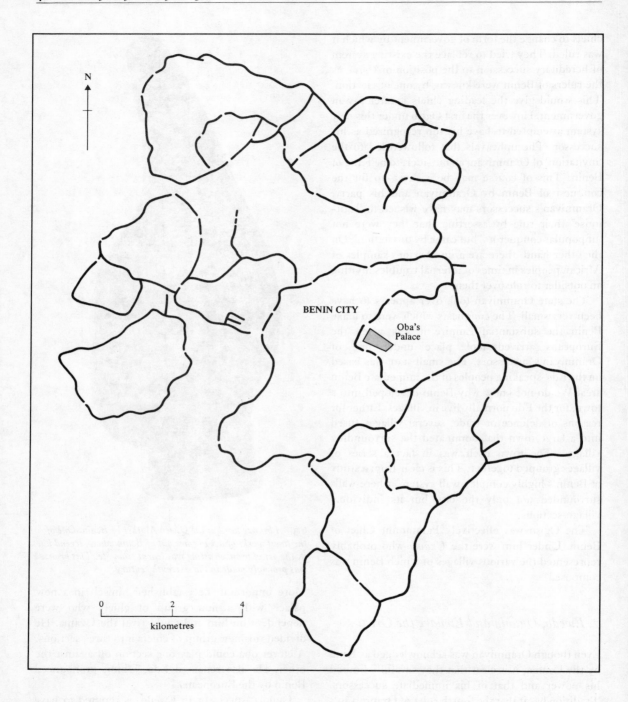

N

BENIN CITY

Oba's
Palace

0   2   4

kilometres

Map 6.3   The complexity and extent of the Benin City walls is clearly demonstrated in this schematic map based on research by Graham Connah.

The history of Oguola's successors is obscure until the reign of Ewuare who came to the throne in the mid-fifteenth century. He introduced major changes into the state, the most important of which was the creation of a new group of chiefs, the town chiefs. Ewuare was clearly trying to obtain support for himself in the town as well as in the palace. By controlling so many titles, he gained great strength. A. C. F. Ryder, a historian of Benin, has written: 'much of the political history of Benin turns upon the strivings of important men and families to win place and advancement in the hierarchies of town and palace and upon the efforts of rulers and pretenders to the throne to consolidate followings in these associations'.

Ewuare is associated with the conquests which turned Benin from a small state into an Empire: under him, parts of Ekiti, Ikare, Western Igbo, Owo and Akure came under Benin rule. It seems clear that it was not only military prowess that sustained Ewuare. Chief Jacob Egharevba, the historian of Benin, describes him as 'powerful, courageous and sagacious'. He was also reputed as a magician. The elaborate rituals performed by the oba even to this day indicate strongly the divine nature of the kingship in Benin.

8 The great city of Benin

Benin must have been a forest terminus of the trans-Saharan caravan trade. Before the coming of the Europeans it looked northwards rather than to the sea. This, as in the case of Ife, would explain the pre-European source of supply of copper for the Benin bronzes. The elaborate houses that so impressed the first European visitors, the delicately carved ivories, the carved doors and stools, all needed an elaborate economy to support their manufacture.

Ozuola, who succeeded Ewuare's immediate successor as Oba of Benin, was the first King of Benin to meet the Europeans. They described his capital as 'the great city of Benin', for in size and buildings it compared with the cities of their homeland, Portugal.

6.4   *Benin city as it appeared to a European visitor in the seventeenth century.*

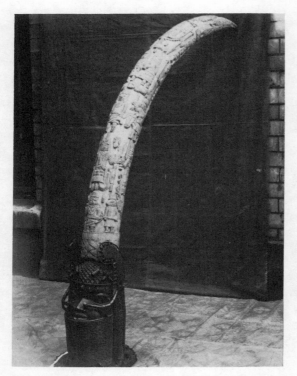

6.5   *Above: a memorial to a past Oba of Benin in the main compound of the palace of Benin. This memorial is to Oba Eweka II, father of the present oba. When the British sacked Benin in 1897 they took most of the bronze memorials to former obas as well as many other treasures with them as loot. Below is one example: a beautiful bronze plaque depicting an oba's servants.*

9 Oyo

During the period we are considering Oyo remained a small state. Founded by Oranmiyan in the northern savannah of Yorubaland near the Niger, it cannot strictly speaking be considered a forest kingdom like Ife and Benin. Nevertheless it had its origins in the forest and its ideas on government came from the forest state of Ife which it continued to look on as the ancestral home.

Oyo was placed strategically in a part of the savannah relatively free from tsetse fly so horses could be used for transport and for war. The basis of Oyo's power was to be its cavalry. It had easy access to the Niger as well as the coast through the savannah corridor to Badagry and Porto Novo. It did not exploit this latter advantage until well after the European trade had been established on the coast. For the time being it acted as an entrepôt for trade between Yorubaland and the Hausa states.

Tradition holds that, after leaving Benin, Oranmiyan entered Borgu where he consulted with the King of Bussa as to where he and his followers

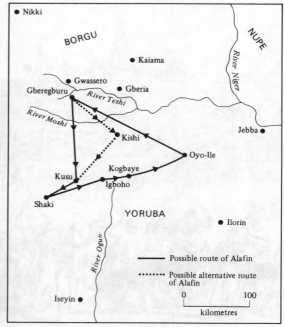

Map 6.4   The journeys of the Alafins of Oyo while establishing their kingdom.

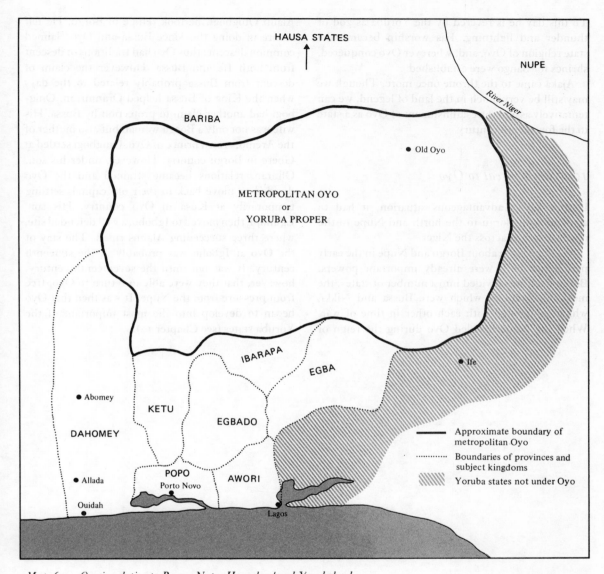

Map. 6.5   Oyo in relation to Borgu, Nupe, Hausaland and Yorubaland.

should settle. The King gave him a charmed serpent and told him to settle where the serpent first halted, which was at Oyo. From there Oranmiyan moved to Oko, which remains unidentified, and stayed there for many years. At the end of his life Oranmiyan returned home to Ife, where, according to Oyo traditions, he is said to have become Oni, and where he was buried. Ajaka, Oranmiyan's son, who had acted as regent in his absence, succeeded him as

Alafin. However he soon handed over the throne to Sango, his stronger younger brother. Sango moved the seat of government back to Oyo. Sango was a famous warrior and a great magician. His dabbling in the magical arts was to have tragic consequences. Showing off his power to control thunder and lightning he brought the latter down on his own palace by mistake. His palace, wives and children were destroyed and he committed suicide in shame.

To this day he is revered by the Yoruba as god of thunder and lightning. His worship became the state religion of Oyo, and, wherever Oyo conquered, shrines for Sango were established.

Ajaka came to the throne once more. Though we may still be very much in the land of legend, we can tentatively assign the establishment of Oyo as a state to the fourteenth century.

10 Nupe's threat to Oyo

Despite Oyo's advantageous situation, it had to contend with Borgu to the north and Nupe to the north-east, just across the Niger.

We know little about Borgu and Nupe in the early period but both were already important powers. Borgu itself was divided into a number of states, the most important of which were Bussa and Nikki, which cooperated with each other in time of war. When the Nupe invaded Oyo during the reign of Alafin Onigbogi, he took refuge in Borgu. He felt secure in doing this since Bussa and Oyo claimed common descent: thus Oyo had traditions of descent from both Ife and Bussa. However the claim of descent from Bussa probably related to the days when the King of Bussa helped Oranmiyan. Onigbogi had another claim to protection by Bussa. His wife was not only a Borgu woman but also mother of the Aremo, crown prince of Oyo. Onigbogi settled at Gbere in Borgu country. However, under his son, Ofinran, relations became strained and the Oyo decided to move back to their old capital, settling temporarily at Kusa in Oyo country. His son, Egunoju, then moved to Igboho, a well defended site, where three succeeding Alafins ruled. The stay of the Oyo at Igboho was probably in the sixteenth century. It was not until the seventeenth century, however, that they were able to return to Oyo, free from pressure from the Nupe. It was then that Oyo began to develop into the most important of the Yoruba states (see Chapter 12).

7 Songhai, Hausaland and Borno: 1450–1600

1 The Central and Western Sudan: 1450–1600

The sixteenth century in the history of the Western and Central Sudan was dominated by Songhai. At the height of its power in the early sixteenth century

Songhai was the largest empire ever created in tropical Africa, stretching from the borders of modern Senegal in the west, northwards to Taghaza in the Sahara, eastwards to include the Sultanate of Aïr and the Hausa states. Its southern frontiers marched with those of Borgu, Mossi and the remains

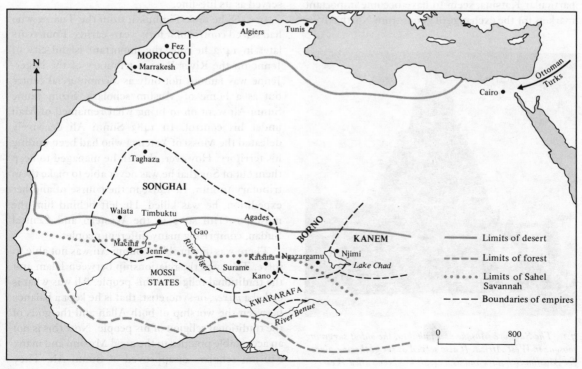

Map 7.1   North Africa and the Central Sudan.

of the great Mali Empire which Songhai replaced as the most powerful state in the Sudan.

The only Sudanese state in the sixteenth century which could in any way compare with Songhai was Borno which lay to its east. The Sefawa rulers were now firmly settled in Borno, and were looking westwards to the Hausa states and Aïr for expansion of their influence. In this they became rivals of Songhai. But for a time control of these states was wrested from both these rivals by Kebbi which had hitherto been a dependent state of Songhai.

To the north of Songhai lay Morocco whose Sultan, towards the end of the sixteenth century, was contesting leadership of Muslim Africa with the powerful Ottoman Empire in Turkey, whose influence extended to the northern frontiers of Borno.

Though the independence of the Hausa states was threatened, and on several occasions taken from them during the sixteenth century, this was a period of considerable growth and prosperity for Katsina and Kano. There was a large increase in the volume of trade across the Sahara Desert, and Kano, and in particular Katsina, seem to have become important markets for the exchange of goods from North Africa

7.1 *The Sankoré Mosque at Timbuktu, the oldest surviving mosque in West Africa. It also served as the gathering place for Muslim Scholars and as a result has been called West Africa's first university.*

with those of West Africa. This growth of trade with North Africa was accompanied by an increasing involvement of the Sudanese states with the Muslim world. Both Songhai and Borno strengthened or established diplomatic relations with Morocco and the Ottoman Empire. Islam itself attracted more and more converts. Kings built mosques and introduced Muslim law into their states. The number of people able to read and write in Arabic script grew. Most important for the historian, a number of scholars wrote down the history of their times so that we have contemporary documents available as evidence of the history of their part of the world in the sixteenth century.

2 Songhai under Sunni Ali

Before the reign of Sunni Ali (1464–1492), Songhai was just a small state on the Niger. In less than thirty years Sunni Ali turned his small Kingdom into a great Empire based on the River Niger, which served as its life-line.

In 1468 he took Timbuktu from the Tuareg who had seized control of it forty years earlier. Four years later in 1472 he took the important island city of Jenne on the River Bani, a tributary of the Niger. Jenne was famous not only as a commercial centre but as a home of Muslim scholars. From Jenne Sunni Ali went on to bring what remained of Mali under his control. In 1483 Sunni Ali decisively defeated the Mossi of Yatenga who had been raiding his territory. However, though he managed to keep them out of Songhai he was never able to make them tributary to him. In 1492, in the course of another expedition, he was killed. He left behind him the most powerful state in the Western and Central Sudan, comprising many different peoples.

There was one problem Sunni Ali was not able to solve. That was the relationship between Islam and the traditional religion of his people. Ali was what is called a *mixer*, or syncretist, that is he kept a balance between the worship of both Allah and the gods of the traditional religion of his people. Now this is not an acceptable practice to the good Muslim and many Muslim scholars disapproved of Sunni Ali. They wrote that he persecuted Muslims. Sunni Ali's son,

Baru, who succeeded him was more of a mixer than his father. However when he came to the throne he was challenged by one of the generals of the Songhai army, Muhammad. Muhammad asked Baru to declare himself a Muslim and deny the traditional gods. This he refused to do and on 12th April 1493 Muhammad attacked Baru. At his first attempt he failed, but at the second he defeated him in battle and became ruler of Songhai.

This dispute between the pure Muslim and the mixer is very important in the history of West Africa. The pure Muslim says that you shall worship no other god but Allah, whatever the circumstances. If you do worship other gods, you are not a Muslim but a pagan and it is legitimate for the pure Muslim to wage *jihad* or Holy war against you. Many kings in West African history, however, whilst they became Muslims, felt that to keep the loyalty of *all* their subjects, Muslims and non-Muslim alike, they had to maintain their role as head of the traditional religions of their states.

3 Songhai under Askia Muhammad

After the defeat of Baru, Muhammad took the title of Askia of Songhai and established his capital at Gao. Hitherto, under Sunni Ali, Songhai had had no fixed capital. Askia Muhammad next set about organising the administration of the large Empire Sunni Ali had built. He divided the Empire into a series of provinces and usually placed a member of his own family in charge of them. The major towns of Timbuktu, Macina, Jenne and Taghaza were placed in the charge of a Governor. He also placed officials in his court in charge of various special tasks such as Master of the Fleet, which was vital to an Empire whose main life-line was the River Niger; Master of the Royal Household; and officer in charge of relations with traders from North Africa.

Muhammad was a devout Muslim and in 1496 he made the pilgrimage to Mecca. His Empire was so secure that he felt able to leave it in the charge of his brother during his absence of nearly two years. In Cairo the Abbasid Caliph made him his deputy for the Western Sudan and, on his return, he began to wage *jihad* against his non-Muslim neighbours.

Throughout his reign he had to conduct campaigns to preserve the Empire he had seized from Sunni Baru. For a time he extended the Empire to include the Hausa states. However this was taken from his control by the rising state of Kebbi.

Towards the end of his life, Muhammad became blind and his eldest son seized the throne after entering Gao on 15th August 1529. Muhammad's reign was the most important in Songhai history. Not only did he consolidate the territories acquired by Sunni Ali, but he organised its administration. Islam flourished under him: many mosques were built, and Muslim law was introduced in the chief towns of the Empire.

Most of Askia Muhammad's successors had brief reigns, due to rivalries between Askia Muhammad's descendents. Only one had a long reign, Askia Dawud (1549–82), who is recorded as being very learned. He was responsible for establishing the Great Mosque of Timbuktu.

While Songhai's rulers changed frequently, it nevertheless remained unchallenged as the most important power in the Western Sudan. The threat to Songhai's position was to come from across the desert (see page 51).

7.2 *The interior of the tomb of Askia Muhammad of Songhai at Gao.*

4 Borno in the sixteenth century

Mai Ali Gaji of Borno, whom we have seen was responsible for establishing a new capital at Ngazargamu and putting an end to internal strife in his country, died in about 1503. He was succeeded by Idris who drove the Bulala out of Njimi on two occasions.

Throughout the sixteenth century the Bulala of Kanem remained a threat to Borno. Indeed, Leo Africanus, the great Arab explorer, who visited the Central Sudan in the early sixteenth century, considered neighbouring Gaoga more powerful than Borno. The Bulala were not the only threat to Borno. To the west the Hausa states, particularly Kano and Katsina, were growing in importance. In the early sixteenth century they had been occupied by Songhai, which brought this great Empire to the very borders of Borno. Later, the rising power of Kebbi occupied Hausaland and for much of the century proved very troublesome to Borno. For instance in about 1561 Borno had to send an expedition against Surame, the capital of Kebbi, in reprisal for Kebbi's attacks on its tributary of Aïr. The Tuareg sultanate of Aïr, with its capital at Agades, proved a problem for Borno throughout the century since both Songhai and Kebbi coveted it. To the south Borno was concerned about the growing power of Kwararafa, centred on the Benue River Valley, which with its swift cavalry made long distance raids on Hausaland and Borno. Over and above this, the Mais of the sixteenth century still had the problem of resistance of the peoples into whose lands they had moved from Kanem.

5 Mai Idris Alooma

In 1569/70 Idris Alooma, the most famous of Borno's mais, came to the throne. This does not mean to say he was the most important. It just happens that we know more about him than any other mai because his Imam, Ahmad Ibn Fartua, wrote at length about his reign and wars.

Idris Alooma secured the frontiers of Borno by defeating the Teda and Tuareg to the north and north-west, and reduced internal opposition to the rule of the Sefawa. He employed a corps of Turkish musketeers and military advisers and had camels which could go on long range campaigns.

Over and above his success as a military leader, Mai Idris Alooma was a great administrator and a devout Muslim. He built mosques and employed Qadis (professional judges) to administer Muslim law. He also continued the policy of his predecessors in developing diplomatic relations with North Africa. Borno already maintained diplomatic relations with the Turks in Tripoli, which the latter had occupied in 1551. However, in 1577 Turks occupied part of the Fezzan, which was considered Borno's territory. So in 1582, Mai Idris Alooma decided to play off the two great rivals in North Africa, the Sultan of Morocco and the ruler of the Ottoman Empire who now controlled most of North Africa. The Sultan and the Ottoman ruler both claimed that they were the supreme head of the Muslim community. Mai Idris, to gain an ally against the Turks, therefore offered to recognise Sultan al Mansur of Morocco as supreme head.

By the time Mai Idris died in about 1603, Morocco had conquered its most powerful rival, Songhai, but had failed to consolidate its conquests, as we shall see. Mai Idris thus left Borno the most powerful state in the Sudan.

6 Hausaland, Kebbi and Aïr

The Hausa states, though they shared a common culture, had not found any unity before the sixteenth century. Kano and Katsina had emerged as the two most important Hausa states. Their rulers had become Muslims trying to reorganise their administration according to Muslim law. *The Kano Chronicle* for instance records that Muhammad Rumfa, King from 1466 to 1493, was 'a good man, just and learned; he can have no equal in might from the time of the founding of Kano until it shall end'. Trade between the Hausa states and what is now northern Ghana had been opened up, bringing the kolanut in as an important item of trade.

In the early sixteenth century Songhai, as we have seen, invaded and occupied Hausaland making its kings tributary to it. In 1516 the Kanta of Kebbi,

7.3 *Agades, capital of the Tuareg Sultanate of Aïr.*

they created a Sultan who would settle their disputes, fix dues to be paid by caravans and also deal with foreigners. The Sultan had his capital at Agades, on which Songhai, Borno and Kebbi all cast greedy eyes. Throughout the sixteenth century the Sultanate of Aïr was threatened by these powers. In 1501 it was taken by Askia Mohammed of Songhai and though, soon after in 1532, it seems to have become tributary to Borno, Songhai remained its common language. Thereafter, Borno was to be constantly troubled by Kebbi in the exercise of its rule over Aïr.

7 The Moroccan invasion of Songhai

As we have seen, Songhai's frontiers extended across the desert right up to Taghaza, which was valuable because of its salt mines. These mines lay on the very borders of Morocco which was jealous of Songhai control because salt was a major item in North African trade with the Western Sudan. However the Moroccans were too preoccupied with wars with Spain and Portugal before the end of the sixteenth century to be able to do much about Taghaza. Sultan Ahmad al-A'raj of Morocco had demanded that the tax on salt leaving the Taghaza mines for metropolitan Songhai be paid to him and not the Askia. Askia Ishaq replied by sending 2,000 Tuaregs to plunder a Moroccan town.

In 1578 Sultan Ahmad al-Mansur came to the throne after a great Moroccan victory against Portugal in which his brother, the reigning Sultan, had died. Although Spain blocked his expansion to the north, he was secure enough on his throne, and powerful enough to try and extend his influence southwards. In 1583 he sent an expedition to occupy the oases of Tuat and Gurara which would give him control of an important share of the trans-Saharan trade. His long term ambition was to conquer Songhai, for then Morocco would not only control the salt and gold trade but also Sultan Ahmad would be leader of the greater part of Islamic Africa. As a result he would be in a better position to press his claim as Caliph or leader of the Muslim world against the Ottoman ruler.

In 1589 Sultan Ahmad sent a demand to Askia Ishaq II for payment of tax on salt leaving Taghaza.

who paid tribute to Songhai, quarrelled with his overlord over the share of booty due to him after an attack on Agades. He declared his independence and thereafter Songhai was unable to subdue him. Kebbi remained independent right up until the Fulani jihad of 1804 (see below page 78). For part of the sixteenth century Kebbi controlled much of Hausaland.

An important reason for rivalry between Kebbi and Borno, as we have seen, was the Sultanate of Aïr. This was not a state like the other states we have been considering. It consisted of a federation of nomadic Tuareg transporters who controlled the Saharan trade routes. Very often these Tuaregs quarrelled among themselves over the dues they would charge on caravans passing through their territories. Also, having no common leader, they had no way of dealing as a group with neighbouring states. So, at some point in the fifteenth century,

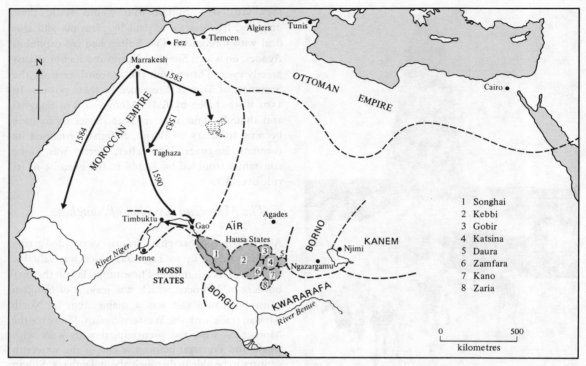

Map 7.2   The Moroccan invasion of Songhai.

Ishaq replied with an insulting refusal. So, on 16th October 1590, a large Moroccan army led by Judar Pasha, a Spanish prisoner of war who had been converted to Islam, set off across the desert. 4,000 soldiers, 600 engineers, 10,000 camels and 1,000 pack horses crossed the desert in two months and advanced on Gao. With their firearms they defeated the larger Songhai army at Tankodibo. They then moved on to Timbuktu, which they occupied and made the capital of a new Moroccan Pashalik. The Songhai Empire disintegrated and through much of the Western Sudan a state of insecurity was produced as a result of the Moroccan conquest.

The Moroccans controlled the main Songhai centres of Gao, Timbuktu and Jenne, but their hold over the countryside was not strong. In Timbuktu the merchants and scholars were very resentful of their new overlords who suppressed opposition by arresting some of the leading scholars, including Ahmed Baba, the distinguished Muslim Jurist. He was sent across the desert in chains to Marrakesh.

The Askia himself retreated with the remains of his army to Dendi which lies to the north of Borgu. There the Songhai army was able to fight off the Moroccans and the Askia re-established his court though he now ruled over only a fraction of his former Empire.

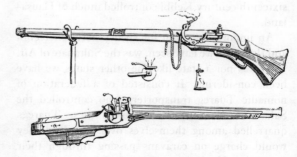

7.4 *A Moroccan arquebus – superior Moroccan weapons, in particular firearms, enabled their small invasion force to overcome the vastly larger Songhai army.*

8 West African coastal states and their hinterlands: 1500–1800

1 West Africa and the coming of the Europeans

Before the sixteenth century the coast of West Africa had been relatively unimportant in its history. Few people lived on the coast, and those that did were occupied with fishing and panning salt from the sea and coastal lagoons. West Africa's contact with the outside world was not across the Atlantic Ocean but across that great sea of sand, the Sahara. Trade over the Sahara supplied West Africa with much needed salt in exchange for gold and slaves which they sold to the Arab merchants of North Africa. Now gold formed the basis of currency not only for the Arab world but also for Europe, which had to obtain its gold from the Arabs. Europeans also had to obtain spices and fine cloths from India through the Arabs. If they could obtain direct access to the sources of supply in both cases, they would be able to avoid paying heavy duties to the Arabs. They therefore tried to get to India by sea, that is by going round the southern point of the African continent. If they could do this, not only could they open up trade direct with India, but also they could buy gold from West Africans direct. By the end of the fifteenth century the Portuguese, who started this enterprise, had explored the whole of the West Coast of Africa and had already started trading in gold from what came to be known as the Gold Coast. From Benin they also sent peppers to Europe, though once they had reached India, trade in African pepper gave way to that in Indian pepper. The Portuguese also bought human beings from the Africans they met on the coast to supply labour for their new colony of São Thomé. Soon afterwards they bought slaves to work for them on their plantations in America which Colombus reached in 1492.

During the sixteenth century trade in gold and slaves from the West Coast grew and provided new economic opportunities for Africans living in the area. They could buy cheap iron, cloths, copper and brass from the Europeans and more especially firearms which they used to defend their states and also to conquer neighbours. As a result towns and states developed on or near the coast as powerful as the great states of the savannah. But we must not see the opening up of the Atlantic coast as the one and only cause of the rise of these states. Benin and Ife we know, had flourished long before the Portuguese arrived. We also know that Oyo was founded before the arrival of the Europeans. But its access to the sea through the savannah corridor to Porto Novo did prove very important to its development. Trade in slaves was a major factor in the rise of the states of the Niger Delta – Old Calabar, New Calabar and Bonny. Dahomey also owed much of its prosperity to trade in slaves with the Europeans, while Asante grew from trade in gold as well as slaves.

2 The slave trade

By the seventeenth century slaves had become the most important item in trade between Europe and

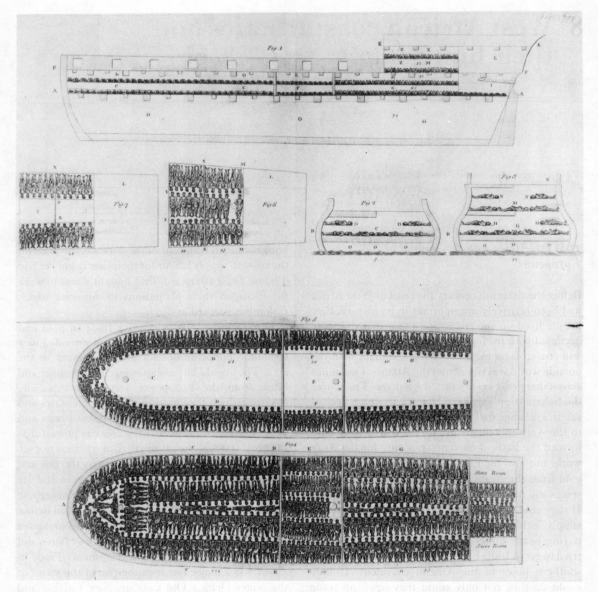

8.1 *Slaves were packed as close together as the slave traders could get them to make maximum use of the space in the ships. They had barely room to move as this plan for 'storage' of slaves in ships shows. As a result of the inhuman conditions in which they were transported across the Atlantic many slaves died, but this did not worry the slave traders who still made large profits on the remainder of their cargo.*

Africa, far surpassing that in gold. During the four centuries when this terrible traffic in human beings was conducted, some ten million or more Africans were shipped across the Atlantic to work on the plantations as slaves. Why did Europeans buy Africans, and why did Africans agree to sell their fellow human beings? When, in the sixteenth century, Spain and Portugal were trying to open up

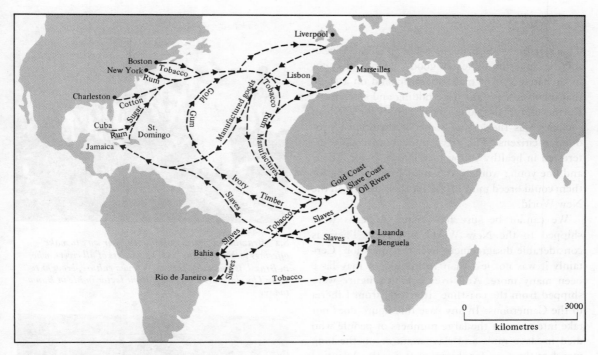

Map 8.1   Atlantic trade in the eighteenth century.

their territories in America, they tried to mine silver and grow sugar with labour supplied either by the indigenous Indians or by Europeans. However, they soon found that the Indians died from new European and African diseases which the Spanish and Portuguese brought with them. On the other hand it was found that Africans who went to the New World survived both its diseases and those of Europe much better than Europeans did. Africans in the Americas were three times more resistant to the diseases there than Europeans. So it was decided by the Europeans to import Africans as slave labour rather than use the local Indians or import Europeans.

Why, you may ask, did the Europeans not establish plantations in Africa itself and save themselves the trouble and high cost of shipping Africans to the New World, especially since sugar and cotton both grow in West Africa? The most important reason was Africa's diseases: malaria and yellow fever, which killed off Europeans at a great rate. Between 400 and 600 out of every 1,000 Europeans

died during their first year in West Africa. With a high death rate, and with Africans resisting fiercely attempts at European occupation, the simplest solution was to take Africans to America. This was helped by new developments in sailing techniques that made it quite cheap to carry slaves across the Atlantic and sell them at a profit for about £20 each in the middle of the seventeenth century.

Why did some Africans agree to sell their fellow men? First, we must remember that nearly every society in history has practised slavery and the idea was not foreign to the Africans from whom the Europeans bought them. Secondly, Africans wanted the goods the Europeans brought. And, just as they had found with the Arabs, apart from gold, the main thing the Europeans wanted to buy was slaves. For lack of any other commodity to exchange with the Europeans, they sold men and women. Usually these were criminals or prisoners of war from other tribes, so they were not people whom the sellers wanted to keep.

3 *The effects of the slave trade*

This terrible trade brought profit to some African societies in terms of the new goods and guns they got in exchange; but it made them depend on a trade that involved constant slave raiding and slave wars. Furthermore, the long term result for African societies was the loss of some of their most productive citizens. The slave traders were only interested in healthy young men and boys for labour and fine young women who apart from working for them could breed more slaves for their owners in the New World.

We cannot be sure how many Africans were shipped to the New World as slaves. There is considerable disagreement over this question. Certainly it was not less than 10 million: it may have been many more. And over half this figure were shipped from the coastline stretching from Liberia to the Cameroons. In any case this figure does not take into account the large numbers of people who died in slave raids and slave wars or on the long march to the coast for shipment across the Atlantic.

The results of this evil trade that reduced human life to the level of goods and chattels were grave for those African societies involved in it. The main lasting result was the spread of the Negro race across North and South America and the Caribbean, where it now forms one tenth of the population. There, Africans suffered bitterly in slavery, and even when this was abolished, in most countries of the New World they were treated, though free, as second class citizens. But in the face of this difficulty, Africans in the New World kept their pride in their race, and in many cases preserved their culture and religion. In Brazil today, and in Cuba, many black people still follow the religion of their Yoruba ancestors.

For Africans in Africa the slave trade brought about a commercial revolution. The coast of West Africa was opened up to trade with Europe and America. New items of trade were introduced such as liquor, tobacco, cloths from India, metal pots, copper and iron bars. Above all Europeans brought in firearms as items of trade. In return Africans exported some of their natural products such as gold, timber and ivory. But by far the most important item was slaves. Not all commercial revolutions are

8.2 *Brazilian devotees in Bahia on their way to make offerings to Yemoja, the Yoruba goddess of all rivers, who, in Brazil, is goddess of the sea. Yoruba culture, brought to Brazil by slaves, is a very important factor in life in Bahia today.*

8.5 *Christiansborg Castle, a Danish trading fort on the West Coast of Africa. When the British occupied the Gold Coast, Christiansborg Castle in Accra became the residence of the British Governors.*

8.3 & 4 *The Portuguese introduced firearms to coastal West African States which used them to raid neighbours for slaves. The Benin bronze (bottom left) depicts a Portuguese soldier firing a gun, while the wooden figurine above shows an African soldier doing the same.*

beneficial and the period of 1500–1800 on the West Coast of Africa has been called 'The Era of Firearms and the Slave Trade'. The imported firearms enabled Africans to secure more slaves for sale. The manpower exported produced cotton and sugar in the New World instead of in Africa. Even imports such as iron, salt, pots and cloth were only substitutes for locally produced items. The Europeans brought little to Africa which improved the quality of life for Africans. Unlike the Muslim traders from North Africa, who also traded in slaves but on a much smaller scale, they did not bring any cultural benefits to West Africans. Very few Africans learnt to read or write, or were taught mathematics. It is

ironic that the Asantehenes, though not Muslim, and with their capital situated so close to the Gold Coast trading forts, employed literate Muslim Africans in their administration, not Africans trained by the Europeans. This was because there were none available.

Some African merchants prospered greatly on the proceeds of the slave trade, and some societies expanded considerably on the basis of the profits gained from it. But they did so at the cost of untold human suffering. And with firearms at their disposal, and the capture of slaves as their objective, they were continually fighting bloody wars.

Whatever passing benefits individual traders and societies may have gained, generally the slave trade weakened African societies. The value of human life was reduced to that of the goods it would fetch from the European traders. The development of legitimate export crops such as cotton, sugar, palm-oil was delayed. So generally we can say that the commercial revolution brought about by contact with Europeans during the period 1500–1800 was without benefit to Africans.

Let us now look at some of the states that developed partly in response to trade with Europe.

We must, however, avoid the common error of thinking that this trade was necessarily the most important thing in the history of these societies at this period. Just as with any other state, trade formed only one aspect of society.

4 States of the Niger Delta and their hinterland 1500–1800

At the mouth of the Niger Delta a number of small Ijo-speaking states were able to profit from the slave trade as a result of their position on the coast. So too were Old Calabar at the mouth of the Cross River and Benin through its port of Gwato on the Benin River. We have seen that Benin had existed before the arrival of the Europeans, so that the slave trade cannot be held up as the cause of its growth. However, some authorities believe that the Ijo states of the Niger Delta developed in response to the European demand for slaves. Small fishing villages,

which were suitable as ports for European ships, grew into powerful states which controlled the trade in slaves with the Europeans. Other historians believed that these states, New Calabar (Elem Kalabari), Nembe, Bonny and Okrika already existed before the arrival of the Europeans. The cause of their growth, they say, was trade along the creeks of the Niger Delta. If you look at the map you can see that canoes can travel along creeks right from Bonny to Lagos. Also, trade developed between the Ijo-speaking peoples of the coast and the Igbo and Ibibio speaking peoples of the interior. The Ijo exchanged fish and salt for vegetables, meat, cloth and iron tools from the Igbo and Ibibio. Later, when the slave trade developed, they exchanged cheap imported iron tools, salt, dried fish and cloth, in exchange for slaves as well as vegetables, thus supplanting much of the earlier local trade. The Igbo and Ibibio for the most part lived in small villages and did not develop states. However, in the northern parts of Igboland, on either side of the

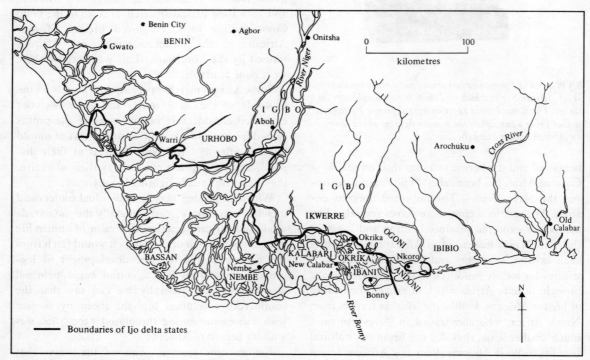

Map 8.2   The Niger Delta from Benin to Old Calabar.

8.6 *A ceremonial bronze wine bowl or cup excavated at Igbo-Ukwu in south-eastern Nigeria. It was probably made in the ninth century AD and demonstrates a high quality of workmanship as well as great beauty.*

River Niger, some Igbo states did develop. Some of these were under Benin influence. At Igbo-Ukwu remains of the culture of one such kingdom have been discovered. Beautiful bronze and terra-cotta pots show how highly developed the culture of these Igbo peoples was.

The Ijo states, as well as Old Calabar, whose people are Efik-speaking, and Warri, which is near Benin grew prosperous on the slave trade. The strength of the Ijo states was based on the large thirty-seater war canoes with which they dominated the creeks of the Niger Delta. Each canoe was manned by men from what was called a *house*. Its leader sat on the council of state. Any trader, once he had enough money and followers to equip a canoe, could found a house. As the Ijo areas were sparsely populated, slaves were not only bought to sell to Europeans but to help man canoes. Such slaves had to learn Ijo and behave exactly as if they were born as Ijos. If they did they could become house heads themselves.

Trade with the Europeans was controlled by the king and the house heads. The Europeans were not allowed into the interior to trade directly with the suppliers of slaves. The Ijo thus acted as go-betweens, or middlemen, in this trade. The Europeans would give house heads, who they trusted, advances with which to purchase slaves. The Europeans also had to pay the king customs duties on their goods.

Because of the wealth produced by this trade, there was strong rivalry among the Ijo peoples and also Warri to dominate it. This often led to wars between the Delta states.

5 Oyo and Dahomey

Early in the seventeenth century Oyo was able to establish itself once more in its old capital at Oyo Ile. Free from Nupe attacks, Oyo began to expand southwards into the Yoruba forest and into the Aja country of modern Dahomey. By the eighteenth century it had become one of the most powerful states, if not the most, on the West African coast. Not even mighty Asante could rival Oyo as it found to its cost in 1764 when a body of 2,000 Asante soldiers strayed into Oyo dominated territory near Atakpame and was destroyed by an Oyo army.

Oyo developed a highly efficient cavalry which it used to extend its power to the coast. It does not seem to have used guns on a large scale until the middle of the eighteenth century. It thus seems that the slave trade was not important as a factor in the rise of the Oyo Empire, since as we have seen one of the main reasons slaves were sold was to obtain guns. If the slave trade was not at first important for Oyo, it was vital for the Aja states. In the early seventeenth century a number of European countries established trading posts along the Aja coast, in particular at Ouidah, Allada, Grand Popo and Badagry. Soon, more slaves were exported from this stretch of the coast than anywhere else in West Africa. Indeed it became known as the Slave Coast.

The Aja states on the coast became very prosperous as a result of the slave trade. At the same time they became very jealous of each other and fought to obtain control of the trade with the Europeans. Within the Aja states, princes vied with each other to become kings because of the wealth the position would bring them.

In 1625 two brothers fought for the throne of Allada. The younger, Dogbagrigenu, won and exiled his elder brother. However, the latter returned and overthrow Dogbagrigenu who in turn was sent into exile with his followers. He trekked north to Abomey where he founded the new state of Dahomey.

Dogbagrigenu and his successors were among the most powerful of African kings. While other kings shared their power with leading chiefs, the Dahomeyan king centralised authority on himself. What is more, the Dahomeyan state demanded complete loyalty of its citizens. It was likened to a water pot with many holes in it. The citizens of Dahomey showed their loyalty by plugging the holes with their fingers so the water would not escape. By the beginning of the eighteenth century Dahomey comprised 40 towns and villages and became a threat to the coastal Aja states. In 1708, Agaja came to the throne and decided to take advantage of the strife amongst the Aja states. He strengthened his army by having all young boys trained in the art of warfare. He also employed regular spies to go out and assess the strength of the enemy.

In 1724 he invaded Allada. This angered Oyo, which resented the growing power of Dahomey in the area. Already, in 1680–2, Oyo had shown both Dahomey and Allada who was master by invading them both. Now, again in 1726 Oyo invaded Dahomey. Though Agaja had guns and Oyo did not, his soldiers were no match for the swift Oyo cavalry, which could run them down whilst they were reloading after the first discharge of their guns.

This defeat did not deter Agaja who, in 1727, took Ouidah, thus making himself supreme ruler of Aja country. But jealous Oyo again invaded Dahomey in 1728. But this time Agaja offered no resistance. Instead he destroyed his capital, removed his subjects and all food supplies into the forest out of reach of the Oyo cavalry. Short of food, and unable to find the Dahomeans, the Oyo army retreated. But in 1729 this method did not work for the Oyo army was well prepared. Finally Agaja sued for peace and agreed not only to move his capital to Allada but to be tributary to Oyo. While he kept Ouidah and Allada, a new port under Oyo's direct control was established at Porto Novo (which means New Port).

Relationships between Oyo and Dahomey remained strained. On several occasions Oyo had to invade Dahomey to ensure it obtained its yearly tribute. In 1748, however, Dahomey finally agreed to a treaty with Oyo that was satisfactory to both parties.

The slave trade dominated the economy of Dahomey. Agaja even appointed a special representative at Ouidah, called the Yevogan, to deal with the European slave traders. The slave trade itself became a royal monopoly. To strengthen his army, which was his means of obtaining slaves, Agaja created the famous corps of women warriors known as Amazons.

Up until the end of the eighteenth century Oyo had not been directly concerned with the slave trade on a large scale. However, trade between the coast and Hausaland was an important factor in the

8.7 *Portrait of Agaja, King of Dahomey, from Archibald Dalzel's* History of Dahomey *published in 1793. It was he who created the famous corps of Amazons, or women warriors.*

growth of the Oyo Empire, of which Dahomey of course formed part. The Alafins or rulers of Oyo in the eighteenth century were mostly traders and by the late eighteenth century the slave trade became of increasing importance to them.

The Oyo Empire was not as centralised in its authority as the Dahomeyan state. The Alafin shared power with the Oyo Mesi, a council of seven chiefs headed by the Basorun. Conflict arose between the Basorun Gaha and the Alafins. Between 1754 and 1770 he had four Alafins murdered. However in 1770 Abiodun came to the throne, and while outwardly doing what Gaha wanted, quietly plotted his downfall. In 1774 he had the Basorun and most of his large family put to death so he could rule in fact as well as name. Though Oyo prospered under Abiodun, no further additions of territory were made to the Empire. Indeed the tensions between the Basorun and Alafin were only a sign of disasters to come. The Egba revolted, and the Bariba and Nupe, until now docile, attacked Oyo's northern frontiers. In 1791 Oyo was actually defeated by Nupe.

Abiodun's successor, Aole, or Awole, who came to the throne in 1789, was a weak ruler and, as we shall see later, his reign saw the beginning of the collapse of the Oyo Empire.

6 Asante and its neighbours

In the forest of southern Ghana there grew up in the seventeenth century the last and the greatest of the Akan states, the great Asante Empire. At the height of its power in the early nineteenth century, Asante controlled most of what is today the Republic of Ghana. Asante's wealth was based on gold which it sold to European traders on the coast and to African traders, known as Dyula, who carried it to Arab traders in Jenne and Timbuktu. They in turn took it across the desert for sale in North Africa. Kolanuts and slaves also became important items in Asante's foreign trade.

The Asante were an Akan-speaking people as were most of the peoples of Southern Ghana. Long before the foundation of Asante in the 1670s by Osei Tutu, there had been a number of important Akan states which prospered from the gold trade.

These states did not grow as a result of the opening up of trade with Europe in the fifteenth century. When the Portuguese reached what the Europeans came to know as the Gold Coast, they found that there were a number of small kingdoms which had already developed the gold mining industry. Valentin Fernandes, writing of his visit to the Gold Coast in about 1500, remarked that 'The mines are very deeply driven into the ground. The kings have slaves whom they put into the mines. . . .'

Before the arrival of the Europeans gold was either exported north to the markets of the Western Sudan or used by the kings and important people for ornaments. When the Europeans arrived seeking to buy gold, they opened up an important new market for the Akan peoples. But trade with the north continued and during the succeeding centuries the Dyula founded trading centres on the northern routes such as Kong, Bobo-Dioulasso and Wa. By the eighteenth century, an important new trade route to Hausaland had been opened up to carry both gold and kolanuts.

The importance of the new European market was two fold: it made the Akan look towards the coast as well as the savannah for their trade; the added prosperity it brought made the rise of large new states possible. The most important of these were Denkyira, Akwamu and Fante, and of course later the great Asante Empire. To begin with the Europeans were mainly interested in gold. However, in the eighteenth century, they were as anxious to buy slaves for the plantations of America as they were gold, which they now obtained from Central and South America. The coastal peoples of Ghana would not let the Europeans go to the mines to get gold. They would only allow them to establish forts on the beaches. The people of the interior brought the gold to the peoples of the coast who bought it and sold it to the Europeans. Thus the Abrade people of the Akwamu Empire brought gold to the market at Abonsa, where it was purchased by the Accra people who sold it to the Europeans. This system operated all along the coast where some 45 forts were established by Portuguese, English, Dutch, French, Swedes, Danes and Brandenburgers. In return for gold and slaves the Europeans sold the same commodities as they did in the Niger Delta, most important of which were firearms.

Whilst the Ijo were able to control the middleman market in slaves in the Niger Delta, there was a constant struggle by the peoples of the interior of Ghana to obtain direct outlets to the coast. Thus in 1667 the Akwamu Empire conquered Accra, to whose king it had previously been tributary. Thereafter, until its collapse, it traded direct with

the Europeans. Later, the rising state of Asante sought its own outlets on the coast and as a result was often at war with the coastal Fante.

By the 1670s immigrants began to flood into the wealthy trading centre of Tafo, now part of modern Kumasi. A struggle for control of the town developed between earlier settlers, in particular the Domaa who had migrated from Akwamu, and the Oyoko, new arrivals from Adanse country. The latter

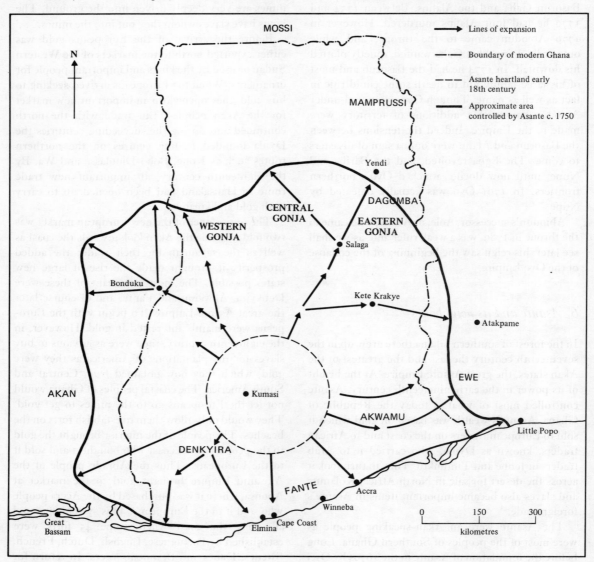

Map 8.3   Asante and its neighbours.

were led by Obiri Yeboa, who was killed in a battle with the Domaa. The Oyoko immigrants then chose Osei Tutu to lead them. With assistance from Akwamu, Osei Tutu defeated the Domaa. He then occupied Tafo and began to group a number of Akan Chieftancies around him to form the basis of the Asante Empire. He established his capital near Tafo at Kumasi and from there engaged in wars of expansion. In 1701 at the battle of Feyiase he defeated Denkyira, and thereafter he pushed towards the western stretch of the Gold Coast in order to obtain supplies of firearms. Osei Tutu also led his armies northwards and by 1717, when he is reported to have died in a battle with Akyem Kotoku to the south, the Asante Empire was firmly established. Direct trade was maintained with the Dutch and British. The Akan states which had joined with Osei Tutu in the foundation of his new Empire, or had been made tributary to him, acknowledged the supreme authority of the Golden Stool. This stool, which was said to have been 'conjured from the sky' symbolised the supremacy of the ruler of Kumasi over all the tributary states of Asante.

By the time of Osei Tutu's death Asante had become a powerful state, but it was no larger than the Akwamu Empire of Nyanaose. His successor, Opoku Ware, who reigned from 1717 to 1750, brought most of southern Ghana under Asante control and conquered Gonja and Dagomba to the north (see map).

Opoku Ware spent much of his time in battle; his successor, Osei Kwadwo, devoted great energy to building an efficient administration. Most important of all he tried to create an independent civil service, entry into which depended on merit, not birth. He also used literate Muslims to help him govern his huge Empire and tried to bring the many provinces under firmer central control.

7 The Mossi states

It is easy to think of Asante as a forest state, mainly dependent on trade with Europeans. Not only did Asante have important trading links with Timbuktu, Jenne and Hausaland through Dyula traders, it also controlled a great deal of northern savannah territory including the Mossi state of Dagomba, and parts of Gonja.

The Mossi states which lay to the north of Dagomba and south of the Niger bend were never very prosperous. Today Upper Volta, which includes the bulk of Mossi land, is one of the poorest states in Africa. The trade routes from the Akan Forest, north-west to Jenne and Timbuktu and north-east to Hausaland, by-passed them. The Mossi had to rely primarily on slaves to obtain imported goods and with their cavalry they raided the largely defenceless peoples living in societies without rulers to be found all over this area. There were seven Mossi kingdoms: Wagadugu, Tekodogo, Yatenga, Fada N'Gurma to the north and Mamprussi, Da-

8.8 *The first day of the Yam festival at Kumasi witnessed by Bowdich, head of the British mission to Osei Bonsu, the Asantehene, in 1817. Bowdich and other members of the mission can be seen on the right. Notice the Muslim dignateries in their turbans at the extreme right.*

gomba and Nanumba to the south. They treated each other as members of the same family and rarely attacked each other. On the other hand if one was attacked by an outsider, the others came to its aid. It is a measure of the strength of Asante by 1744–5, that it was able to occupy Dagomba. The great

Songhai Empire had, as we have seen, driven the Mossi off its territory, but had been unable to occupy them. Thus Asante became a powerful savannah as well as forest state. The only other state to achieve this was Oyo.

9 The Western and Central Sudan in the seventeenth and eighteenth centuries

1 The seventeenth and eighteenth centuries in the history of the Western Sudan

It is usually supposed that the Moroccan invasion of Songhai led to a breakdown of authority in the Western Sudan. It is also commonly supposed that Borno, the greatest state of the Central Sudan, declined during this period. Indeed these two centuries have been characterised as 'the dark ages' of West African history which preceded the revolutionary years of the nineteenth century during which reformist Islam and new Christian ideas were widely spread.

While the seventeenth and eighteenth centuries did not see the growth of a major state to fill the vacuum left by the collapse of Songhai, they were not centuries of chaos as is commonly supposed. Islam spread slowly into new areas, and Islamic learning became more widespread. Traders opened up new trade routes, particularly to the south. New, but smaller states, replaced the old Songhai Empire. Even when these states were not Muslim, their rulers often used the services of Muslims who could read and write in their administrations. This was true also of some of the states of the forest areas like Asante.

During the eighteenth century many West African Muslims became inspired by the reformist ideas that were stirring throughout the Muslim world at the time. There was a demand for a return to the ideals of law and government of the early

Caliphate. These ideas inspired jihads, or holy wars, which swept away corrupt Muslim governments and conquered peoples who did not believe in Islam. The first of these jihads took place in the eighteenth century in the Futa Djallon and the Futa Toro. The importance of these two early jihads was as forerunners to the great jihads that brought much of West Africa under Muslim control in the nineteenth century.

2 States of the western Atlantic coast

One area of the Western Sudan that did not come under strong Muslim influence until the nineteenth century was the western Atlantic coast. Few of the peoples living on or behind the stretch of the West African coast from the River Gambia to the Western borders of Asante had organised states. They were either ruled by petty chiefs, such as the Mende and Temne of Sierra Leone, and the Mandinka of the Gambia, or lived in non-centralised societies, as did the Bete, Kissi, Dan and Kru peoples of modern Liberia and Ivory Coast. We have already discussed such peoples in Chapter 3. In Senegal, however, when the Portuguese first reached it in 1445, there had already been established the large Wollof Empire, and further in the interior the state of Futa Toro. The only other important state to emerge south of the Western Sudan and west of Asante was that of Futa Djallon in the eighteenth century.

3 The Wollof Empire

The Wollof Empire at the time of the arrival of the Portuguese covered most of modern Senegal. To the north it was bounded by the River Senegal across which were to be found the Moors of present day Mauritania. To the north-east it was bounded by the semi-desert Ferlo, beyond which lay Futa Toro. To the east it was bounded by states which came under the rule of Mali. To the south it was bounded by the River Gambia where the Mandinka inhabitants lived in small chieftaincies.

The Wollof Empire consisted of six states. The most important was Djollof whose ruler, the Bourba Djollof, was paramount over the other five: Walo, Cayor, Baol, Sine and Saloum. The majority of the inhabitants of this Empire were Wollofs or Serers. The capital of the Empire was at Linguère, some 150 kilometres inland.

With the arrival of the Portuguese, the coastal kingdoms of the Empire, Walo, Cayor, Baol, Sine and Saloum, began to be more important than Djollof itself. The Portuguese started trading for gold which was brought to the coast from Bambuk and Bure, which had previously supplied the Mali Empire with its gold. The Portuguese also bought slaves, but not on such a large scale as they did further down the coast, for the peoples of this region

9.1   *A drawing of a Wollof trader made in the early nineteenth century by the Senegalese Abbé Boilat.*

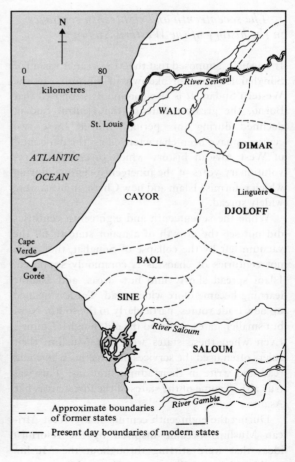

Map 9.1   The Wollof Empire.

were found not to make such good slaves as those from the Gold Coast or the Niger Delta.

It seems that as a result of the growing prosperity which trade with the Europeans brought these coastal kingdoms, they were able to gain their independence from the Bourba Djollof. By the seventeenth century all of them were independent and the Bourba Djollof himself was paying tribute to Futa Toro. This important state, successor to Takrur, lay along the fertile valley of the River Senegal.

The Wollof Empire was distinguished by a very special social organisation. Society was divided into castes, and people in one caste could not marry people from another caste. First there were the royals. Then came the free men which included non-royal nobles, known as *guer*. Beneath them were the artisan castes: blacksmiths, jewellers, weavers and leather-workers. Another separate group were the *griots*, whose duty was to remember to sing the traditions of their masters. A final group were the slaves. These were divided into two classes: those who belonged to particular families, known as domestic slaves, and those who could be sold freely. Some of the domestic slaves became very powerful, since their masters felt they were more reliable than free-men. Indeed in all the states of the Wollof Empire the slave bodyguards of the king, known as

the *Tiedo*, became so powerful that they formed a new nobility. In the nineteenth century they largely controlled the Djollof and Serer Kingdoms.

The history of the former Wollof Empire in the seventeenth and eighteenth centuries is largely that of continuing struggle between its former states. A major factor in this struggle was the growing influence of Islam in the area. Those who had become Muslims followed leaders called *Marabouts*, men who were devout and often learned Muslims. The Wollof and Serer kings saw them as a threat to their position and often persecuted them. We shall see, in following chapters, that this conflict between Muslim reformers and their rulers, which began in the eighteenth century, was to change the course of West African history in the nineteenth century.

4 Futa Djallon and Futa Toro

The first successful jihad led by Fulani Muslim reformists was in the Futa Djallon in the Guinea highlands. Non-Muslim Fulani had been migrating into this area over a long period of time. By the end of the sixteenth century they were spread all over the Futa Djallon, living peacefully alongside their Mande neighbours, the Dialonke, Susu and Malinke. However, towards the end of the seventeenth century a large number of Fulani came to settle in the Futa Djallon from Macina because of the unsettled situation there. This sudden increase in the number of Fulani settlers, some of whom were Muslim, upset the non-Muslim Dialonke. As a result there were clashes between the two groups.

In 1725 one of the Fulani Muslim leaders, Karamoko Alfa, called on his people to revolt against the non-Muslim Dialonke. For over half a century the Fulani Muslims did battle with the Dialonke, while establishing a state based on the principles of the *sharia* or Muslim law. Their ruler was called the *Almami* or chief priest or judge. When he was turbanned he was told 'Futa is balanced on your head like a pot of fresh milk. Do not stumble or else the milk will spill'.

Karamoko Alfa was succeeded by his cousin Ibrahima Sori. Thereafter the office of Almamy rotated every two years between the family of

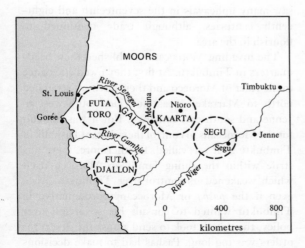

Map 9.2   Futa Djallon, Futa Toro, Segu and Kaarta.

Karamoko Alfa (*Alfaya*) and Ibrahima Sori (*Soraya*). However, there was great rivalry between the two families which, despite the rule of change every two years, did not like to see the other family in office. This led to much strife between them including civil war. However, the state survived this because of the unity Islam gave it. By the end of the eighteenth century the state was firmly established and its rulers were able to raid for slaves and these, with gold from Bure, enabled it to carry on a flourishing trade with the Rivières du Sud (Rivers of the South).

The second successful jihad by Muslims against non-Muslim rulers was in Futa Toro in the Senegal River valley. The Denianke rulers were non-Muslim Fulanis, whilst the Torobe were the Fulani Muslim faction. Led by Suleiman Bal, the Torobe rose in revolt against the *Silatigui*, or pagan king, and overthrew him and the Denianke in 1776. Once the Muslims were in power they built mosques in every village and Islam became the state religion.

While Suleiman Bal refused to become head of the new Muslim state, when he died, his companion, Abdoul Kader, became spiritual and political leader of Futa Toro with the title of Almamy. He reigned until 1804 when he was murdered at the age of eighty-one.

5 Segu and Kaarta

To the east of Futa Toro and to the north of Futa Djallon lay the Bambara states of Segu and Kaarta. Though their rulers were mainly non-Muslims, Islam was an important influence in the administrations of these states. While the majority of the inhabitants of Segu were Bambara, the most powerful group were the Massasi, a mixture of Bambara, Fulani and Berber. The leading Massasi family was the Koulibali. Another important group in the Segu region were the Marka who were Muslim traders with their headquarters at Kirango.

In 1740 Mamari Koulibali, who was partly Marka, attacked Kirango and founded the Segu State. The secret of his strength was the way he made all his followers and all the men in his state his personal slaves. He governed his people with the assistance of a special corps of slaves known as the ton-dyon. These slaves owed absolute loyalty to him and as a result he became practically a dictator of his state. However, when he died in 1755 his successors found it difficult to control the ton-dyon. Several rulers were assassinated by them. It was not until 1766 when a powerful military leader from the Diara clan took the throne that peace was restored to Segu. Ngolo Diara, who reigned from 1766 to 1790, succeeded in replacing the Koulibali by the Diara. It was his son, Mansong, whom Mungo Park met when he visited Segu.

To the north of Segu another group of Massasi were settled at Beledugu. In 1753 they clashed with Mamari Koulibali who nearly wiped them out. The survivors of the battle moved into the Kaarta region where they established a second Bambara state. They eventually built their capital at Guemou. Desse Koro, who ruled Kaarta from 1788 to 1799, tried to attack Segu on several occasions. Though at first they were successful because of the disorders in Segu, when Mansong came to the throne of Segu he drove them back and destroyed Guemou. Till the end of the eighteenth century, then, Segu remained the more powerful of the two Bambara states.

6 The Niger Bend area

The region east of Segu and west of Hausaland which had been the heartland of the Songhai Empire saw many upheavals in the seventeenth and eighteenth centuries, although trade continued to flourish in the area.

The invading Moroccans established their headquarters in Timbuktu. At first they owed allegiance to the ruler of Morocco and their territory stretched north to Marrakesh, east to Gao, south-west to Jenne and south-east to Mossi. But it was difficult for the Moroccans to control their distant Pashalik of Timbuktu as it was called. Furthermore, there was strife within the ruling family in Morocco itself which weakened its control over Timbuktu. Also, even if the *pasha* or Moroccan representative in Timbuktu wanted to consult his sovereign over policy, the time it took to send across the desert for orders was too long. Pashas had to make decisions quickly, especially as the people they had conquered

9.2 *Timbuktu as seen by Rene Caillié the French traveller and first white man to visit Timbuktu in 1823 and then return to Europe. His account of Timbuktu was widely disbelieved. Some Europeans believed the city was much larger than he described it.*

often tried to revolt against them. By 1660 the Moroccans of Timbuktu, who became known as the Arma, were effectively independent of Morocco.

Their rule was not strong. Tuaregs and Berber living in the desert were attracted by the rich lands held by the Arma. Two major groups of Tuareg, the Aulimaden and the Tadmakka began to seek control of rich lands of the Niger bend. The Arma leaders of Timbuktu weakened their position by calling on Tuareg, Berber and Bambara mercenaries to support them in their attempts to gain the office of Pasha. By 1734 the Tuareg were at the gates of Timbuktu and in 1737, after raiding the city on several occasions, the Tadmakka Tuaregs made Timbuktu their tributary.

9.3 *Tuareg warriors. After the conquest of the Songhai Empire by the Moroccans the Tuareg became militarily and politically more influential on the Niger.*

9.4 & 5 *Kano City walls seen from the inside (left). They were entered by gates which could be closed in times of attack (right). Today the wall is crumbling badly but some of the gates have been restored.*

The Tadmakka and Aulimaden Tuareg now controlled the rich heartland of the former Songhai Empire. While the Tadmakka controlled Timbuktu, the Aulimadan gained control of Gao.

7 Hausaland 1600–1800

The seventeenth and eighteenth centuries saw the rise of Zamfara and then Katsina to the position of the most important trading cities in the Central Sudan. They were strategically placed on the trans-Saharan trade route through Agades to Tripoli. This same period saw the decline in power of Kebbi which was under constant attack by Zamfara, Gobir and Aïr.

Before 1650 Katsina's prosperity was threatened by its constant wars with Kano but around 1650 the two settled their differences and there were no more wars between them. The main threat to Katsina came from its western neighbour, Gobir, which was extending its power southwards and eastwards. Though Zamfara was at first more important than Gobir, it was preoccupied with fighting Kebbi. Gobir, however, was able to attack both Kebbi and Katsina. Another threat to Katsina's security were the long-distance raids by the Kwararafa from the Benue Valley.

Despite all this, Katsina prospered commercially and became a major centre for Islamic scholars.

However, it was not within the rich city of Katsina that the first major demands for Islamic reform came, but in neighbouring Gobir. By the end of the eighteenth century, Gobir had at last established itself as the most powerful state in Hausaland. But this had resulted in the peasants being heavily taxed and there was considerable discontent among them. Not only the peasants were discontented, but also the growing class of Muslims in the state. They saw the rulers of Gobir and indeed of all the Hausa states as corrupt and bad Muslims. Soon they began to call for change and in this they were lead by a learned scholar, Usman dan Fodio. It was he who, as we shall see in the next chapter, was to overthrow the Hausa kings, known as Habe, and establish a pure Muslim state over all Hausaland.

8 Borno 1600–1800

During the seventeenth and eighteenth centuries in West Africa the only state that could properly be called Muslim was Borno. Mai Idris Alooma had ensured the internal security of Borno and had made it respected over a wide area. His successors in the seventeenth century consolidated the frontiers and many states placed themselves under Borno's protection. The invasions of the Kwararafa in the seventeenth century failed to weaken the state but the continual raiding of the northern frontiers by the

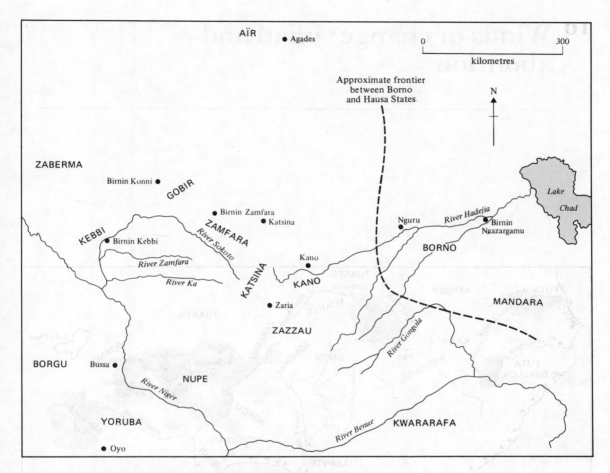

Map 9.3   Hausaland and Borno in the seventeenth and eighteenth centuries.

Tuareg led to large-scale population movements. The rulers of Borno in the eighteenth century were pious and have often been accused of lethargy in defending their inheritance but it seems that they frequently led their armies to war even if they became less and less successful on the battlefield. Military weakness seems to have been accompanied by economic decline as emigrant Kanuri and others established more efficient trading networks to the east and west of Borno.

Throughout this period Islam spread and flourished. Borno was a great centre of scholarship under the patronage of the mais – themselves frequently fine scholars – many of whom made the pilgrimage. It was only after Borno had aided the rulers of the Hausa states against the forces of the jihad that dan Fodio accused the mais of unbelief. An occusation rejected by another great scholar, Muhammad el-Amin El-Kanemi who was to take over the reins of government from the mais.

10 Winds of change: jihad and abolition

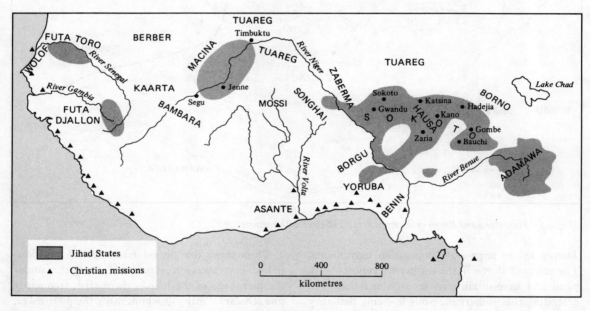

Map 10.1   Nineteenth century jihad states and missionary outposts before 1880.

1 The nineteenth century jihads

In 1804 a learned Fulani scholar, Usman dan Fodio, declared a jihad against the Habe kings of Hausaland. He and his followers were determined to reform society in Hausaland where the practice of Islam was not pure. They accused the rulers of Hausaland of being pagans, and declared that though they called themselves Muslims they did not obey the sharia or Muslim law. Within a decade most of Hausaland as well as parts of Borno and what are now Bauchi and Adamawa came under the control of the jihadists.

From their new capital at Sokoto, the leaders of the jihad set about reforming government in the lands they had conquered along the lines laid down by the sharia. What they sought was a return to the standards of government and justice maintained by the first four Caliphs who ruled the Muslim world after the death of the Prophet Mohammed. Already, as we saw in Chapter 9, there had been jihads in Futa Djallon and Futa Toro in the eighteenth century where the Fulani had overthrown the ruling dynasties in order to set up Muslim governments organised according to the sharia. There had, indeed, been a number of other small revolutions in which Muslims tried to take over control of non-Muslim governments before the jihad of Usman dan Fodio. And soon after his jihad, another was launched in Macina by Seku Ahmadu (also known as Ahmad Lobbo), who looked to Usman dan Fodio for inspiration. Seku Ahmadu established a state governed strictly according to the sharia. Macina was swallowed up some fifty years later by another jihad, that of Al Hajj Umar, a Tukolor from the Senegal River valley who became leader of the Tijanniya order of Muslims in West Africa (see p. 123). He claimed that on 6th September 1852, God commanded him to conquer all those who refused to accept his call to Islam. By the time of his death in 1864, he had carved out a huge Empire stretching from the eastern Senegal River valley to the borders of Sokoto. Other smaller jihads were launched in the Senegambia with the same object of establishing governments under Muslim law. But before the end of the nineteenth century, just at the time of the European conquest, another great Muslim leader emerged to bring vast areas, in which hitherto indigenous African religions had reigned supreme, under Muslim government. This was Samori Toure who established his authority at one time or another over areas stretching from the borders of Futa Djallon in the west to Asante in the east, to Bamako in the north and the forests of Ivory Coast and Liberia in the south. There is some dispute among scholars as to whether Samori Toure can be considered a jihadist in the same sense as Usman dan Fodio and Al Hajj Umar. But we will discuss this later (see p. 126). What is important is that he, like the others, brought large areas of West Africa under systematic Muslim government. Thus, on the eve of the European conquest, nearly two-thirds of West Africa was ruled by Muslim governments. One of the most important themes in nineteenth century West Africa, then, was the fact that the Muslim way of life was spread both through missionary zeal and by the use of force over a huge area.

2 *The abolition of the slave trade*

In 1807, when Britain abolished slave trading by its own nationals, another revolution, inspired by missionary zeal and later to be carried on by force, was underway. At the time, the British Parliament which passed the act abolishing the slave trade could hardly have seen that it would have as great long term effects on West Africa as did the jihads. The impact of the jihad was felt at once by those against whom it was launched. If they lost to the jihadists, they were either forcibly converted to Islam or at least subjected to rule by Muslims. On the face of it the simple act of abolition of the slave trade by Britain merely stopped slave traders of one European nation trading in slaves with Africans. But the matter was not so simple. In the first place the slave trade was so profitable for some British sea captains that they would risk execution to continue buying and selling Africans. So the British, to enforce abolition, sent out naval ships to intercept British ships carrying slaves. Later, when Britain had persuaded other European nations to abolish the slave trade, it made treaties with them whereby the British navy could search their ships for slaves. Such ships were taken to Freetown, capital of the new British Colony, and their captains were tried before a Court of Mixed Commission, that is a court on which judges from both Britain and the European nation concerned sat. The freed slaves, like those from the British slavers, were settled in Freetown.

The abolition of the slave trade suited the interests of many of those who supported the Bill in the British Parliament because they wanted to trade in West Africa's natural resources rather than in its men. They also wanted, as one historian has put it, to deal with Africans as customers rather than as merchandise. The industrial revolution in Britain, by producing cheap manufactured goods on a large scale, made it necessary to look for new markets. Africa provided one such market. It also provided important raw materials for the new industries of Britain; in particular palm-oil. But commerce was not the only motive for abolishing the slave trade. There were devout Christians who had come sincerely to believe that to enslave men and to buy and sell them was a sin against God. Therefore the slave

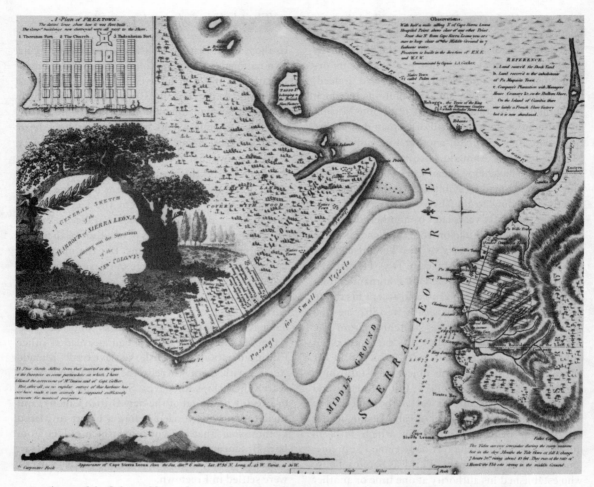

10.1 *A map of the Colony of Sierra Leone made in 1795. Sierra Leone was first established as a settlement for freed slaves at the end of the eighteenth century. Later, with the abolition of the slave trade by Britain, it became the headquarters of the anti-slavery patrol.*

trade should be stopped by force if necessary. Not only did the humanitarians, as such people came to be known, want to stop the slave trade but they wanted to abolish *all* forms of slavery. In 1833, largely due to their pressure, the status of slave was abolished in all British possessions. But of course this did not apply in those areas of Africa outside British control. And in 1833 Britain had very few, and only small colonies in West Africa: the Gambia, Sierra Leone, and a few trading castles along the Gold Coast. So the humanitarians sponsored missionaries to go out to Africa and preach the gospel of Christ in the hopes that through conversion Africans would give up trading in their fellow human beings and give up other practices they considered undesirable such as human sacrifice, cannibalism and twin-murder. Though here, we must point out that the missionaries greatly exaggerated the prevalence of such practices.

Just as the Muslim reformers of Sokoto had at first tried to introduce Muslim reform by preaching, the Christian missionaries used preaching to introduce the Christian way of life. By the end of the nineteenth century, however, the Christian govern-

10.2 & 3 *Sierra Leone also became the headquarters for British missionary activity in West Africa. Many of the slaves freed by the anti-slavery patrol were settled in Christian villages near Freetown, like Bathurst (left), where Bishop Crowther gained his first education and Regent (right), where he was schoolmaster in 1830.*

ments of Western Europe were to use force to bring Africa under their rule. While, as we shall see later, the reasons for the European conquest were many and varied, the forcible subjection of Africans, whether Muslim or non-Muslim, to their rule can be seen as not dissimilar to the approach of the jihad leaders. At the end of the nineteenth century most Europeans were still Christian. While Church and State were separate, the occupation of West Africa was justified in part by the fact that 'civilisation', or

the European-Christian way of life, was being brought to Africans. That is they would be subjected to the standards of government and law acceptable to Christian Europe.

Of course, as we have seen, there were strong economic motives for the occupation; the missionaries themselves supported the traders and industrialists who wished to open up Africa to European commerce. They believed strongly in the virtue of labour. Slavery would only disappear if Africans had alternative methods of gaining a livelihood: they believed this would be supplied by trade with Europe in 'legitimate' goods, as distinct from illegal slaves. Accordingly they encouraged legitimate trade in palm-oil, groundnuts, cotton and timber.

Missionaries, too, supported the European conquest of Africa because in the end, they came to see it would be easier for them to spread the gospel under the protection of European rather than African governments. And, indeed, as a result of the European occupation many thousands of Africans did become Christians.

3 The jihadists and humanitarians compared

What is important to appreciate in the study of nineteenth century West Africa is that there were close parallels between what the jihadists and

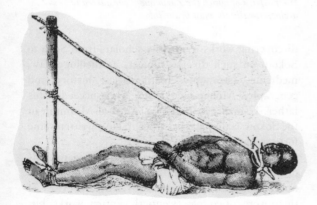

10.4 *Despite the efforts of the Anti-Slavery patrol the export of slaves continued from West Africa until the mid-1860s. John Baptist Desalu, pictured here after his capture, was an Egba Christian convert, who was taken prisoner in 1851 after the Dahomeyan attack on Abeokuta. He was sold to slave dealers and shipped to Cuba where, on the intervention of the British Government, he was set free.*

humanitarians were trying to achieve. Both sought to impose their ideas on how life should be lived on the peoples of West Africa. But here there was a major difference: the leaders of the jihads were themselves West Africans, while for the most part the humanitarians were Europeans or Americans. Both wanted to establish as supreme, religions which acknowledged one God, and in this case the same God although worshipped differently. Most Africans who were neither Muslims nor Christians, whilst they believed in a High God, also believed in many other lesser gods. That is they were polytheists (believers in many gods) rather than monotheists (believers in one god). Both Muslims and Christians believed that their way of life was the best possible and that it was their duty to impose this way of life on those not fortunate enough to share it. Both Christianity and Islam are missionary religions. Now most African religions, with one or two notable exceptions, were not missionary religions. Rather, each ethnic group had its own religion and did not seek to impose it on other ethnic groups. With both Islam and Christianity went a system of government and justice which was derived either directly or indirectly from their Holy Books, the Koran and the Bible. In the case of the Christians, their legal and governmental systems were only indirectly based on the teachings of Christ. But in the case of the Muslims, the Koran provided the rules for good government and departure from these rules meant that a government was not strictly speaking, Muslim.

Both Islam and Christianity are religions of the Book: the Koran and the Bible. Thus literacy was inextricably tied up with both. Both religions believed in the virtue of literacy since it helped converts to read their Holy Books. Both, too, have great educational traditions associated not only with the deepening of understanding of their Holy Books, but with the operation of government and law and of the trade that supported the state. One of the results of the jihads of the nineteenth century was the spread of education in Arabic throughout the Western Sudan. We have seen that this had been important before the jihads of the nineteenth century, but as a result of these jihads education spread at an unprecedented rate. We are still, for instance,

10.5   *The great Mosque at Zaria. As a result of the jihads of the nineteenth century a great many mosques were built in West Africa of which the Zaria one is considered to be architecturally the most beautiful.*

discovering works written by scholars from Segu to Sokoto on such diverse subjects as theology, law, medicine, astronomy, mathematics, history and geography. Mohammed Bello, who succeeded his father, Usman dan Fodio, as Amir-al-Muminin of the Sokoto Caliphate, is known to have written some forty works.

The Christian missionaries, too, became indirectly responsible for the production of a large number of books and articles by Africans. Most of them were, of course, twentieth century works, but those of Samuel Johnson, Samuel Ajayi Crowther, Abbé Boilat and Carl Christian Reindorf to name a few of the nineteenth century, are an impressive testimony to the impact of Christian education.

Both religions taught that all men are equal in the sight of God, and that a man's colour, tribe or language did not matter. Thus, in an ethnically fragmented continent, they provided a major unifying force. Both jihadists and European conquerors established states where a uniform system of law prevailed and within whose frontiers trade and movement were secure. Finally, both religions, being world religions, brought their converts into a wider world community which looked beyond the shores of Africa.

4 Conclusion

As a result of these two reforming movements, most West Africans today are either Muslim or Christian.

The surprising fact emerges that whereas all West Africans came under Christian-European rule in the twentieth century, Islam made greater progress than Christianity. A number of factors may account for this. Islam had been established in West Africa since the tenth century, and by the twentieth century nearly all Muslim missionaries in West Africa were West Africans. Despite the fact that Christian

Europeans had been trading with West Africans since the fifteenth century, until the nineteenth century they showed little interest in converting them to their own religion. In the nineteenth and twentieth centuries most Christian missionaries were foreigners. Christian missionaries required potential converts to undergo a period of instruction in their religion before they could be accepted as Christians. For someone who wished to become a Muslim it was sufficient to declare himself one. Very important, too, Islam accepted polygamy which European Christianity did not. What could the potential Christian convert do if he had more than one wife?

We have discussed in considerable detail the impact of two world religions and their way of life on West Africa in the nineteenth and twentieth centuries. But we must be careful not to think of these as the only two important factors in the history of this period. As we shall see in succeeding chapters there were many areas of West African life that were not affected by them. But they did introduce radical new ideas into West Africa which no history of the area can afford to ignore.

11 The Sokoto Caliphate and Borno in the nineteenth century

1 Usman dan Fodio's jihad

The greatest and certainly the most influential of the nineteenth century jihads was that of Usman dan Fodio. He was a Fulani of the Torodbe clan which had migrated to Gobir, in north-western Hausaland, many generations before. He was born in 1754 into a scholarly family and he and his younger brother, Abdullahi, were given a broad Islamic education.

At the time of his youth Gobir, as we have seen, had become the most powerful of the Hausa states, dominating in particular Zamfara and Kebbi. Gobir's domination was hated. The people generally resented the heavy taxation that was used to maintain the armies and to make the big men in society greater and richer than before. The weak feared enslavement by the strong. Though the Habe kings thought of themselves as Muslims, they did not always follow Muslim law and often tolerated and even participated in 'pagan' practices. The Muslim communities of Hausaland deeply resented the 'paganism' of their rulers and their failure to observe the sharia. Many ordinary people resented the oppressions of their rulers so that when Usman dan Fodio, at the age of twenty, returned to Gobir from Agades, where he had been taught by the Muslim revolutionary teacher, Jibril, there were many who were willing to listen to someone who would attack their rulers.

Usman dan Fodio was a fine teacher and as a preacher could hold the attention of large crowds. When he criticised the Hausa rulers for their bad government he found an eager response from his listeners.

Furthermore, at that time many believed in prophecies that the end of the world was near. It was said that in the thirteenth century after the Prophet Mohammed, the Mahdi would come to prepare the way for the end of the world. Usman dan Fodio denied that he was the Mahdi, but said he was his fore-runner.

In such circumstances, many flocked to join Usman dan Fodio who was becoming a major political force in Gobir. So much so that Bawa, King of Gobir, recognised his community and the right of his followers to wear the distinguishing clothes of a Muslim, turbans in the case of men and veils in the case of women. Usman established his community at Degel on the borders of Gobir and Zamfara. It was effectively independent of Gobir, and provided an example of what good Muslim government should be, contrasting strongly with that of Gobir.

Bawa's successor, Nafata, felt himself threatened by Usman dan Fodio's growing community and tried to reduce his influence. He forbad the Muslims to wear turbans and veils and attacked Usman's followers. It was Nafata's son, Yunfa, who really tried to rid himself of Usman dan Fodio's influence. He summoned him to his court and shot him with a pistol. But it backfired and burnt Yunfa's face. Although he failed to kill Usman, Yunfa attacked and seized his disciples. On one occasion a group of Muslim captives passing near Degel was freed by Usman dan Fodio's followers. A critical situation

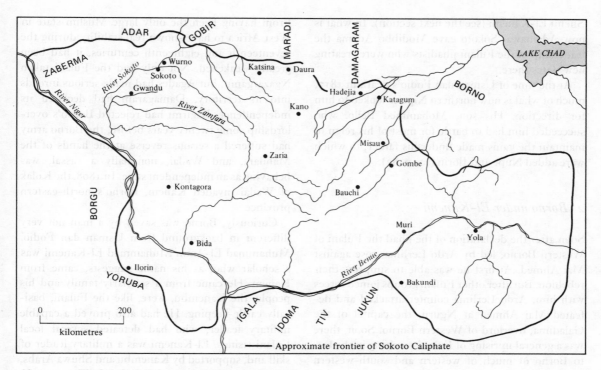

Map 11.1   The Sokoto Caliphate and Borno under El-Kanemi.

had now developed. Yunfa ordered dan Fodio and his followers to leave Degel. Usman therefore told them they would emigrate, or perform the *hijra* as the Prophet had from Mecca to Medina, but in Usman's case from Degel to Gudu, beyond the borders of Gobir. From there the Muslims would launch a jihad against their oppressors.

Usman dan Fodio was elected Amir-al-Muminin or Commander of the Faithful by his followers in February 1804 and they began to arm themselves for war. Meanwhile Yunfa's forces pursued him and at Tabkin Kwatto they were defeated in a remarkable battle where the heavy cavalry of Gobir proved no match for the small band of Muslims who had greater mobility and a deadly weapon in their Fulani bows with poisoned arrows.

Usman dan Fodio now proclaimed jihad against all the 'pagan' Hausa rulers. He sent letters to them saying they should reform or else face the consequences. Only Zazzau (Zaria) responded to his call. Muslim leaders, mainly Fulani, from all over northern Nigeria came to Usman dan Fodio to get

his blessing for their own revolutions against their 'pagan' overlords. To these leaders he gave flags which they should carry into battle against their oppressors.

It took the Shehu, as Usman dan Fodio was known, four years and several reverses before he finally took Alkalawa, the capital of Gobir, in 1808. During those years the war leaders became more important than the scholars, and the Fulani became the dominant group among the jihadists. Indeed some Hausa Muslims, in disgust at the dominating role of the Fulani and the pillaging of the land by the jihadists, joined the Habe rulers.

But these difficulties apart, the jihad swept the savannah like a fire. Its success was due largely to the unity, leadership and strength of support possessed by the jihadists and the lack of co-operation among the Habe rulers. In 1809 Zaria, which now had a ruler who rejected dan Fodio's call to reform, Katsina and Kano all fell to the jihadists. In 1808 the Mai of Borno was driven out of his capital, though he was later reinstated by a Kanembu Sheik, known as

Shehu El-Kanemi (see the next section). In what is now Adamawa, Sokoto gave Modibbo Adama the leadership of the Fulani jihadists who were creating new states there.

At the time of Usman dan Fodio's death in 1817, much of what is now northern Nigeria looked to him for direction. His son, Mohammed Bello, who succeeded him had to battle for most of his reign to maintain the gains made under his father, to which were added Nupe and Ilorin (see p. 82).

2   *Borno under El-Kanemi*

Soon after the declaration of the jihad the Fulani of Western Borno, led by Ardo Lerlima, rose against Mai Ahmed. At first he was able to suppress their rebellion. But after other Fulani groups joined forces with him, Ardo Lerlima counter-attacked and defeated Mai Ahmed at Nguru, the capital of the Galadima, overlord of Western Borno. Soon, there was a general uprising of Fulani resulting in the loss to Borno of much of western and south-western Borno. The new Fulani emirates of Katagum, Gombe, Misau and Hadejia were carved out of Borno territory. In 1808 the Fulani actually took the Mai's capital of Ngazargamu. It seemed then that Borno would fall to the Fulani and become part of the Sokoto Caliphate.

In 1808 Borno was in a weak position indeed.

From having been the only large Muslim state in West Africa to have shown real stability during the seventeenth and eighteenth centuries, it had been greatly weakened. Not only had the Fulani taken Ngazargamu, but Agades had made serious inroads into its territory, Damagaram had declared its independence, Bagirmi had rejected Borno's overlordship some twenty years before, the Borno army had suffered a serious reverse at the hands of the Mandara, and Wadai, nominally a vassal, was behaving as an independent state. In 1808, the Kolak of Wadai invaded Kanem, Borno's north-eastern province.

Curiously, Borno was saved by a man not very different in background from Usman dan Fodio. Muhammad El-Amin Muhammad El-Kanemi was a scholar who, as his name suggests, came from Kanem. He came from a scholarly family and his people, the Kanembu, were, like the Fulani, basically cattle-keeping. He had also proved a capable military leader, who had defeated several local Fulani risings. El-Kanemi was a military leader of skill and, supported by Kanembu and Shuwa Arabs, he re-took Ngazargamu for the Mai.

After the fall of Ngazargamu, Mai Ahmed, who was very old and blind, retired from the throne in favour of his son, Dunama. It was Dunama who called on El-Kanemi to assist him in re-capturing the capital. For his help he was rewarded handsomely by the Mai. However, he preferred to return

11.1   *El-Kanemi, Shehu of Borno.*

11.2   *Kanembu warriors. They and Shuwa Arabs formed the backbone of El-Kanemi's army when he came to the aid of the Mai of Borno against the Fulani.*

11.3 *Kukawa, the capital of El-Kanemi, as seen by the traveller, Heinrich Barth, in 1851.*

to his home at Ngala, rather than live in the Mai's court.

Again in 1809 the Fulani took Ngazargamu, and after El-Kanemi retook it Dunama was deposed in favour of his uncle, Muhammad Ngileruma. Like Dunama, Mai Ngileruma relied heavily on El-Kanemi for support, and the latter now became a major power in Borno. Indeed, he plotted successfully with Dunama to restore him to the throne in return for a large area of land which he would administer. Dunama was now very much a puppet of El-Kanemi, who even built his own capital thirty kilometres north of the Mai's new capital at Birnin Kufela. Mai Dunama then tried to ally with Bagirmi against El-Kanemi, promising its ruler his independence if he could rid him of his rival. Unfortunately for Dunama, his letters were intercepted by spies of El-Kanemi, who thus discovered his battle plans and was able to defeat his army and kill the Mai himself. From then on the real ruler in Borno was El-Kanemi. As Commander Clapperton, the British explorer, remarked in 1820 when he visited El-Kanemi 'The Sultanship (Mai) of Borno, however, is but a name. . . . .'

After the second battle of Ngazargamu, Sokoto made no further attacks into Borno. They did however continue to believe that the jihad against Borno, even though it was a Muslim state, was

justified. Mohammed Bello and El-Kanemi entered into bitter correspondence in which Bello accused Borno of tolerating pagan practices and persecuting Muslims. El-Kanemi replied that by Bello's definition of what constituted a Muslim not even Egypt could be considered a Muslim country. He also told Sokoto that the best way to teach people the true way of Islam was not to attack them, for the accidental killing of Muslims in a jihad was far worse than allowing unbelievers to continue their pagan practices.

El-Kanemi and the mais successfully defended Borno against further inroads by the Fulani largely because the bulk of the Kanuri peasantry remained loyal to the Mai, and also the scholars, led by El-Kanemi, supported him. Where scholars, cattle nomads and much of the peasantry supported Usman dan Fodio against the Hausa kings, by and large scholars, peasants and cattle nomads, like the Kanembu and Shuwa – though of course not the Fulani – supported the mai against the jihadists.

El-Kanemi was content to rule Borno in fact rather than name. The Mai of Borno had become largely a ceremonial figure like the Queen of England today. By keeping the Mai on the throne, he also secured the good-will of many who might have regretted the passing of the Sefawa dynasty. In 1837 El-Kanemi died and was succeeded by his son,

Umar, who like his father took only the title of Shehu. However, in 1846 Ibrahim, successor to Dunama as Mai, tried to restore the authority of the Sefawa dynasty. In that year there was a revolt in Damagaram, which was once again under Borno, and while Shehu Umar was preoccupied with this, Mai Ibrahim called on the ruler of Wadai for support. Ibrahim's treachery was discovered and he was executed. But Wadai successfully invaded Borno and sacked Kukawa installing Ali, the teenage son of Ibrahim, on the throne.

Umar negotiated his return and the withdrawal of Wadai while the young Mai was killed in an ensuing battle. No new Mai was appointed and an end was brought to the thousand year old Sefawa dynasty. Umar was now ruler of Borno in name as well as in fact. Later we will discuss the changes in the administration of Borno brought about by Umar and his father.

3 The jihad in the south

The first objective of the jihadists had been the overthrow of the Habe kings of Hausaland. Then they attacked the Caliphate of Borno. However, their ambitions extended beyond those areas of northern Nigeria in which Islam had long been established. In 1806 Modibbo Adama travelled from the Benue River valley area, where many Fulani had settled, to obtain a flag from Usman dan Fodio. On his return he and his followers subdued the diverse 'pagan' ethnic groups of what is now called Adamawa, after his name, and created the Emirate of Fombina with its capital at Yola. Further south, in about 1833, Hammaruwa established the Emirate of Muri, also in an area largely inhabited by non-Muslims, and comprising some of the northern territories of the Jukun. In what is now Bauchi, Yakub, the only non-Fulani flag-bearer, founded the town of Bauchi in 1809 as headquarters of a huge new Emirate that comprised a largely non-Muslim population.

To the south, in Nupeland, a Fulani scholar, called Mallam Dendo, took advantage of civil strife in the ancient Nupe Kingdom and eventually took it over in the name of the jihad. When Muhammad,

Etsu or King of the Nupe, died, his son Majia succeeded as Etsu but was challenged by his cousin Jumadu. Mallam Dendo, who had been a court adviser, backed by the considerable number of Fulani who had settled in Nupe, skilfully played one faction off against the other. When Majia defeated Jumada, he gave his support to the latter's son Idris and together they drove Majia out of his capital. Mallam Dendo became the real power in Nupe but it was not until after his death in 1832 that the Fulani were finally able to take over the state.

At the time of the Fulani jihad the great Oyo Empire was on the verge of collapse (see below p. 86). Around 1817 Afonja, the Are-ona-Kakanfo or Commander in Chief of the Oyo armies, who was based in Ilorin, declared his independence of the Alafin. To achieve this, he joined forces with a powerful Muslim of Ilorin, Solagberu. But to maintain his position he had to rely on soldiers supplied by Mallam Alimi, a Fulani scholar who had settled in Ilorin.

Although Mallam Alimi was not a flag-bearer of the jihad, the fact that Afonja and Solagberu had to rely on his support meant that the Fulani had gained an indirect foothold in Ilorin. On his death, his son, Abdulsalami, tried to seize power and with the aid of Solagberu, turned on Afonja. The latter was defeated, and soon after Solagberu was killed by Abdulsalami. The result was that Ilorin became the southern outpost of the Fulani jihad, though Abdulsalami was not given a flag until about 1829. We shall discuss later the battles Ilorin fought with Oyo and its allies to maintain its independence.

4 The administration of Sokoto

By about 1830 the Sokoto Caliphate had established the frontiers it was to maintain roughly intact throughout the nineteenth Century. The credit for this is largely due to the Caliph Mohammed Bello. At all points where there was danger of invasion by rulers who had been driven out of their kingdoms by the jihads, *ribats* or fortified towns were established. For instance, a series were built on the north-western frontier to deal with the Zamfarawa, Gobirawa and Kebbawa. During his reign, Mohammed

Bello was as often at war as he was in his capital administering the Caliphate. And this situation continued under his successor right through the century until the British conquest.

There is so much information about the Sokoto Caliphate during the nineteenth century that it would be impossible to summarise it in this introductory history. What we can do is look at the way this huge Empire was organised. The capital, Sokoto, was situated in the extreme north-western corner, as was Gwandu, the twin, but subordinate capital, ruled by the successors of Abdullahi, the brother of the Shehu. While the Caliph at Sokoto was supreme overlord, the western emirates of Ilorin, Bida (Nupe) and Kontagora, founded in about 1859, were administered from Gwandu whose ruler was thus a super-Emir.

As we have noted, the Caliph at Sokoto was fully occupied in defending his capital against Kebbi, Zamfara, the Tuareg and, of course, Gobir. He certainly did not have the time nor the troops to suppress rebellions, or attempts to assert their independence on the part of his subordinate emirs. How then, did he control emirs as distant as Bauchi and Yola? To understand this we must appreciate that the Caliph's control of his emirs was based not on his military superiority but on his religious authority. The emirs had sworn their allegiance to him as their Amir-al-Muminin or their Commander of the Faithful. As good Muslims, to break that allegiance would be to commit a sin. Thus it was, that right through the century the Caliph controlled the appointment of emirs, received tributes from them as well as military support, and once a year received them all in his court at Sokoto to pay him homage. His Waziri, or Vizier, made frequent tours of inspection of the emirates directly under Sokoto as did the Waziri of Gwandu of those emirates in the Western sector. When there was a dispute as to who should succeed to an emirship, the claimants would travel to Sokoto to have the Caliph settle it. They also feared that if they did not go to Sokoto, the Caliph might give a flag to someone to carve a new emirate out of their own territory, or else support rivals against their son's claims to succession. The spiritual position of the Caliph thus was the glue that held this series of otherwise semi-independent

emirates together in one of the largest political entities ever to have been created in the Western Sudan.

The advantages to the merchants and city dwellers resulting from this were many. This new political system greatly enlarged upon the states built up by the Habe rulers and provided wider opportunities for the acquisition of wealth. Trade and movement were made safe over a large area. New towns were founded; old towns like Zaria, Kano and Katsina expanded rapidly. Kano, in particular, became the most important market in the Western Sudan. See how the great explorer, Heinrich Barth, described Kano in the middle of the century:

> The great advantage of Kano is that commerce and manufactures go hand in hand, and that almost every family has its share in them. There is really something grand in this kind of industry, which spreads to the north as far as Murzuk, Ghat and even Tripoli; to the west, not only to Timbuktu, but in some degree even as far as the shores of the Atlantic, the very inhabitants of Arguin dressing in the cloth woven and dyed in Kano; to the east, all over Borno, although there it comes into contact with the native industry of the country, and to the south it maintains a rivalry with the native industry of the Igbira and Igbo, while towards the south-east it invades the whole of Adamawa, and is only limited by the nakedness of the pagan *sansculottes*,* who do not wear clothing.

Apart from the rapid growth of trade in the Sokoto Caliphate, another major development was education. During the nineteenth century the class of scholars, who in the late eighteenth century had provided the propaganda for the jihad, and judicial personnel grew rapidly since the administrations of the emirates needed not only judges to administer the law but clerks to help work the complex machinery of government. The literacy rate increased and we have a large number of original works written by inhabitants of the Sokoto Caliphate

---

* This is a French term originally used to describe republicans during the French revolution who were usually poor people. Here it can be translated literally as meaning 'without trousers'.

11.4 *A letter written by Caliph Mohammed Bello of Sokoto(1817–1837) in the possession of the Waziri of Sokoto. It gives the date and place of a rendezvous for a military campaign to 'Umar Dadi of Kanoma.*

during the nineteenth century as a result of the increasing emphasis placed on education which, in turn, was a result of the jihad.

But while the jihad had been fought to impose Muslim law on the people, many of the successors of the emirs to whom Usman dan Fodio gave flags became guilty of the very abuses he had attacked in the rule of the Habe kings, and lived lives of luxury and did little to spread the Muslim faith among their subjects.

5 The administration of Borno

Shehu Umar, who ruled Borno with only one brief interruption from 1846 to 1881, took over an empire much reduced in size from the eighteenth century. While the Sokoto authorities instituted a radically new system of administration in their new Caliphate, Shehu Umar, in his administration, was largely influenced by that of the Sefawa. In the first place he went into seclusion from his subjects just like the mais. His main contact with the people was through his Vizier, or Waziri. He appointed his mother Queen Mother with the old Kanuri title of *Yon Magira* and his senior wife as *Yon Gumsu*. Those Kanuri fiefholders who were prepared to swear allegiance to him were allowed to retain their lands. The lands of those who fled were given to his followers. The advisory council of six which had been so important in the court of El-Kanemi, now became largely ceremonial. He did, however, appoint a Chief Qadi to take over some of the judicial duties of the former mais.

Though he reigned for nearly forty years, Shehu Umar was not a very strong ruler. His main interests were in scholarship, and he left the day to day running of the Kingdom to his trusted Waziri, Al-Hajj Bashir. Unfortunately Al-Hajj Bashir was widely hated by his subjects, and in particular by Shehu Umar's relatives and chief fiefholders. In 1853 Umar's brother, Abba Abdurrahman, who had helped restore him to the throne in 1846, and who hated Al-Hajj Bashir, led a successful revolt and became Shehu. He allowed Umar to live peacefully in Kukawa, and promised Al-Hajj Bashir, who had fled, a safe conduct back. However, when Al-Hajj Bashir returned, he was immediately executed.

Abba Abdurrahman proved an unpopular ruler and once again Umar took over the throne. This time Shehu Umar chose his Waziri carefully and Laminu Ntijiya served him wisely until his death in 1871. For the next ten years, the ageing Shehu relied largely on his son, and eventual, successor, Bukar, as his chief adviser.

Though Umar's reign was long, it did not provide stability. There was constant intrigue among the royal family and the nobles. The Shehu does not seem to have had the same sort of authority over his subordinates as did the Amir-al-Muminin in Sokoto. Where the latter played an active part in the administration of the Caliphate, Shehu Umar lived largely in seclusion.

Worst of all the foreign policy of Borno was such that it did not secure the trade routes on which Borno so much depended. Wadai, now independent, competed with Borno for control of the trade routes, with the smaller independent states of Kanem and Bagirmi entering into the struggle. In these circumstances, Borno was never again able to exercise its traditional monopoly over the northward Fezzan-Tripoli trade route or the eastward trade and pilgrim route to Darfur.

Indeed, by the time of Umar's death in 1881, the major trans-Saharan trade routes passed from Tripoli to Kano and from Benghazi to Wadai, while that to the east, though passing through Kukawa, also passed through independent Wadai. While trade did flourish in Borno in the nineteenth century, it was no longer the major commercial centre it had been in the eighteenth century. The Sokoto Caliphate and Wadai had diverted the main trans-Saharan trade-routes westwards and eastwards respectively.

1 Afonja's rebellion against the Alafin

While Oyo reached the height of its power in the eighteenth century, it was, as we saw in Chapter 8, a deeply divided Empire. The strains in the Oyo Empire became more pronounced under Alafin Abiodun's successor, Aole, or Awole, who reigned from 1789–96. To the north the Borgawa and Nupe, who seem to have been in a tributary relationship to Oyo, asserted their independence. Worse still, they not only raided into northern Oyo but cut off its supply of horses, so essential to its cavalry. Oyo appears to have had difficulties in obtaining regular supplies of firearms from the coast. Furthermore, it has been suggested that Oyo's increasing involvement in the slave trade disrupted economic life by shifting the centre of trade southwards, which resulted in increasing economic difficulties when Britain abolished the slave trade in 1807 and began to intercept the slave ships visiting the coast.

Awole, who is described as a man 'too weak and mild for the times' by Samuel Johnson, the great Yoruba historian, had increasing difficulties with his Basorun and his army commander, the *Kakanfo*, who eventually mutinied against him. They forced him to commit suicide but before doing so he cursed the mutineers and shot arrows to the north, the south and the west to indicate the directions they would be sold into slavery. There is an Oyo song which sums up the desperate situation in which the Empire now found itself. 'In Abiodun's day we weighed our money in calabashes; in Awole's reign

we packed up and fled.'

Soon after Awole's death, the Egba, under Lishabi, asserted their independence in about 1797, and twenty years later, Dahomey, under King Ghezo, ceased to pay tribute.

Added to all these troubles was another major problem for Oyo: the Sokoto jihad.

The main cause of the collapse of the Oyo Empire, however, was the rebellion of Afonja, the Are-ona-Kakanfo, or leader of the Oyo armies. He was a member of the royal family, though born of a slave mother. He had built up a strong headquarters at Ilorin, and decided to declare his independence. As we have seen, he called on the support of a Fulani preacher, Mallam Alimi, who was able to persuade Muslim Hausa and Fulani slaves to join Afonja. Chiefs who had grievances against the Alafin also joined Afonja, and such were the divisions in Oyo at this time, that even part of the army sent to crush Afonja, joined him.

Ilorin now became an independent state under Afonja, supported by Mallam Alimi and his Hausa and Fulani Muslims and Solagberu, leader of the Yoruba Muslims. Afonja himself did not become a Muslim, and soon the Muslims in Ilorin combined against him and he was overthrown and killed in about 1823–4. After that the Fulani Muslims and the Yoruba Muslims under Solagberu clashed, and the latter was killed. Abdulsalami, the son of Mallam Alimi by a Yoruba wife, then took control of Ilorin as its first Emir, and Ilorin became part of the Sokoto Caliphate.

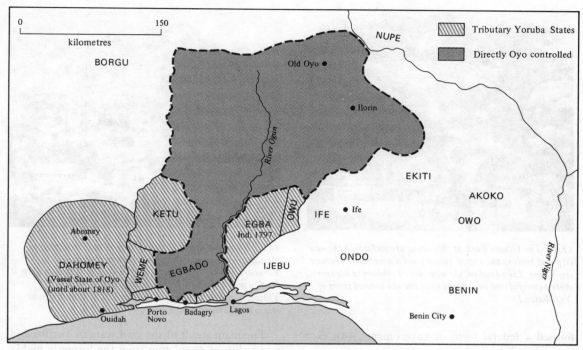

Map 12.1   Oyo and other Yoruba states in about 1825.

2 The break-up of Oyo

Ilorin continued to put pressure on Oyo, particularly on the capital, Old Oyo. Between 1831 and 1833 the Fulani sacked Oyo. In a desperate attempt to crush the Fulani of Ilorin, Alafin Oluewu joined forces with Borgu whose armies were led by the King of Nikki. The Oyo army and its allies were crushed by Ilorin, Oluewu was killed and Old Oyo was abandoned in about 1835.

Already as a result of the wars with Ilorin and the Fulani inroads into Oyo's populous territory, many people had fled in search of new homes to the less populous south and east. They moved into towns under Oyo control as well as into areas which had never been subject to Oyo. Slaves, which had never been an important item of export from Yorubaland, now became a major source of profit for coastal traders in Lagos. Where Yoruba had rarely sold Yoruba, now as a result of the flood of prisoners and homeless, they were readily sold in Lagos and Badagry, which at this time were not effectively patrolled by the British navy.

Oyo refugees had become a complicating factor in the long drawn-out dispute between Ife and Owu over control of the important market town of Apomu. In about 1811 Owu was ordered by the rulers of the Oyo provincial towns of Ogbomosho and Ikoyi to attack Ife, because the Ife had kidnapped Oyo traders in Apomu. The Ife, joined by the Ijebu, attacked and besieged Owu. In 1816 the Ife and Owu were again at war and this time the Ife were joined by Oyo refugees from the north as well as the Ijebu. For five years they lay siege to Owu, which finally fell around 1821–3. The Owu fled and the Ife and their allies marched into the now independent Egba territories.

This resulted in a great upheaval of population. The Egba and Owu fled to the south-western parts of Egbaland under the leadership of Sodeke, a famous hunter, and finally settled at Abeokuta, the town under the rock. Abeokuta comprised several communities, the Egba-Alake, the Egba-Oke-Ona, the Gbagura and the Owu refugees. Together they

12.1   *The Olumo Rock at Abeokuta around which the new city was built in the 1820s, taken from a nineteenth century engraving. Like Ibadan, the new city of Abeokuta became more powerful and important than the old capital cities of Yorubaland.*

12.2   *Ibadan in the 1850s as seen by Anna Hinderer, an Anglican missionary who spent seventeen years in Yorubaland. Barely thirteen years old at the time she drew it, Ibadan was already a large city and capital of a new Yoruba Empire. Today it is the largest city of indigenous origin in Tropical Africa.*

formed a federal form of government, with each community's leader having a say in decisions.

At about the same time as Abeokuta was founded, Ife, Ijebu and Oyo forces settled at the small Gbagura village of Ibadan under the leadership of Okunade, the Maye of Ife. Thus were founded the two most important nineteenth century cities of Yorubaland.

When Oyo was abandoned in about 1836, Ibadan and Abeokuta had become the strongest towns in Yorubaland, if we except Ilorin under Fulani control. In these towns, the traditional crowned rulers were unimportant: what mattered in these war-torn times was military leadership. Typical of these new developments was the founding of Ijaye in northern Egbaland by Kurunmi, a great military leader. But while he exercised dictatorial control over Ijaye, Ibadan was governed by a council of war-chiefs led by the most able among them. A former slave, if he showed military prowess, could rise to the highest office of state.

Many other new towns were founded as a result of the upheavals in Oyo. The small provincial town of Ogbomosho grew so rapidly as a result of im-migration by refugees that in 1960 it was the third largest town in Nigeria after Lagos and Ibadan.

The main result of the civil wars in Yorubaland was a shift of population from the formerly highly populated savannah of metropolitan Oyo to the thinly populated forest areas south of Ibadan. Interestingly this shift of population coincided with the pattern of as yet hidden wealth that was to be exploited under colonial rule. It was in these forest areas that the cocoa tree was to be cultivated.

3 The Ibadan Empire

The result of the fall of Oyo was the sudden expansion of Ife as a power. An Ife leader controlled Ibadan. Ife made successful incursions into Ijeshaland and Ondo. But the arrogance of Okunade, as leader of Ibadan, led to his downfall and the end of Ife's short-lived Empire. The Oyo replaced Ife as the leaders of Ibadan. Ibadan invaded Ife, and the Oyo founded settlements in Ife territory, including Modakeke at the very gates of Ife.

While Ibadan and Ijaye grew in power, Oyo, as we have seen, was under continual pressure from the Fulani and was finally abandoned. The capital of Oyo was re-founded at present day Oyo by Atiba, who succeeded Oluewu as Alafin. He built a palace

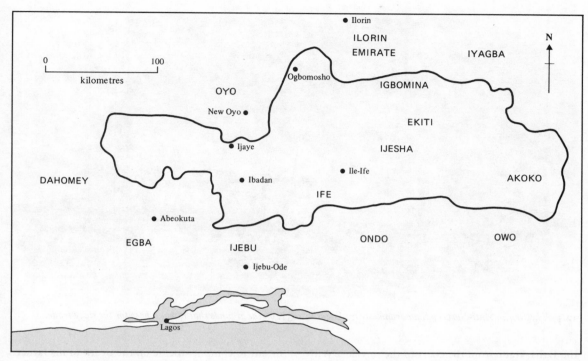

Map 12.2   The Ibadan Empire at its height.

at New Oyo just like that destroyed at Old Oyo. He also tried to re-create the Oyo system of government with himself as divine king. But in this he had to contend with the fact that the power-base of Oyo lay

12.3 *Atiba, Alafin of Oyo, nominal overlord of Ibadan, receives the Anglican missionaries Townsend and Mann at Oyo on 28 September 1853.*

now in Ijaye and Ibadan, both led by men whose leadership depended not on heredity but on military skill. If he were to continue successfully to resist Ilorin, he must gain the cooperation of both Ijaye and Ibadan. So he made Kurunmi, the Are-ona-Kakanfo of Oyo, and the leader of Ibadan, the Basorun. Ibadan's principal task was to deal with the Fulani, while Kurunmi's task was to deal with the Egba and Dahomey. In about 1838 Ibadan defeated Ilorin at the battle of Oshogbo and drove the Ilorin back to Offa. Thereafter the Ilorin-Oyo boundary was fixed at Offa-Ikirun.

As a result of its defeat by Ibadan, the emirs of Ilorin turned their attention to north-eastern Yorubaland, as indeed did Nupe. Ibadan also looked eastwards for expansion into areas which had traditionally come under Benin influence. By 1860, after Ilorin had been driven out of Eastern Yorubaland, the Ibadan Empire controlled Ife, Ijesha, Ekiti, Oshun, Akoko and Igbomina.

To the south of Ibadan the Ijebu were becoming more and more important, controlling, together with

12.4 *The British Anti-Slavery Squadron destroys Lagos in 1851, on the grounds that it was a base for the slave trade.*

the Egba, trade from the coast to the interior. With Ilorin cutting off supplies from the north, Ibadan became increasingly dependent on these routes for arms and supplies.

Lagos, the small island-port, once under Benin control, became important as a base for the slave-trade. To suppress this trade the British attacked Lagos in 1851 and deposed its ruler Kosoko in favour of Akintoye, who was sympathetic to them.

Christian missionaries who had moved into Abeokuta supported the British action, since they wanted to promote legitimate trade in place of the slave trade. In 1861, after further troubles at Lagos, the British again attacked it and occupied it and made it a British Colony. From Lagos, the British Governor began to interfere in the internal affairs of Yorubaland, and was often supported by British missionaries who had established missions in many parts of the country. In 1851, missionaries had even assisted Abeokuta against an invading Dahomeyan army.

In 1860 Ibadan went to war with Ijaye. The reason given was that when Alafin Atiba was dying he had nominated Adelu, his son and Crown Prince, as his successor. Formerly the Crown Prince was meant to commit suicide on the death of his father. As a result Kurunmi of Ijaye refused to recognise Adelu, but the leaders of Ibadan did. In fact, Oyo had been growing jealous of Kurunmi's increasing power and it suited the new Alafin to try and eliminate him. Though Kurunmi was joined by the Egba, Ilorin and Ijebu, the Oyo armies with Ibadan at their head completely destroyed Ijaye. Ibadan was now in truth the New Oyo, though the Alafin continued to hold his traditional position as ruler of Oyo.

4 The fall of the Ibadan Empire

Ibadan, whilst it defeated Kurunmi, was unable to deal with the Ijebu or Egba who frequently closed the trade-routes to the coast. This denied Ibadan gunpowder and weapons which had to be brought round a long and difficult route through the Delta and Eastern Yorubaland. The closing of the routes by the Egba and Ijebu, however, also blocked the development of legitimate trade which both the missionaries and the British Government at Lagos wanted to develop. The British thus tended to support Ibadan despite Egba's complaints that if Ibadan had easy access to arms and ammunition they would be the sufferers. In 1865, when the Egba besieged the Remo town of Ikorodu, which was strategic for supplies for Ibadan from the coast, Glover, the British Governor of Lagos, drove off the Egba in an attempt to open the roads. Such was the resentment at Abeokuta against British interference that in 1867 they expelled the British missionaries and their converts. In 1871 Glover actually called a conference of Yoruba rulers to try and open the roads to Ibadan. But it was not successful and that year Glover left Lagos for another appointment.

While the British supported Ibadan, its rule in the interior was becoming increasingly unpopular. Its provincial administrators, the *ajele* or official messengers, and its military leaders, for the most part extorted what they could from the population for their own personal gain. Thus in 1877 when Ibadan tried once and for all to break the Ijebu-Egba stranglehold on the trade-routes to the coast, the eastern provinces rebelled. They formed the Ekitiparapo comprising the Ekiti, Ijesha, Akoko and Igbomina provinces. The Ekitiparapo was joined by the Egba and Ijebu as well as Ilorin, ever anxious to stir up trouble for Ibadan. That Ibadan was able to hold off this formidable alliance for nine years is some indication of its immense strength. Ibadan's position was further complicated by the attacks made by Dahomey into the Upper Ogun area and the fact that it had less than full-hearted support from the Alafin, who felt very much overshadowed by his theoretical subordinate.

The war was brought to a partial close by British intervention. Indeed the war was finally ended as a result of the European 'Scramble for Africa'. In 1886 Lagos sent delegations to the interior to persuade the warring factions to accept a peace-treaty. A cease-fire was arranged between Ibadan and the Ekitiparapo and between Ife and its Oyo settlement of Modakeke which in fact controlled the town. At a conference in Lagos, Ibadan accepted the independence of its eastern provinces. Modakeke was to be rebuilt in Ibadan territory. A small Hausa force from Lagos then set off to ensure disbandment of the war camps.

Although the war in the east had ended, the wars in the west, north and south continued. Dahomey continued to harass from the west and was not subdued until the French occupation of 1894. The Ilorin harassed from the north and were only taken out of the conflict when the Royal Niger Company occupied it in 1896. Meanwhile, Ijebu and Egba continued to close the roads. The British invaded Ijebu in 1892 thus opening the roads; once the Ijebu roads were open, there was little point in Abeokuta continuing to close their roads. They too sued for peace and with the exception of troubles from Ilorin and, for a short while, from Dahomey, Yorubaland was restored to peace.

5 The rise of Dahomey

While Oyo was breaking up in the nineteenth century, its former tributary, Dahomey, enjoyed unprecedented strength and unity. Taking advantage of the troubles at Oyo, Dahomey seized its independence in 1818 under the leadership of its new King, Ghezo. He and his son, Glele, ruled Dahomey for seventy-one years: Ghezo from 1818 to 1858, and Glele from 1858–1889.

The independent kingdom of Dahomey was very small compared with that of Oyo or its successor Ibadan. It numbered less than a quarter of a million

12.5 *King Ghezo of Dahomey with his son Prince Badahun, who succeeded him as King Glele, pictured in 1856.*

people and covered a relatively small area of modern Dahomey and parts of Togo. It was a highly centralised kingdom, administered by an efficient bureaucracy. The king was much more powerful than most other African monarchs, but some historians have tended to picture him as a dictator. Like other kings he had to take into account the wishes of powerful chiefs and factions in the state. He was also not above the law, and on one occasion Glele was fined for breaking it.

Several factors made nineteenth century Dahomeyan kings more powerful than most African rulers. In the first place their state was of a manageable size, so that the king could know what was going on within it. Secondly, the Dahomeyan kings had the backing of a powerful standing army that grew from about 3,000 in the early eighteenth century to 12,000 in the mid-nineteenth century. Part of this army consisted of Amazons, or women soldiers, who were dedicated to their king. Very few other African states had a regular trained army.

The Dahomeyans had also developed a highly efficient centralised form of administration. The king, who ruled the metropolitan province of Abomey, was assisted by ministers who were appointed for their ability, not just because they came from a particular family. The Mingi, who sat on the king's right hand, was responsible for justice; the Meu, who sat on his left hand, for financial affairs. The Yevogan, who governed the coastal province of Ouidah, was responsible for overseas trade. Five other provinces – Atakpame, Savalou, Zagnanado, Adja and Allada (see Map 18.3, p. 140) – were ruled by provincial governors. But there was little chance that these provincial governors would try to assert their independence. The provincial capitals were all within easy marching distance of the capital, and each governor had a female counterpart resident in his court who reported back to the king on the governor's administration.

6 From slaves to palm-oil

At first the British anti-slave patrol could do little to stop the trade on the Dahomeyan coast, known to European traders as the Slave Coast. But in 1839,

the British signed Equipment Treaties which allowed them to search Portuguese and Brazilian ships and seize them if they had equipment that showed that their object was to trade in slaves. In 1851, when the British occupied Lagos and established a Consulate there, it became a base from which to check the export of slaves from the Dahomeyan coast.

The greater part of Dahomey's revenue came from the slave trade, so it was vital that an alternative source of income be found. In the late eighteenth century Dahomeyan kings had established palm-oil plantations, and during the first half of the nineteenth century these were greatly expanded. Slaves captured in war or on slaving expeditions, instead of being sold on the coast, were now employed on these plantations. After 1851, revenue from palm-oil exports became the substitute for that from slaves. Indeed, one of the motives for Dahomey's incursion into Egbaland and the Upper Ogun was to extend her territory into the rich Yoruba palm-oil producing areas.

The Dahomeyan state taxed the palm-oil producers at a third of the value of their production. The central administration kept a census not only of the people but of the number of palm-trees and livestock in the kingdom. By the time of the French conquest it was reckoned that there were some forty million palm-trees in Dahomey.

Dahomey's oil was shipped through its ports at Ouidah, Cotonou and the Popos. Porto Novo, which was once more independent, also shipped oil. Now for foreign traders Porto Novo had the advantage of charging much lower duties than the Dahomeyan ports or the British port of Lagos. So Porto Novo began to drain away trade from both, and sought French protection against Dahomey as well as the British in Lagos, who naturally resented the fact that it was taking away their trade. Dahomey, however, cut off Porto Novo from the sea by establishing customs posts on its beaches. This time the French were not strong enough to protect Porto Novo. But in 1883, they had more forces at their disposal in West Africa and took it under their protection. At the same time palm-oil prices were dropping on the world market because of plentiful supplies. Thus, Dahomeyan revenues suffered because of both loss of trade to Porto Novo and falling prices. Furthermore, in 1889 the French demanded that Dahomey abandon its control over Cotonou. They sent a mission to achieve this to Glele's capital at Abomey. With falling revenues and the French at his door, Glele, in despair, committed suicide. He was succeeded by his son, Behanzin, who decided to try and drive out the French, but he was conquered by them in 1892 after a fierce struggle. (See Chapter 18.)

13 The Niger Delta and its hinterland in the nineteenth century

1 Slave trade versus palm-oil trade

The history of the Niger Delta and its hinterland during the nineteenth century is very complex. We can discern two main trends: the replacement of the slave trade by the palm-oil trade; and the replacement of the Niger Delta states by British merchants as controllers of the trade with the hinterland.

No other area of West Africa was so immediately affected by Britain's abolition of the slave trade as the states of the Niger Delta and their suppliers in the hinterland. The presence of the British navy in the easily accessible ports of Old Calabar and Bonny forced the Delta middlemen and their suppliers to look for an alternative commodity for exchange with European goods. The wild palm-oil trees that grew in profusion in the Igbo and Ibibio hinterland supplied the answer. And in Old Calabar, the ruling Ekpe society settled slaves on oil-palm plantations, just as the Dahomeyans did, to ensure a steady supply of the commodity.

The abolition of the slave trade by Britain did not bring an end to slave trading by the Delta states – it merely made it more difficult. The Delta rulers, too, must have found it odd that white men who had for two centuries vigorously supported the slave trade, should now just as vigorously oppose it. If the British had suddenly come to see it as wrong, the Delta rulers had not, and nor had many other European traders. Indeed the slave trade became even more profitable. Since slaves were now more difficult to obtain because of the activities of the

British navy, the price for them rose. What is more, the slave-operated plantations in America, Cuba and Brazil were expanding and this increased the demand for slaves. Thus in 1826, nearly twenty years after the abolition of the slave trade by Britain, twelve slavers and twelve merchant-ships were seen in Bonny waters. Indeed the volume of slaves exported from West Africa increased rapidly. In 1842 it was calculated that 24,800 slaves were exported while in 1847, 84,300 were taken across the Atlantic. But the slaves came increasingly from ports to which the British navy did not have access. In the Delta, Brass, which had a concealed port, became the chief slaving outlet while Old Calabar, Bonny, Elem Kalabari and the Itsekiri concentrated increasingly on the export of palm-oil.

The chief feature of the nineteenth century history of the Delta and its hinterland was the changeover from an economy based on slaves to one based on palm-oil. But this did not mean that the hunt for slaves ceased. Instead, Igbo and Ibibio slaves were now used as porters to carry the palm-oil to the river ports where the Ijo middlemen bought it. In Calabar, slaves were used on plantations in a manner not very different from the American slave plantations. But in this case the slaves led a successful revolt against their masters, the members of the Ekpe Society. In protest against the harsh treatment they received on the plantations and the use of slaves as sacrifices on the death of their kings, they formed a secret society of Blood Men. In 1851, the Blood Men invaded Old Calabar and threatened to burn the town if the Ekpe did not release slaves they had seized. The next year, when King Archibong died, Blood Men again invaded Old Calabar, and prevented sacrifices of slaves for his funeral.

During the nineteenth century, with the high prices to be obtained for both slaves and oil, there was fierce competition between the Delta states for control of the hinterland trade. Trade along the Cross River and Calabar River, giving access to the Ibibio areas, was in the hands of Old Calabar. Trade up the Imo River, was dominated by Bonny and gave it access to rich Igbo and Ibibio areas. Elem Kalabari controlled trade along the Sombreiro

River, while Brass Nembe controlled trade up the Niger to the Igbo Kingdom of Aboh. Further up the coast, the Itsekiri traders of Warri controlled trade on the Ethiope and Warri Rivers. The Delta states were essentially waterborn traders. As far as Old Calabar, Bonny and Elem Kalabari were concerned, the land trade was handled by the Aro. The Aro maintained settlements at major points on the trade routes which linked Bende with the north and the coast (see Map 13.2). The fact that they were able to establish settlements, some of which actually controlled the political and religious life of the surrounding people, is due to two factors. First, Ibini

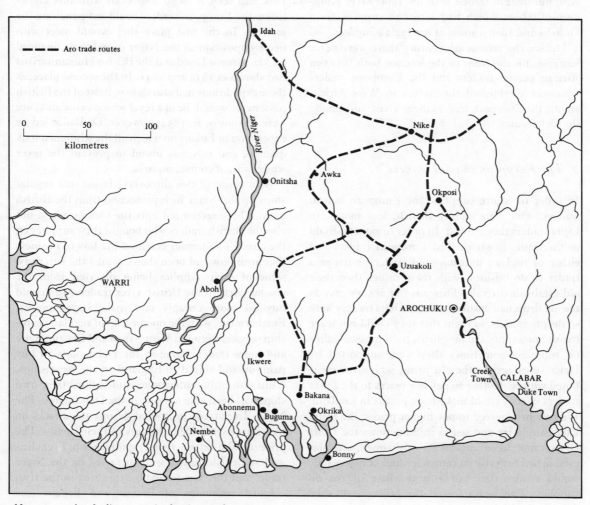

Map 13.1   Aro trading routes in the nineteenth century.

Okpabe, the oracle of Arochukwu, was widely revered in Igboland, and among the Efik, Ibibio and Ijo. The Aro traders and settlers were considered by these peoples to be the children of Ibini Okpabe and therefore they should not be harmed. Secondly, the Aro strengthened their position further by the threat of force: they had at their disposal bands of mercenaries using firearms who could discipline any village which did not respect the Aro's special position. Though they maintained trade routes throughout much of Igboland, the Aro never brought or tried to impose political unity on it. Of the Delta states, only Brass did not trade with the Aro, but instead traded with the Igbo River Kingdom of Aboh, which had access to supplies from Onitsha and Idah, capital of the Igala Kingdom.

During the nineteenth century there were fierce struggles for the trade of the interior both between African coastal traders and the European traders who now established themselves in West Africa; among the European traders themselves, and among the Delta states.

2   The European coastal traders

In order to secure supplies, the European coastal traders, who were mainly British, lent money to Delta traders they trusted. In order to get a foothold in the trade, newly arrived European traders had either to find an uncommitted trader or tempt a trader to do business with them rather than their old-established rivals. This was not always easy as the old firms had ensured that the Delta traders were so deeply in debt to them that they could not leave them. Sometimes the new firms tried to seize palm-oil supplies. Sometimes they were supported by Delta kings against the old firms, who often combined with each other to pay low prices to the Delta traders so they could make huge profits in England. If a new firm agreed to pay higher prices, the Delta kings would try and sell to it. Sometimes the Delta kings came to arrangements with one particular established firm that in return for higher prices they would ensure they got a large share of the oil supplies. This again forced the other established firms to pay higher prices.

The European traders also wanted to get at the source of the supplies of palm-oil direct, without having to use the Delta middlemen. If they could do this, they could buy more cheaply, since they would not have to pay the charges of the Delta middlemen for bringing supplies to the coastal ports. They were not able to do this until two things had been achieved. In 1830 Richard and John Lander, the British explorers, proved to their country-men that the River Niger flowed into the sea through the numerous small rivers that criss-cross the Niger Delta. Nobody had believed that these small rivers led into the mighty Niger which Mungo Park had seen at Segu. But even with this knowledge, the European traders could not penetrate the interior. In the first place they would meet with fierce opposition as the Niger expeditions financed by MacGregor Laird and the British Humanitarians had shown in 1832 and 1841. In the second place, as these expeditions had also shown, most of the British passengers would die of a fever whose cause and cure were unknown. In 1854, however, Dr Baikie led an expedition to Lokoja on which all the whitemen took quinine, and this was found to prevent the fever which was, of course, malaria.

As a result of this discovery, Laird sent regular ships up the Niger with protection from the British navy. This angered not only the Delta traders, but also the British traders who bought their supplies on the coast. The former resented the loss of business that until now had been theirs, whilst the latter saw some of their supplies being diverted from the coastal ports to the British river traders who could buy oil more cheaply and make larger profits. Furthermore, with the opening up of regular steamship services between West Africa and Britain, more and more traders came to the Delta ports to buy palm-oil and ship it to England on the steamships. Until now only traders who could afford their own ships had been able to trade in the Delta states. The Niger River trade prospered despite the attacks on the ships by the Delta traders of their agents. The price of palm-oil was rising rapidly. Soon, French as well as British traders were attracted by the Niger trade, and this was to involve this area in the rival colonial ambitions of France and Britain (see opposite page).

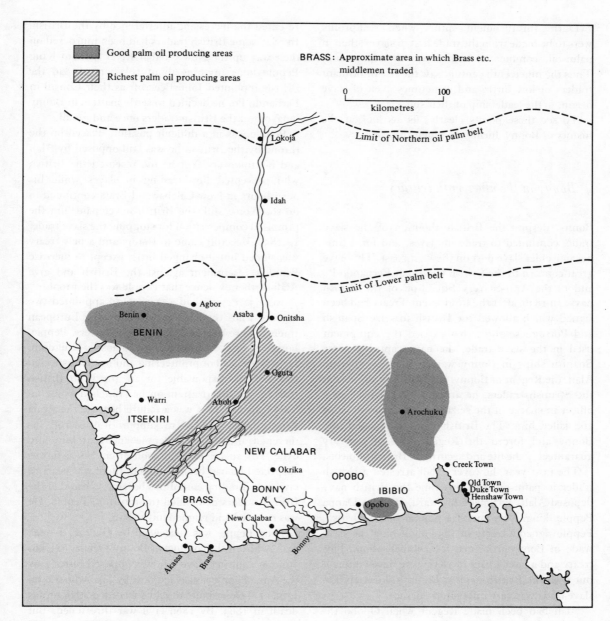

Map 13.2   The Niger Delta.

3   Struggles in the Delta states

The struggles between the Delta states for control of the rich palm-oil trade led to many wars during the century. Within states there was rivalry between houses as to which could make the most profits from the trade. In two cases this led to civil war – Elem Kalabari, and Bonny.

Furthermore, these struggles, together with continued slave trading and stoppages with the European traders, involved the British Consul at Fernando Po in the internal affairs of the states.

During this turbulent century, when great profits were to be made from the trade first in slaves, then in palm-oil, commercial ability was at a premium. Thus the nineteenth century saw the rise of brilliant traders of low birth, and sometimes even of slave origin, to the leadership of their states.

To see these points clearly, let us look at the history of Bonny during the nineteenth century.

4 Bonny in the nineteenth century

Bonny, despite the British abolition of the slave trade, continued to trade in slaves, and for a time became chief slave port on the west coast. This gave great concern to the British Consul at Fernando Po and to the Anti-Slavery Squadron of the British navy. In 1836, after the Equipment Treaty had been signed which allowed the British to seize Spanish and Portuguese ships that carried the equipment used in the slave trade, the navy captured some Spanish ships in Bonny waters. This so angered Alali, the Regent of Bonny, that with the support of the Spanish traders, he arrested the British naval officer in charge of the seizure of the Spanish ships and jailed him. The British navy then sailed into Bonny and forced the Regent to sign a treaty guaranteeing the life and security of British subjects.

The next year, however, Alali arrested a British trader in palm-oil, and this time the British navy deposed Alali, and made his ward, William Dappa Pepple, king. Very much a puppet of the British, Pepple signed a treaty in 1839 abolishing the slave trade in Bonny in return for compensation. This treaty and a later treaty of 1841 were never ratified, but with the British navy at Bonny's doorstep, the slave trade was very difficult to pursue.

Alali had been made Regent when Opobo the Great died in about 1830 because his heir, William Dappa Pepple, was under-age. Alali was a slave by origin who, because of his ability, had become head of the powerful Anna Pepple house. Once deposed as Regent, he gathered support from all those who resented British interference in Bonny's internal affairs. At the same time, King Pepple himself also

resented the increasing interference by the British. In 1847 some British traders had been murdered on their way up the New Calabar River without King Pepple doing anything about it. When, in 1849, the British appointed John Beecroft as their Consul in Fernando Po, he decided to settle matters in Bonny in favour of the British traders once and for all.

Pepple was in a difficult position. Placed on the throne by the British, he was still opposed by Alali and his followers. Yet he too resented the British who prevented him trading in slaves while his neighbours in New Calabar and Brass continued to do so. Worse still, the British never paid him the promised compensation for stopping the slave trade. In 1850, Beecroft came to Bonny and a new treaty was signed but it changed little, except to increase Pepple's resentment against the British and give Alali further evidence that Pepple was their tool.

In 1852 Pepple had a stroke and appointed two regents who, though supported by the European traders, were resented by Alali's followers. Pepple, however, recovered but he faced a hostile Kingdom. He was accused of profiteering and it was suspected that he was responsible for an attack on British traders. To divert attention he launched a war on New Calabar. This was a failure because the Anna Pepple house refused to support it. Beecroft intervened and deposed Pepple and sent him into exile. His successor died soon after. Since it was suspected he had been poisoned, there was nearly a civil war. Trading conditions became so bad that the British traders demanded the return of Pepple. He was restored and reigned until 1865.

King Pepple was succeeded by George, a weak man, who left the conduct of Bonny's affairs to Oko-Jumbo, a former slave. He was opposed bitterly by the Anna Pepple house, led now by Jaja, who was an Igbo of slave origin and had succeeded Alali on his death in 1863. By 1869 civil war threatened. But Jaja, rather than fight Oko-Jumbo, who had heavy guns, did a much cleverer thing. He and the Anna Pepple house moved up river and established themselves in Andoni country where he cut Bonny off from its source of palm-oil. Despite the British Consul's warnings, the British traders dealt with Jaja, since he now effectively controlled Bonny's

13.1 & 2 *King Jaja of Opobo in traditional dress (on the left) participates in a ceremony connected with the water spirits. The picture on the right shows him when he was still head of the Anna Pepple House of the Kingdom of Bonny from which he successfully seceded.*

trade. Even though the British Consul threatened him, Jaja successfully established his new Kingdom of Opobo in 1870. There he and his people grew rich until the British intervened in 1887 and seized and deported Jaja for blocking British trade.

We have dealt with the history of Bonny in detail for three reasons: first it shows the increasing interference of the British in an independent African state; second it shows the cut-throat competition between British traders; thirdly it demonstrates clearly the rise of the new men.

5 The other Delta states: Brass, New Calabar and Itsekiri

Before the nineteenth century Brass had not been actively engaged in the slave trade like its neighbours, Bonny and New Calabar. Once the British navy blockaded exports of slaves from Bonny and, less successfully, from Elem Kalabari (New Calabar), Brass, whose capital was secluded deep in the Delta, and whose port of Twon was difficult for the British navy to get to, became a major exporter of

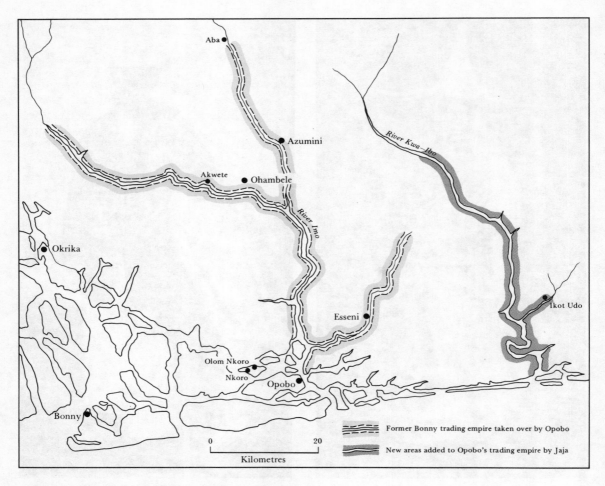

Map 13.3   How Opobo cut off Bonny from its hinterland.

slaves. Because its port was protected by a confusing series of creeks, it was difficult for the British navy to know from which one slave ships would emerge. When, by the 1860s, the slave trade had come to an end because of the lack of demand in the New World, Brass switched successfully to exporting palm-oil.

New Calabar suffered in its trade as a result of competition from Brass and Bonny, and later Opobo. Within the state, the ruling Amakiri dynasty was challenged by the Barboy house. This resulted in civil war in the 1880s and New Calabar broke up into three separate states: Abonema, Bakana and Buguma, which became the capital of the Amakiri

dynasty. This civil war brought to an end the already declining fortunes of New Calabar in the Delta trade.

The Itsekiri were also troubled by civil strife and in 1848 the Itsekiri monarchy was overthrown. Thereafter, trade on this part of the coast suffered a setback. However, by the 1870s the Itsekiri re-organised themselves on the Benin River, where Ebrohimi became the chief trading port, replacing Warri. The Itsekiris elected a wealthy trader, Olomu, as their leader. The British Consul re-cognised Olomu as the Governor of the Benin River, that is the Itsekiri leader through whom the British would deal in trade matters.

13.3 *Nana Olomu of the Itsekiri photographed in Accra after he was defeated and exiled there by the British.*

On the death of Olomu in 1883 he was succeeded by his son, Nana, who extended his control over the Ethiope, Warri and Jamieson Rivers. Trade prospered in Nana's state, which now included Urhobos as well as Itsekiris. Relations with the British traders were peaceful, and the Consul had no occasion to bring in his gunboats. In 1885 Nana even signed a Treaty of Protection with the British. But, because he would not allow the British to trade independently of him, he stored up trouble for himself and eventually the British attacked and exiled him.

6 The establishment of the Royal Niger Company

Despite opposition from the traders of the Delta states and of the European traders on the coast, British firms succeeded in establishing themselves on the Niger River. British factories were opened up at Onitsha and Aboh, from which palm-oil was shipped direct down the Niger to Liverpool. Four British firms had established themselves by 1879, when George Goldie Taubman arrived on the Niger as head of the Central African Trading Company. His aim was to create a monopoly of trade for his firm on the Niger. He persuaded the three other British firms on the Niger to join with his Central African Trading Company to form the United Africa Company. Now, instead of competing with each other, they formed a common front to deal with the African sellers of palm-oil. This meant they could buy palm-oil at the price they decided, since there was no-one else for the Africans to sell to. At that time, however, the French also became interested in the Niger trade. By 1882 two French firms, of almost equal strength to the United Africa Company, had established themselves on the river. This now meant that if African traders did not like the prices paid by the United Africa Company, they could try and get better prices from the French. Goldie tried to combat the French by getting the British Government to grant him a Charter. This would mean his company would have British protection as an officially recognised company which could administer the areas in which it traded on

13.4 *Sir George Goldie, head of the United Africa Company, later the Royal Niger Company, who was responsible for establishing British rule over much of southern and parts of northern Nigeria.*

behalf of Britain and impose taxes on the French companies. The British Government did not agree to this, so Goldie then tried to persuade the French companies to join him. They refused. He then decided to kill the trade of the French companies by using his capital reserves to buy palm-oil at prices above that which the French could afford to pay if they were to make a profit. He also sold goods to African traders at prices below that which the French could afford to sell if they were to make a profit. This meant, of course, that his company, now named the National Africa Company, did not make

a profit. However, he achieved his aim of forcing the French out of business in 1884. Thereafter he could charge whatever prices he wished for his goods and buy palm-oil at the prices he fixed. Thus he was able to recover the losses he had made in the commercial war with the French. He was also now in complete control of the Niger trade. In such a strong position he was able to take over the government of the areas in which he traded and in 1886 his company was given a royal charter as the Royal Niger Company to govern on behalf of the British Crown.

14 Asante and Fante in the nineteenth century

1 Asante gains control of the coast 1801–1816

In 1801 Osei Bonsu, a ruler as remarkable as Osei Tutu and Opoku Ware, was enstooled as Asantehene. Not only did he continue improvements in the administration begun by his predecessors, he also tightened his hold on the kingdoms they had conquered and made into provinces of the Asante Empire. He appointed men to offices in the administration not because of the families they came from but because of their ability. He employed literate Muslims as clerks to keep the records of his administration.

Before Osei Bonsu came to the throne, the rulers of the kingdoms conquered by Asante were allowed to continue governing their kingdoms as long as they paid tribute to the Asantehene and helped him in war when he asked for their assistance. Now Osei Bonsu sent residents from Kumasi to oversee the governments of the provincial rulers, thus strengthening his control of them.

Asante, at the time of Osei Bonsu's reign, covered nearly all of modern Ghana and parts of Togo, Upper Volta and Ivory Coast. But it did not include the collection of twenty Fante states which controlled the coastline where most of the European trading forts were situated. Asante's only major coastal trading outlets were Elmina and Accra.

Asante resented Fante control of the coastal trade for two main reasons. Firstly, the Fante made rich profits as middlemen handling the gold-dust and slaves sent by Asante to the European forts, and then on the European goods which they in turn sold to Asante. Secondly, Asante needed a supply of European firearms to maintain its hold over its outlying provinces which would try to gain their independence at the slightest opportunity. It did not like depending on the Fante for its firearm supplies as they often gave assistance to states anxious to free themselves from Asante rule.

The European merchants – British, Danes and Dutch – based in their forts on the Fante coast found themselves in a dilemma. They depended on Asante for their supplies of gold-dust and slaves, but they feared the establishment of a monopoly on trade by Asante which would mean that Asante, being the only suppliers, could charge whatever prices they liked. The British, however, were more fearful of an Asante monopoly than the Danes and the Dutch. In particular the British believed that if Asante conquered the Fante, the Dutch, who had always been very friendly with the Asantehenes, would gain most of Asante's trade. Furthermore, the British forts were all based on the Fante coast, so the British had always needed to be friendly with the Fante.

In 1806 Osei Bonsu sent his army into Fante, because it had given refuge to two rebellious chiefs. The Fante were defeated in Abora, a Fante state which had common frontiers with Asante. The Asante army then marched to the coast and besieged the British fort at Anomabo which was protecting a large number of Fante.

Though the British had at first assisted the Fante

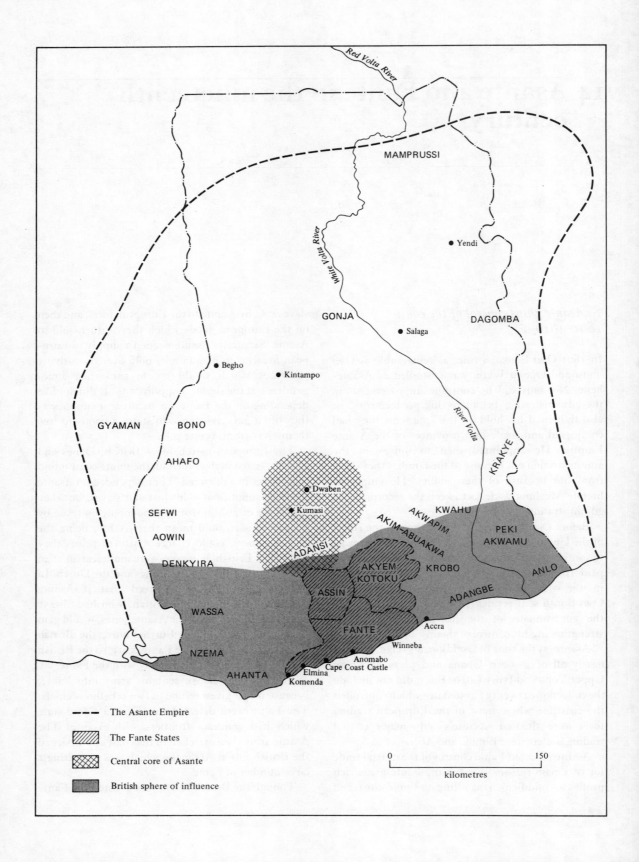

Red Volta River

MAMPRUSSI

White Volta River

● Yendi

GONJA

River Volta

● Salaga

DAGOMBA

● Begho

● Kintampo

GYAMAN   BONO

AHAFO

KWAHU

SEFWI

Dwaben

AKWAPIM

AKIM-ABUAKWA

PEKI
AKWAMU

KRAKYE

● Kumasi

AOWIN

ADANSI

DENKYIRA

AKYEM
KOTOKU

KROBO

ANLO

WASSA

ASSIN

ADANGBE

NZEMA

FANTE

Accra

Winneba

AHANTA

Anomabo

Cape Coast Castle

Elmina

Komenda

- - - - The Asante Empire

▨▨▨ The Fante States

▧▧▧ Central core of Asante

▓▓▓ British sphere of influence

0   150

kilometres

against the Asante, Colonel Torrane, Governor of the British Forts, feared that the British Fort William at Anomabo could not hold out against the Asante attacks. He also feared that if Asante did gain control of the coast, British trade would suffer. So he placated the Asantehene by handing over one of the rebel chiefs to him, as well as half the Fante who had taken refuge in Fort William.

The Asantehene thus triumphed over his Fante enemies. At Winneba he waded into the sea and when he returned to the shore he took the name of Bonsu, meaning whale, because he had not even found an enemy in the sea who could repel him. But in 1807 an enemy which respects no man, smallpox, forced him to return to Kumasi.

In 1809 the Fante attacked the Asante coastal outlets of Accra and Elmina. But Osei Bonsu replied in 1811 by invading Fante once again. One army was sent to aid Accra, another to break the Fante blockade of Elmina. However, the tributary rulers of Akim Abuakwa and Akwapim joined with the Fante against their Asante overlords and after long drawn out fighting the Asante armies withdrew to Kumasi.

In 1814 Osei Bonsu again sent armies into Fante, Akim-Abuakwa and Akwapim to establish once and for all his domination of the coast. By June 1816 he had crushed the rebellious tributary states and overrun Fante where he posted his own commissioners. Asante now controlled most of what is now Ghana.

2 The first Asante war with the British

The Fante did not accept Asante rule readily. The British Company of Merchants, while they sympathised with the Fante, had of course to ensure that they continued to have their share of trade with the interior. They feared that, because the Dutch had for long been friendly with Asante, they might now gain a trading advantage over them. The British Company of Merchants therefore sent a mission to Kumasi to secure a treaty. After lengthy negotiations, a treaty was secured which ensured British trade with Asante, and by which the British re-

Map 14.1 (opposite) Asante and Fante in the nineteenth century.

14.1 *Elmina Castle, showing its draw-bridge, from a present-day photograph.*

cognised that the Fante were subjects of the Asante and promised to investigate any Asante complaints against their Fante subjects.

The British Governor resented this last provision of the treaty and when in 1818 the Fante of Komenda insulted Asante messengers he did nothing about it. The Asantehene, citing the treaty he had made with the British, insisted that the Governor deal with Komenda and threatened war if he did not.

At the time of this dispute, the British Government in London appointed a Consul to represent it at the court of the Asantehene. He was independent of the British Governor and was much resented by the British merchants who saw him as a rival source of British authority. The Consul, Joseph Dupuis, was at Cape Coast when the Asante messengers threatened war if the Governor did not take action against Komenda. However, when they learnt of Dupuis' appointment as British Consul to Kumasi, they decided to delay action and refer this new development to the Asantehene.

In February 1819 Dupuis set out for Kumasi where he drew up a new treaty by which the Asantehene withdrew his complaints against the Governor. The Fante were recognised as subjects of

14.2 *The British Consul in Kumasi, Joseph Dupuis, visits the Asantehene to try and settle the dispute between the Asantehene and the Governor of the British Company of Merchants.*

the Asante. The British Governor however refused to accept that the Fante were subjects of the Asante. Asante–British relations became worse and worse.

In London there was growing criticism of the administration of the British Council of Merchants. It was said they had not stamped out the slave trade effectively; that their forts were not strong enough to resist attacks; and that their policies had harmed trade. So in 1821 the Company was abolished and the British forts were placed under Sir Charles Macarthy, Governor of Sierra Leone. Macarthy arrived in the Gold Coast to take over the forts in April 1822. He quickly formed a bad opinion of the Asante, believing them to be 'barbarians' with whom it was impossible to conduct trade. He thus decided to prepare for war.

When Macarthy was away in Sierra Leone a policeman serving the British at Anomabo quarrelled with an Asante trader who insulted the British Governor. In turn the policeman insulted the

Asantehene. When news of this reached the Asante authorities the policeman was kidnapped and taken inland to Dunkwa. As soon as Macarthy learnt of this he sent an expedition to rescue the policeman. But the Asante surprised the troops and they retreated.

It was now only a question of time before full-scale war broke out. Macarthy prepared his army and the Asante moved southwards. In January 1824 a battle was finally fought but Macarthy's forces were no match for the Asante army and he himself was wounded. Macarthy killed himself rather than be captured. That same day Osei Bonsu himself died, but not before he learnt of the British defeat. When he died the Asante Empire was as powerful as it had ever been or would ever be again. The British army had been defeated, as too had the rebellious tributary states of Wassa and Denkyira.

Two years later the British, determined to revenge their defeat of 1824, led a combined British

14.3 *George Maclean, appointed Governor of the British Company of Merchants in 1828, arrived on the Gold Coast in 1830. He was to have a profound influence on both the Asante and the Fante States.*

and Fante army, and overcame the Asante. Asante never really recovered from this defeat. After long negotiations Asante signed a treaty in April 1831 by which it agreed to deposit six hundred ounces of gold with the British as well as send them two princes as security for Asante's good faith. Trade was to be free, and the independence of Denkyira, Assin and the Fante states was recognised.

3 The Fante states and the British 1826–1863

Although the British had defeated Asante in 1826, and the Fante states were free, the British Government decided to withdraw from the Gold Coast. The British merchants protested against this decision but were allowed once again to take over the administration of the British forts. In 1828 the merchants appointed Captain George Maclean as their Governor and in 1830 he arrived to take up his appointment.

Maclean proved to be a remarkable diplomat, one of whose first actions was to finalise the peace treaty with Asante. From the time of his arrival until the end of his administration in 1843 his primary concern was to maintain peace on the coast so that trade would be uninterrupted. He gained the trust of both the Asante and the Fante, and over the latter he began to extend an informal British administration. He stationed his policemen in their towns and settled their disputes. Above all he ensured they did not do anything to provoke the Asante. The measure of Maclean's success is that between 1831 and 1840 imports in Cape Coast rose from £131,000 to £423,000 and exports from £90,000 to £325,000.

But Maclean made enemies among the merchants and some accused him of not doing anything to stop the slave trade and domestic slavery. Others said he misused his powers. In truth there was no basis for his extension of British-style law and order to the Fante states. In 1841 the British Government sent a Commissioner, Dr Madden, to the Coast to investigate the charges against Maclean. He confirmed them. However, the Select Committee of the British

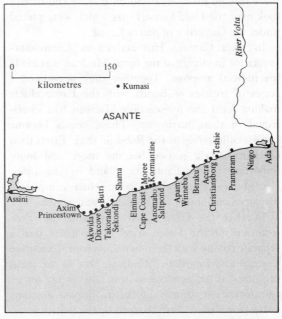

Map 14.2 British, Dutch and Danish forts on the West Coast.

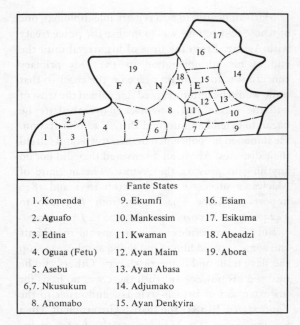

Map 14.3   The Fante States.

Fante States		
1. Komenda	9. Ekumfi	16. Esiam
2. Aguafo	10. Mankessim	17. Esikuma
3. Edina	11. Kwaman	18. Abeadzi
4. Oguaa (Fetu)	12. Ayan Maim	19. Abora
5. Asebu	13. Ayan Abasa	
6,7. Nkusukum	14. Adjumako	
8. Anomabo	15. Ayan Denkyira	

Parliament which met in 1842 did not find Maclean guilty, but recommended that his administration of the Fante be made legal. So once again the British took over the Gold Coast Forts which were placed under the Governor of Sierra Leone.

In 1844 Captain Hill arrived as Lieutenant-Governor in charge of the forts. Maclean was made his judicial assessor. Together they negotiated a series of treaties or bonds with the Fante chiefs making legal the jurisdiction Maclean had established in their territories. These bonds became known collectively as the Bond of 1844. From then on British-style justice became more and more important in the Fante states and by the 1860s English law and English courts had completely displaced customary law in many Fante states.

In 1850 the Gold Coast forts and the 'Protectorate' of the Fante states were made into a separate colony with their own Governor, Executive Council and Legislative Council. One of the main problems of the new colony was how to pay for its administration. It was difficult to impose customs duties, for if these were charged by the British forts, then all trade would be diverted to the Dutch forts which did not charge duties. The British, who had

already bought the Danish forts, therefore tried to buy the Dutch forts. But this took a long time. So, in 1852, as an alternative source of revenue they imposed an unpopular poll-tax of one shilling a head on all inhabitants of the Gold Coast 'Protectorate'. Many people simply did not pay even when threatened with force and by 1861 the British dropped the tax as not being worth the trouble of its collection.

While Maclean had maintained good relations with the Asante during his administration, under direct British Government control the old abuses of the Fante against Asante traders started once more. In 1853 the Asante attempted to invade Assin and the British became suspicious of their intentions. In 1862 an Asante chief and a runaway slave boy took refuge with the British who refused to return them despite a promise by the Asantehene on the great Asante oath that the chief would not be executed. As a result the Asantehene, Kwaku Dua, invaded the Fante states and twice defeated the Anglo-Fante armies in their third war.

The British defeat led the British Parliament to appoint a Select Committee in 1865 to enquire into the British settlements on the West Coast. The Committee recommended that apart from possibly Sierra Leone, the British should transfer the administration of their West African colonies of the Gambia, Gold Coast and Lagos to their local inhabitants. The Government should not sign any further treaties offering protection to 'native tribes'.

4 *The Fante Confederation*

The Parliamentary Select Committee had recommended that British policy be 'to encourage in the natives the exercise of those qualities which may render it possible for us more and more to transfer to them the administration of all Governments. . . .' However, when, in 1868, the Fante formed a confederation with the expressed purpose of governing themselves, the British opposed it. Nor did they show any signs of withdrawing from the Coast. Indeed, in 1867 the British arranged with the Dutch that they exchange forts so that the Dutch would control all forts west of the Sweet River near Elmina, and the British all forts to the east. Thus the British would be able to charge customs duties without difficulty on their stretch of the Coast.

This arrangement angered the Fante who had not been consulted and who feared the Dutch as friends of the Asante. Furthermore, some Fante, like those of Komenda, would now come under Dutch rule and the Dutch were considered worse masters than the British. These and other grievances against the British had led the Fante kings to form their Confederation at Mankessim in January 1868. The Fante also felt that they had regained their independence from Asante only to lose it to the British. Furthermore British 'Protection' was of little value

14.4 *Surgeon-Major J. Africanus B. Horton, who was a distinguished scholar and adviser to the Fante Confederation.*

in the light of the recent invasion of the Asante army. They had hated the poll-tax and in many cases refused to pay. The British Governor had had King John Aggrey of Cape Coast arrested and deported for complaining to him that 'The time has now come for me to record a solemn protest against the perpetual annoyances and insults that you persistently and perseveringly continue to practice on me in my capacity as legally constituted King of Cape Coast'. Finally the Fante wanted to regain their profitable middleman role between the Asante and the Europeans.

The Fante Confederation was short-lived because of opposition from the British. But it did set up a constitution with the advice of the distinguished Sierra Leonean scholar and doctor, Surgeon-Major J. Africanus B. Horton. It elected a King-President, established an Executive and Legislative Council, appointed a Secretary, Under-Secretary and Treasurer. It raised an army and it collected taxes. It also established its own Supreme Court.

Here was an obvious example of 'natives' exercising the qualities of self-government that the British were supposed to encourage. Instead the British Administrator did his best to drive a wedge between the educated Africans and the kings, and between the kings themselves. Indeed, in 1871 the Acting Administrator, Salmon, arrested members of the Executive Council of the Confederation on the charge of treason. Though he was ordered by London to release them, he successfully ended an early experiment in self-government with Western style institutions which if it had been encouraged by the British might well have succeeded.

5 The fourth Anglo-Asante war

In 1872 the Dutch finally withdrew from the coast, leaving the British in complete control and able to charge customs duties without any fear of rival neighbouring ports that did not do so. Among the Dutch forts transferred to the British was Elmina which the Asantehene, Kofi Karikari, claimed as his. The Asantehene now decided to take back Elmina and win back his former Fante subjects. The Asante army moved southwards.

The British meanwhile decided to deal with

14.5   *Hausa artillery crossing the River Pra in the 1874 British campaign against Asante.*

Asante once and for all and brought from Britain Sir Garnet Wolseley, a distinguished English general, to lead an army against Kumasi. When Wolseley arrived he found an Asante army of some 20,000 soldiers within easy reach of Elmina and Cape Coast. He launched an attack on them and they retreated, not so much because of Wolseley's superiority as because their soldiers were suffering from outbreaks of smallpox and dysentery. Later Wolseley's secretary, H. Brackenbury, wrote of the Asante army that 'the army of a civilised nation need not have been ashamed of a retreat conducted with such skill and such success'.

Wolseley drew up his combined force of African levies, Hausa troops from Lagos, Fante allies, and the recently arrived troops from Britain and set off for Kumasi. He then sent a demand to the Asantehene for an armistice. But negotiations broke down because in the end the Asantehene was unable to

accept Wolseley's conditions which included releasing all prisoners, sending the Queen Mother of Asante and the heir to the Golden Stool as hostages and paying an indemnity of 50,000 ounces of gold.

Wolseley then advanced and fought the Asante army at Amoafo, where the latter fought bravely but were defeated as a result of the superior weapons of the British. One of Wolseley's British regiments made a surprise dash to Kumasi, but found it deserted. Wolseley fired the town and blew up the Asantehene's palace. The Asante had not been defeated but in the face of British power they signed a Peace Treaty at Fomena whereby they recognised the independence of all states south of the River Pra. Not that this meant anything to the Fante who were now formally made a British Crown Colony.

Asante seemed completely broken. Its outlying provinces of Dagomba and Gonja declared their independence. The Brong states and even metro-

14.6 *An Asante war-dance from a contempory engraving.*

politan states like Adansi and Dwaben seized the opportunity to break away from Kumasi's control.

Over the next ten years Mensa Bonsu, who succeeded as Asantehene in 1874, tried to rebuild Asante. He soon negotiated the allegiance of two of the disaffected metropolitan states, Bekwai and Kokofu, but Dwaben, which was given support by the British, refused to rejoin the Confederacy. Mensa Bonsu therefore successfully invaded Dwaben in October 1875. But he was unable to do the same with Adansi and Gyaman and in 1883 he was overthrown because of his greed and his refusal to support Banda in its attempt to invade Gyaman.

There followed five years of civil war which permitted the Brong states to strengthen their newly won independence. When Agyeman Prempe I succeeded as Asantehene in 1888, the Empire seemed finally to have broken up. However, this was to reckon without the forceful personality of Prempe. Within a few months he had brought metropolitan Asante once more under the rule of Kumasi. Soon the Dwaben, who had fled south of the River Pra, returned to Asante.

The British became nervous of Asante's revived power, and feared that the French from their base on the Ivory Coast might gain access to the rich hinterland of Britain's Gold Coast Colony, so they asked Prempe to place his Empire under British protection.

'My Kingdom of Asante' he replied 'will never commit itself to such a policy. Asante must remain independent as of old, at the same time to be friendly with all white men. I do not write this with a boastful spirit but in the clear sense of its meaning'.

But Asante's fate was already sealed. It was only time before the European Scramble would bring it, together with nearly all other African states, under foreign rule (see p. 140).

15 The West Atlantic Coast: African experiments with European ideas

1 Assimilation in Senegal: France's stepping stone to the Western Sudan

Along the West African coast from Elmina to Old Calabar we have seen how trade in the nineteenth century attracted Europeans to the interior. Until the late nineteenth century, however, they found it difficult to penetrate beyond the coast because of African hostility. One exception was on the River Niger, which enabled Liverpool traders with their steamships to establish themselves as far inland as Onitsha. On the stretch of coast from Senegal to the Ivory Coast, which we may for convenience call the West Atlantic Coast, European traders met with the same opposition from Africans to their attempts to penetrate the interior. There were, however, two major exceptions: the Rivers Senegal and Gambia which gave French and British traders at St Louis and Bathurst (Banjul) respectively access to the markets of the hinterland.

The French founded the town of St Louis at the mouth of the River Senegal in 1659. There they traded in gum arabic, used for making dyes fast, and in slaves. The French also established themselves on Gorée, the small island that lies off modern Dakar. During the wars between France and Britain in the late eighteenth and early nineteenth century St Louis was occupied by the British. After 1817, and until independence, it remained in the hands of France and became its main base for the penetration of the interior of the Western Sudan.

During the early half of the nineteenth century the French believed that all men, no matter what their colour or their religion were equal. So in St Louis and Gorée, Africans and Mulattoes, that is people of mixed African and European blood, were treated as though they were Frenchmen. They were given French citizenship and French education, and many became Catholics like the French. A Mulatto became Mayor of St Louis, and the General who headed the French forces that invaded Dahomey was also a Mulatto. When in 1848 St Louis and Gorée were permitted to elect a deputy or representative to the Chamber of Deputies in Paris the Senegalese citizens chose a Mulatto from St Louis called Durand-Valentin. This French policy of treating their African and Mulatto subjects as equal to themselves and giving them the same rights and privileges as French citizens was known as *assimilation*. Later, as we shall see, the French abandoned this policy. But to begin with, inspired by the ideals of the French revolution – Liberty, Fraternity and Equality – they treated all men as equals.

So we find during the nineteenth century that the Senegalese towns of St Louis and Gorée, and later Dakar and Rufisque, were turned into municipalities just like those in France with mayors and councillors. After 1879 Senegal itself was governed by a *Conseil-Général* or General Council just like those in the Departments or major administrative divisions of France. All the inhabitants were citizens with the right to vote for representatives on the town councils, the General Council and the French Chamber of Deputies.

15.1 *A contemporary view of St Louis, headquarters of the French in Senegal, showing the fort.*

After St Louis had been given back to them by the British, the French tried to settle Frenchmen there to cultivate the land. But this did not work as the climate and disease were hostile to them. The French then tried introducing new crops which the Senegalese inhabitants would cultivate for export to France. But these experiments were not very successful and St Louis depended mainly on the trade along the River Senegal. After the abolition of the slave trade, this was mainly in gum Arabic.

The French had a string of forts and trading posts along the River Senegal from which they conducted their trade. However, the Moors, who lived along the River Senegal, often charged high customs dues and interrupted trade. Also, the great Muslim reformer, Al-Hajj Umar, who came from Futa Toro, on the upper reaches of the River Senegal, demanded that the French pay tribute to him not only in Futa Toro but in St Louis which he claimed as his own (see below p. 124).

2 The French push along the River Senegal

To deal with these threats to their trade the French appointed General Louis Faidherbe as Governor of Senegal. He had already had experience in the French conquest of Algeria. He sent expeditions up the River Senegal and crushed the Moors between 1855 and 1858. In 1855 he built a fort at Medina to deal with the threat of Al-Hajj Umar. In 1857 Al-Hajj Umar nearly succeeded in taking the fort, but it was relieved by a Senegalese Mulatto, Paul Holle. Indeed, for the most part Faidherbe used Senegalese troops, the famous *Tirailleurs Sénégalais* or Senegalese Sharpshooters, against the Moors and Al-Hajj Umar.

Though the French never conquered Al-Hajj Umar, they successfully resisted his westward expansion and after they had destroyed his fort at Guemou he turned his attention eastwards to the conquest of Macina (see below p. 124).

15.2   *A drawing made by Governor Faidherbe of Senegal of trade between the French and the Trarza Moors whom he was later to conquer because of their stoppages of trade on the River Senegal.*

The French now controlled a third of modern Senegal. But the main source of their trade came not from their new protectorate along the Senegal River but from the lands to the south. These produced groundnuts in quantity which were exported to France where their oil was extracted for use in cooking and making soap. Despite this, Faidherbe and many of his successors believed that the most important markets for France lay along the Niger in the Western Sudan. It was for this reason that in 1882 the French Government agreed to provide funds for a railway linking Medina with Bamako in the Tukolor Empire. This would bring the wealth of the lands on the River Niger to the River Senegal and hence to St Louis.

The French now no longer ignored the wealthy groundnut areas between St Louis and Dakar and also made funds available to build a railway between these two cities. But Ahmadou, son of Al-Hajj Umar, who succeeded as ruler of his father's Empire, objected to the railway crossing his territory. So too did Lat Dior, Damel of Cayor, through whose lands the Dakar–Saint Louis line would also pass. This as

we shall see led to war.

Meanwhile, the French in St Louis began to have doubts about the wisdom of their policy of assimilation. They did not apply it to their newly won Protectorate for several reasons. They began to doubt whether Muslims could be made into Frenchmen, since they would not give up their religion and accept French private law which forbade polygamy. Also, many Frenchmen, inspired by racist philosophies, began to argue that black men were inferior to white men. As they conquered more and more territory and brought more and more Africans under their rule, the cost of a full scale assimilation policy increased. How could France pay for the education services necessary to turn Africans into 'black Frenchmen'? Finally, if France made all her overseas subjects citizens with the right to vote, the French would be a minority in their own Parliament. Apart from Black Africa, France had colonial possessions in South-East Asia, North Africa, the Middle East and South America. If a full-scale policy of assimilation were followed France would become a colony of her colonies, since there were more colonial subjects in her Empire than Frenchmen. So in Black Africa, outside Senegal, France abandoned her policy of assimilation just as Africans in Senegal were beginning to show that with education and opportunity they could compete on equal terms with their white masters in trade, politics and the professions.

3 Recaptives in Sierra Leone

Before the British abolition of the slave trade in 1807, slavery in Britain had been prohibited. A number of slaves of the American colonists had fled either to Britain or to the British colony of Nova Scotia in Canada. In England, many free blacks were without work and the humanitarian, Granville Sharpe, persuaded the British Government to send 400 of them to settle in Sierra Leone. So in 1787 the Sierra Leone Company was founded to re-settle these former slaves in the Province of Freedom in what is now Freetown. The original 400 were joined in 1792 by free blacks from Nova Scotia who had found the life there very hard and felt Sierra Leone offered them a better prospect. Again in 1796 Maroons from Nova Scotia asked to be settled in Sierra Leone. The Maroons were slaves who had successfully revolted against their owners in Jamaica and taken to the hills a hundred years before. Finally they were defeated by the British and deported to Nova Scotia.

The settlers suffered a great deal. Malaria killed many. The local Temne people were hostile to them and would not give them land. In 1789 the Temne invaded the colony and nearly destroyed it. In 1794 the French, who were then at war with Britain, bombarded and destroyed Freetown. To add to the new colony's troubles, the Company's government was unpopular and in 1800 some of the Nova Scotians rebelled. So in 1807 the British Government took over Sierra Leone as a Crown Colony.

Sierra Leone was now to become home for all those slaves freed by the ships of the British Anti-Slavery Squadron. Of the original settlers more than half had died by the time Britain took over direct control of the colony. But their numbers were swelled as the British navy became increasingly successful in capturing slave ships. In the colony the British pursued a policy not dissimilar to that of the French in Senegal. All of the freed slaves, or recaptives, were to be converted to Christianity, and to be given an English education. They were settled in English style villages with English names like Leicester, Kent, Regent and York.

The re-captives, as the freed slaves were known, came from all parts of the western coast of Africa, but a large number of them were Yoruba, captured and sold as a result of the civil wars. Though most of the freed slaves became Christians, many of them retained their ancestral culture. To this day in Sierra Leone elements of these cultures survive, in particular that of the Yoruba. The language the freed slaves and settlers spoke, Creole, was a mixture of English and African languages.

By the middle of the nineteenth century this mixture of settlers and recaptives had blended into a distinct cultural group known today as Creoles. Though they were western educated, and trained in western techniques such as carpentry, masonry and blacksmithing, they also retained a strong sense of their identity as Africans. Many of them longed to return to their homelands and bring to their people the benefits of their new-found religion and education. Thus Samuel Ajayi Crowther, a Yoruba, and J. I. C. Taylor, an Igbo, returned to Nigeria to help

15.3 *Fourah Bay College, the first western university institution in West Africa, and two of its students. Bishop Crowther was a foundation student at Fourah Bay.*

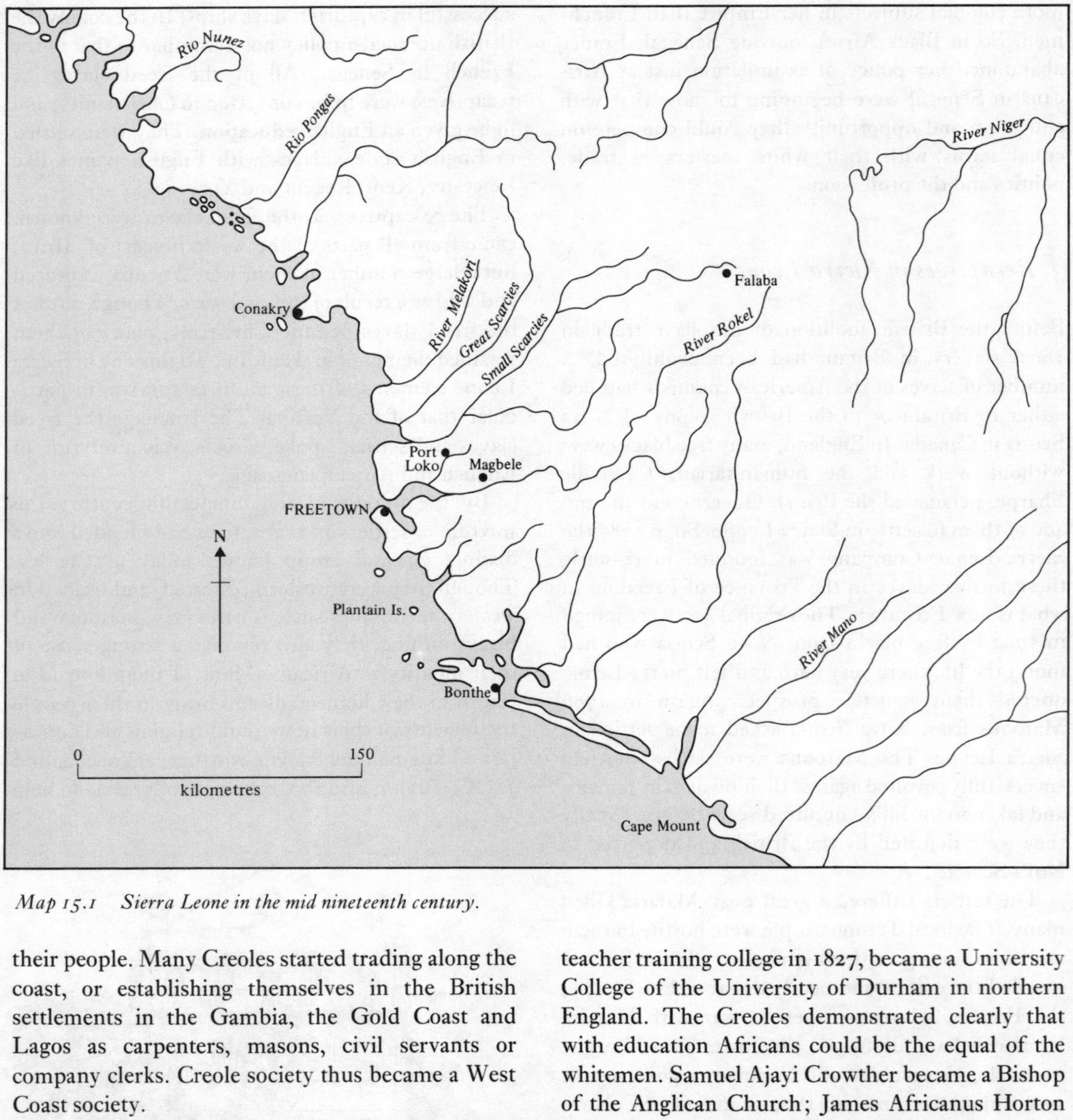

Map 15.1   Sierra Leone in the mid nineteenth century.

their people. Many Creoles started trading along the coast, or establishing themselves in the British settlements in the Gambia, the Gold Coast and Lagos as carpenters, masons, civil servants or company clerks. Creole society thus became a West Coast society.

In 1863 the British introduced a constitution which allowed Creoles representation on both the Executive Councils and Legislative Councils. In 1893 Freetown was made a municipality like St Louis and Dakar. It had a Creole Mayor, Samuel Lewis, who became the first African to be knighted.

Creoles could even attend university in Freetown after 1876 when Fourah Bay College, established as a

teacher training college in 1827, became a University College of the University of Durham in northern England. The Creoles demonstrated clearly that with education Africans could be the equal of the whitemen. Samuel Ajayi Crowther became a Bishop of the Anglican Church; James Africanus Horton became a Surgeon-Major in the British army, and as we have seen wrote the constitution of the Fante Confederation; J.C. Parkes became Secretary for Native Affairs in the Sierra Leone Government; a Creole became President of Liberia; while two Creoles became successively Chief Justices of the Gambia.

Creoles made important contributions to African

15.4 *Bishop Crowther, the first West African to become a Bishop, photographed in his old age. Crowther was a pioneer of Yoruba language studies.*

studies. To mention a few of their works: A. B. C. Sibthorpe's *History and Geography of Sierra Leone*; James Africanus Horton's *West African Countries and Peoples* together with books on tropical African diseases; and Samuel Ajayi Crowther's *Grammar and Vocabulary of the Yoruba Language*.

4 Creole influence in West Africa

One of the reasons for the Creoles trading along the coast, rather than into the interior, was that the peoples of the hinterland were as wary of the Creoles supplanting them in their middleman role as they were of the British and French. It was for this reason, as we shall see, that the Creoles urged the British Government to extend their rule over the peoples of the interior.

The Creoles, like the Senegalese citizens, had their hey-day in the nineteenth century. Towards the 1880s, as the Europeans began to extend their control over the interior, the Creoles found themselves ousted from their senior positions in the colonial governments and replaced by whitemen. Even in the Anglican church, Bishop Crowther and his African clergy were supplanted by white missionaries. Two factors account for this. At the end of the nineteenth century white people came increasingly to believe that the African was inferior to the whiteman even where Africans had demonstrated clearly that they could do any type of work as well as a whiteman could. Secondly, the whitemen felt that they, rather than these 'foreign Africans' as they thought of them, could deal better with the Africans of the interior than they could.

Though the Creoles were displaced by the whitemen, they, like the Senegalese citizens, were to have a major influence over the rise of the nationalist movement under colonial rule. Throughout the colonial period, the Creoles were to be among the leaders of those Africans who rejected the idea that the British were in any way superior to them.

5 Black Americans in Liberia

America's successful War of Independence against Britain from 1775–83 meant that the American colonists were no longer bound by British laws. Thus, while the United States of America was persuaded to abolish the slave trade a year after Britain did, she did not follow Britain in abolishing slavery in 1833. Even though the United States made the slave trade illegal, she did little to stop her subjects from shipping slaves to her ports. It took the bitter American Civil War from 1861–1865 to free slaves in the United States.

Though slavery continued to exist in the United States right up to 1865, there were a number of slaves who had been freed by their masters or who had escaped to states where slavery did not exist. Though they were free, they were treated as second class citizens and resented by the white Americans. In 1816, a group of white Americans founded the American Colonisation Society. Their aim was to solve the problem of these unwanted black Americans by returning them to Africa, their continent of origin. They obtained half-hearted governmental

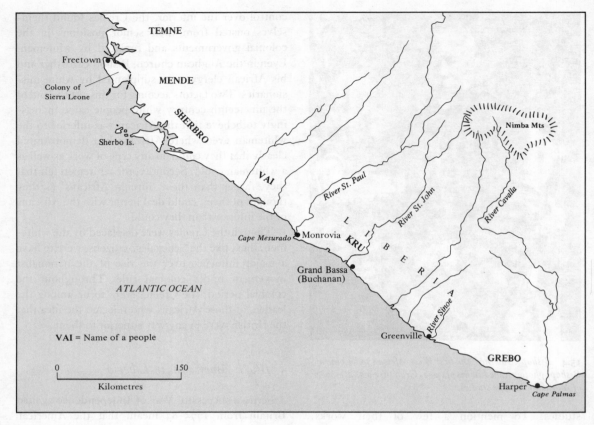

Map 15.2   Liberia in the early nineteenth century.

support for their plans and in 1822 the first group of free black Americans arrived at Cape Mesurado on the coast of modern Liberia. There they founded the town of Monrovia which became the capital of the new Colony of Liberia. The capital took its name from that of the United States President, Monroe, while Liberia was derived from the Latin word *liber*, meaning free.

The American Colonisation Society hoped that their colony would help solve the problem of unwanted free blacks. They also hoped that it would help spread Christianity and American commerce in Africa. But the Society was very small, and it did not have official government backing. Its members often quarrelled among themselves. Thus when in 1847 the Black settlers demanded independence there was little the Society could do about it. Indeed it was quite glad not to have to administer the colony.

Liberia's twenty-four years as a colony were troubled ones. In the first place the death rate among the settlers was very high. Of those of mixed white and black blood – the Mulattoes – nearly 80 percent died. Of those of pure black blood, many of whom had retained some immunity to malaria, 40 percent died. Unlike Sierra Leone, the number of settlers was not increased to any great degree by recaptives. The American navy was not very active in capturing American ships continuing to trade in slaves.

In the second place, while the Black American settlers, or Americo-Liberians as they came to be known, were free, the Society did not allow them full participation in the government of the new colony. They were ruled by white governors, and the Society had the right to deport anyone it wanted from the colony. There was however a governor's advisory council and an elected post of Lieutenant-Governor.

But this did not satisfy the settlers who resented the Society's control over the land they cultivated. They also accused the white Governors of favouring the Mulatto settlers over the Negroes.

In 1839 a conference was called by the settlers to demand self-government. The Society refused it but in 1841 went some way to meet the settlers grievances by appointing a settler as Governor, Joseph Roberts, a Mulatto.

The third major problem of the colony was its status. It was not an independent state, nor was it a colony of a government, or even officially backed by a government as in the case of Granville Sharp's Province of Freedom. Thus when it tried to impose customs dues to raise revenue to run its government, some European traders refused to pay them on the grounds that a Society as distinct from a government could not impose them.

When Governor Roberts held a referendum among the settlers on the question of independence, and the majority favoured it, the Society did not object.

6 Liberia becomes independent

In 1847 the settlers drew up a constitution at the Monrovia Convention and Roberts became first President of the newly independent Republic. While the greater part of Africa was independent at this time, the independent colony of Liberia had a special

15.5 *The residence of Joseph Roberts, President of Liberia, 1871–1877.*

significance. In the first place it was ruled by freed slaves who had come from many different parts of Africa, and in many cases had white blood in their veins. Thus they did not come originally from the land they now made their own. In the second place, they modelled their constitution on that of the United States, not on that of a neighbouring African state. Thus they became agents for the introduction of Western ideas in West Africa. Protestant Christianity was the official religion of their Republic. Its legal system was also based on that of the United States. Finally they introduced western style education.

The new republic was fortunate in being established at a time when the European powers were not very interested in occupying African lands for themselves. Also, up until the 1880s when the European scramble for African colonies threatened Liberia's very existence, prices for Liberia's exports, palm-oil, camwood and raffia were high. The European scramble for Africa coincided with a fall in world prices. Before the 1880s Liberia was not greatly troubled by the peoples of her hinterland. There were no European powers trying to take it away from her. This meant that there was no need for her to occupy the hinterland since the European powers had not yet declared that to claim a colony a power had to occupy it. On the international scene then, Liberia, apart from some minor quarrels with the neighbouring Sierra Leone, was untroubled for the first forty years of her existence. Her merchants prospered, and her ships carried goods to the United States and Europe. (None could have imagined then, that today Liberia would have the largest single fleet of merchant ships flying her flag in the world.)

While from the international point of view Liberia was untroubled, there were deep divisions in her society. First of all there was rivalry between the merchants of the capital and the farmers of the counties, particularly Grand Bassa, which even threatened to declare its independence in 1847. Much worse was the division between the Mulattoes and the full-blooded Negroes. As we have seen the Mulattoes were favoured by the American Society for Colonisation. The first President was a Mulatto, and he gave most of the jobs in government to Mulattoes. Furthermore, when sending new settlers

15.6 *Edward Wilmot Blyden, scholar and West African patriot.*

to the Republic, the Society tended to send Mulattoes. Roberts' party, the Republican Party, became the party of the Mulattoes while the True Whig Party represented the black settlers.

From 1848 to 1869 the Mulattoes dominated Liberian politics. In 1869, however, the True Whig Party led by E. J. Roye, a Black settler, took power. At the time Liberian presidents had only two years in office at a time. Roye and his chief adviser, the brilliant scholar Edward Blyden, felt that this was too short a time to achieve their plans. In particular they hoped to open up the interior. On top of the time factor, Roye faced a hostile Mulatto dominated civil service. When in 1871 he tried to extend his term of office by two years, he was seized by Republicans and put in jail where he died. Blyden narrowly escaped with his life.

From 1871 to 1877 Liberia was again under Republican rule with Joseph Roberts as president. But the Mulatto Republican Party was in the long-term doomed. The American Society for Colonisation no longer financed Mulatto settlers, and the Mulattoes died off at a greater speed than the full-Black settlers whose ranks were swelled by freed slaves and assimilated Africans. In 1877 the True Whigs won the election and since then the party has been in power. When in 1883 H. R. Johnson, who had been supported by both parties for President, declared himself a True Whig, he also replaced the Republicans in the civil service with True Whigs. Thus the main continuing strength of the Republican Party was removed.

Apart from the struggles between Mulatto and Black settlers, Liberia suffered deeply from its system of patronage. When a man became President he shared out offices among his supporters not on the basis of merit but to ensure he kept their loyalty. Thus most offices were looked on as political rewards rather than rewards for excellence. The civil service and government became very corrupt, since officials tried to see how much they could make for their families rather than direct their work for the good of the people as a whole. Education in particular suffered since the Presidency of the main institution of higher learning, Liberia College, was also a political reward.

Despite these problems, Liberia was a remarkable achievement. In a strange land, with little money, and suffering from disease, these settlers who had known the degradation and bitterness of slavery, who had never been allowed to exercise the rights of man in America, established and maintained their new Republic. And, despite the antagonism of Europeans during the Scramble for Africa, it survived as a symbol of African freedom.

7 Postscript

Despite the racist policies introduced by France and Britain in their West African colonies at the end of the nineteenth century, the memory of the nineteenth century experiments in Senegal and Sierra Leone did not die. Africans continued to believe that they were equal to Europeans no matter what the latter said.

16 Three jihads in the Western Sudan

1 The jihad of Seku Ahmadu

At the beginning of the nineteenth century the Bambara of Kaarta and Segu dominated the Western Sudan from the borders of Futa Toro to the borders of Hausaland. They were to be overthrown by two great jihads, those of Seku Ahmadu from

16.1 *Interior of the great Mosque of Jenne.*

Macina and Al-Hajj Umar from Futa Toro. Seku Ahmadu succeeded only in wresting control of the Fulani province of Macina from the Bambara state of Segu. But the loss to Segu was considerable for he took with him Jenne and Timbuktu as well as the fertile lands of Macina itself.

Seku Ahmadu came from a scholarly Fulani family and had spent time with Shehu Usman dan Fodio and even took part in the early stages of the jihad in 1805. Inspired by the Shehu's teaching he returned to Macina and spoke out against the pagan practices of the Muslim *Ardo'en*, as the leaders of the Fulani of Macina were called. He also attacked the non-Muslim Bambara overlords of Macina.

Through his preaching Ahmadu soon gained a following among both Muslim and non-Muslim Fulani in Macina as well as Muslims like the Marka who felt themselves oppressed. For some time he preached and taught in a village near Jenne. But the Arma or Governor of Jenne feared his revolutionary teachings and expelled him. From there he went to Sebera in Macina, denouncing the lax morals of the Ardo'en and their subservience to the pagan Bambara. His aim was to gain independence for the Fulani of Macina. Like Shehu Usman dan Fodio he held out to his followers the prospect of a true Muslim society, in which the sharia would be supreme.

In 1818 some of his students quarrelled with the son of one of the Ardo'en and killed him. This was the signal for the Ardo'en to try and suppress

Ahmadu once and for all. But Ahmadu had a large number of supporters and the Ardo'en found their own Fulani unwilling to fight him. In desperation they called on their Bambara overlords for help, but Ahmadu swept all before him. As encouragement Ahmadu even received a flag from Usman dan Fodio, though he never acknowledged him as his overlord.

In 1819 he established his capital at Hamdullahi in Macina, mid-way between Jenne and Timbuktu. In 1826–27 he conquered Timbuktu itself.

2 The administration of Macina

The Bambara were expelled from their province of Macina, but still posed a threat from Segu. Thus, one of the main problems of Seku Ahmadu was to defend his new state against raids by the Bambara, particularly on the cattle which were one of its principal sources of wealth.

Seku Ahmadu devised a highly efficient system of administration for Macina, carefully observing Muslim law. The state was ruled by a Council of Forty, which was presided over not by Ahmadu, but by one of his two close companions. He himself was just a member of the Council. He did, however, take the title of Amir-al-Muminin, and of course everyone on the Council listened closely to what he said.

The state was divided into five provinces, each governed by an emir. Under them were judges, tax collectors and local army commanders. Ahmadu was determined that there should be no corruption in his state, so he organised a network of official spies to check on the administration. Weights and measures were made uniform.

In many ways Ahmadu's jihad was much more revolutionary than the one in Sokoto. He inaugurated a state education system as well as pensions for old people. State controlled granaries were established against times of war or drought. An official was appointed to oversee public morals so that people caught drinking, smoking, dancing or committing adultery would be severely punished.

Though Seku Ahmadu imposed a strict Muslim regime on his subjects they accepted it for two reasons. In the first place Ahmadu himself was a very humble man. He obeyed the laws just like other men and listened to their opinions. In the second place, the people remained united in face of the threat from Segu. It was not, however, the Bambara who were to overrun Macina, but another jihad leader, Al-Hajj Umar.

3 The pilgrimage of Al-Hajj Umar

Seku Ahmadu died in 1842 leaving to his successors a stable Caliphate whose system of government followed closely the teachings of Islam. For the next twenty years the state flourished until in 1862 it was attacked and conquered by the Tukolor leader, Al-Hajj Umar.

Umar Said Tall was born in 1794 in the Futa Toro. As we have seen (p. 68) the people of Futa Toro had overthrown their lax Muslim rulers and established a truly Muslim state just twenty years before his birth. Umar proved to be a brilliant student and such was his reputation as a scholar that in 1826 he was able to raise enough funds from wealthy Muslims to make the pilgrimage to Mecca. In those days this was a tremendous undertaking, especially starting from St Louis since it meant a long trek of many months across the Western Sudan, through Darfur to Egypt. Anyone who managed to reach Mecca and return enjoyed great prestige amongst his fellow Muslims.

At the time of his departure, Umar had been initiated into the Tijanniya brotherhood. This was a Sufi order that asserted that its members were spiritually superior to all other Muslims. It also promised its members favoured treatment on the day of judgement. The founder of the order, Ahmed al-Tijani, a North African, claimed that he had direct communication with the Prophet. For all members of the order there was the possibility of obtaining *wilaya* or sainthood for it emphasised the equality of men and did not place great importance on scholarship. Furthermore the litany, or prayers, to be said daily by members of the Tijanniya order was very simple. This contrasted with the more complex litany of the Qadiriyya order which was at that time the most widespread in Africa. These factors, combined with Al-Hajj Umar's magnetic personality, account for the wide popular appeal of the new Tijanniya order.

Apart from making the pilgrimage to Mecca, Umar travelled in Palestine and Syria. Scholars there were impressed by his learning and the Tijani leader of the Hejaz appointed him leader of the Tijanis of the Western Sudan.

Al-Hajj Umar returned to the Western Sudan in 1833. He spent some time in the courts of Borno and Sokoto, where he initiated Muslims into his new order. In Borno he so annoyed El-Kanemi by the success of his teachings that he was forced to move on to Sokoto. There he had the sympathy of Sultan Bello, one of whose daughters he married. But when Sultan Bello died, he was forced to leave since other leading Sokoto Muslims resented his preachings. At that time most of the Muslim ruling classes of the western Sudan were members of the Qadiriyya order. They saw the Tijanniya, with its wide popular appeal, as a threat to their own positions.

From Sokoto he travelled to Segu where he was imprisoned by the Bambara ruler. On his release he travelled to his home in Futa Toro. Even there he was treated with suspicion. So he moved on to neighbouring Futa Djallon where he settled at Diagakou. But the Almami was upset by Umar's calls for reform and expelled him. Umar again moved on, this time to Dinguiray, between Futa Djallon and Futa Toro. There he established a fortress where he trained his disciples in the art of warfare and gathered as many weapons as he could, in particular guns.

4 The Tijanniya jihad of Al-Hajj Umar

Once he felt himself strong enough, he decided to launch a jihad against the 'pagan' state of Kaarta. On 6th September 1852 he reported that God had commanded him to conquer all those who refused to accept his call to Islam.

Umar's jihad differs from those of Sokoto and Macina in a number of ways. In the first place he was not revolting against his own rulers, but attacking an independent non-Muslim state. So it was neither a revolution like that of Sokoto nor an independence

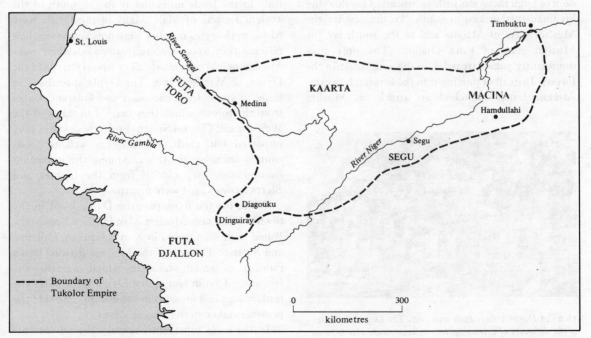

Map 16.1   Tukolor Caliphate under Al-Hajj Umar.

movement like that of Macina. In the second place Umar was to attack and conquer a state that was quite clearly Muslim – Macina. Thirdly, Umar led his jihad against Christians in the form of the French at St Louis.

After conquering Kaarta, Umar turned westwards towards his homeland of Futa Toro where the French were active. He demanded that the French recognise him as ruler of the lands along the River Senegal right up to and including St Louis. They should pay him *jizya*, a Muslim tax due to a Muslim ruler from his non-Muslim subjects who wanted his protection. The French, as we have seen (p. 113), would have none of this and after a series of bloody battles drove him out of Futa Toro.

Umar, having been unable to defeat the French, negotiated a treaty with them which left them in control of the Senegal River west of Medina. The lands to the east were thus free for Al-Hajj Umar. Though the treaty was never ratified by the French, they observed it in practice. Al-Hajj Umar was now joined in his jihad by many Muslims from French-controlled St Louis and Futa Toro.

Once he had conquered the non-Muslim Kingdom of Segu there was little justification for carrying his jihad further east or south. To the east lay the Muslim state of Macina and to the south lay the Muslim state of Futa Djallon. The only predominantly pagan areas lay to the south-east in the forests. Instead of moving into the forests, however, Al-Hajj Umar launched an attack on Muslim

16.2 *A Dogon village built on a cliff. The Dogon, because of the difficulty of getting to their villages, were able to resist the Muslim jihadists and pursue their own religion.*

Macina. The pretext for this was the fact that Ahmadu III, the Caliph of Macina, claimed Segu as his own. With his guns, Umar had little difficulty in conquering Macina in 1862. But soon the Fulani of Macina, the Tuareg of Timbuktu and the Bambara of Segu rose against Umar and besieged Hamdullahi. In February 1864, as Umar was trying to break the siege, he was killed. It was left to his successor, Ahmadu, who was his son by the daughter of Sultan Bello, to quell these rebellions.

From the Muslim point of view it was a major tragedy that two Muslim Caliphates should have clashed when there were non-Muslim lands close by still to bring under Islam. This task was left to the Mandinka, Samori Toure, who established a huge Muslim state bounded in the north by the Tukolor Caliphate, in the west by the Imamate of Futa Djallon, in the east by Asante, and in the south by the forests of Sierra Leone, Liberia and Ivory Coast.

5 The Dyula revolution

For many centuries Dyula had been trading peacefully in the lands immediately to the south of the ancient Empire of Mali. Many of the Dyula were Muslim, though a number were not. Whatever their religion they lived peacefully alongside their non-Muslim neighbours nearly all of whom were, like the Dyula, of Mande origin. The Dyula specialised in trade in goods from the coast and kola and slaves from the forests which they carried to states of the Western and Central Sudan. From these states they imported salt, cloth and cattle as well as goods coming from North Africa. Among the important commodities they carried from the Guinea and Sierra Leone Coast were firearms.

While for the most part the Dyula lived in the towns of the non-Muslim Mande, they had established their own towns in Kong, Kankan, Odienné and Sikasso. The rest of the area was divided into a number of small states in which warfare was frequent. This in fact suited Dyula trade since the traders supplied firearms to combatants and sold the prisoners taken in the wars as slaves.

In the early nineteenth century the movements for Islamic reform sweeping the Western and

16.3 & 4 *Samori Toure, the father of the Mandinka Empire : left, when in power, right after capture by the French.*

Central Sudan began to affect Muslim Dyula. The Dyula Marabout, Mori-Ule-Sise, inspired by the jihads of Futa Djallon and Macina, settled at Madina where a large number of Muslims joined him. Around 1835 he proclaimed a jihad against the non-Muslim inhabitants of the area and founded the Muslim kingdom of Moriuledegu. Later one of his disciples killed him and founded another Muslim kingdom called Kabasarana. Then, reconciling himself with the successors of Mori-Ule-Sise, he joined forces with them and moved up the valley of the River Milo into the Konya country, attacking the non-Muslim Berete.

During these wars the mother of a pagan Dyula, called Samori Toure, was captured with her son in

about 1853 by the Sise and taken to Madina. Samori spent five years with the Sise where he learnt much about the art of warfare. He then left Madina to live among the Berete, but he quarrelled with them so he returned to his own Konya people. There he offered his services to his uncles, and soon had gathered a group of warriors round him consisting of his friends and relations.

In 1865 he allied himself with the Sise of Madina and helped them conquer the Berete. By now Samori Toure had become a major force in the Konya region. Through his Dyula friends and relations he imported firearms and horses to strengthen his corps of warriors. In 1874 he felt strong enough to establish his own capital at Bisandugu, where he declared his

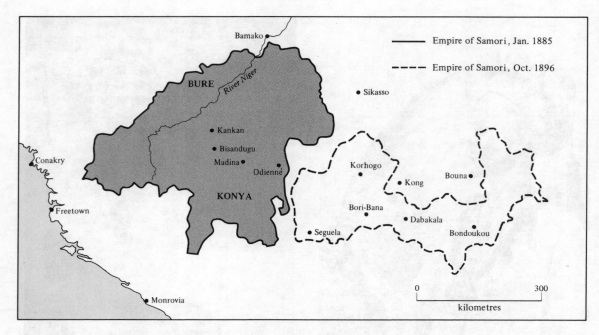

Map 16.2   Samori Toure's first and second empires.

independence from the Konya. He proclaimed that the main objective of his new state was to protect trade. This appealed to the Dyula who often found their trade subject to heavy taxes by local chiefs, who sometimes closed the trade routes.

As proof of his intentions he helped the Muslim Dyula of Kankan to conquer the local non-Muslim chiefs who had closed the city's trade routes. He then conquered territory stretching right up to Bamako, on the borders of the Tukolor Caliphate. He also took the rich gold fields of Bure.

As a result of these conquests Samori now had no shortage of money or men, and turned on the Sise of Madina and on Kankan. By mid-1881, he had established a huge empire for himself, such as had never existed in this area before.

6   *The organisation of Samori's Empire*

Samori Toure had taken as his title as the head of his state the non-Muslim military title of Faama. His early wars had not been undertaken in the name of Islam, but for the sake of keeping the Dyula trade

routes open. In 1884, however, Samori took the title Almami, and made his state a Muslim state. In 1886 he ordered all his subjects to convert to Islam. His state became the third largest Muslim state in the Sudan, after Sokoto and the Tukolor Caliphate.

While Islam played a major part in Samori's new state, the army was the key to its success. Islam could serve as a unifying force amongst peoples of different ethnic groups. But it was the army that held it together.

The leaders of Samori's armies were his close friends. When he conquered a state, he did not sell the captured soldiers, but made them members of his army. They were offered their freedom in return for serving him. His troops were organised not by caste or ethnic group or village of origin but were all mixed up together. This meant that their loyalty was to the army not to any particular group.

The army basically consisted of infantry. In the battle of Sikasso, for instance, Samori had only 3,000 cavalry as against between 30,000 and 35,000 foot-soldiers. But his soldiers were all called Sofas which means literally horse-father. He equipped as many of his soldiers as possible with guns, including rapid firing rifles which he imported from Sierra Leone and the Guinea Coast. His own blacksmiths were able to make guns and repair imported rifles.

He divided his Empire into six administrative units. He himself controlled the metropolitan district, called the *Foroba*, while soldier-administrators, called *Kelitigi*, controlled five provinces. Each Kelitigi had roughly 5,000 soldiers at his disposal. In the Foroba, Samori maintained a central army of between 8,000 and 10,000 men. Throughout his Empire Samori built mosques and established schools. The sharia became the law of the land. Appeals against judgements were heard personally by Samori.

Within a short period of time Samori had built a great Muslim state from a series of feuding little states. He had organised a non-tribal army. He had established workshops that could manufacture guns for his troops. But even as he was building his empire he came into conflict with the French whom he was to fight on and off from 1881–1898 in an attempt to maintain his empire. But for the French, Samori could have turned his organising genius to the task of economic and social development. As it was, as we shall see later, his energies from 1891–1898 were entirely monopolised by concern to defend his Empire.

17 Background to the European occupation of West Africa

1 Explorers, missionaries and traders

Though by the beginning of the nineteenth century the Europeans had a considerable amount of knowledge about the coastal states of West Africa, they were almost entirely ignorant about the interior of the continent. So men were sent off to explore the interior of Africa and bring back information about its peoples, its products and its geography. The main reason for this was to get information about trading possibilities. This is why the early explorers of West Africa were so concerned with the River Niger, which they believed would be the highway to the riches of the interior.

The Europeans thought of themselves as explorers of unknown lands. From the point of view of

17.1 *Richard and John Lander visit the King of Badagry at the start of their famous journey as a result of which Europeans learnt where the beginning of the Niger was. Explorers like the Landers did much to pave the way for eventual European occupation of Africa.*

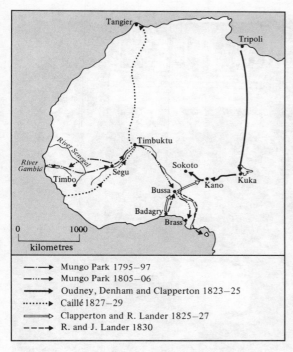

Map 17.1   Early explorers' routes.

the Africans these European explorers were tourists in lands which Africans had known for centuries. As a result of trade, particularly by the Dyula and Hausa, there were groups of Africans who knew a great deal about the geography of their neighbours. In 1826 the Caliph Mohammed Bello of Sokoto was able to tell his visitor, Commander Clapperton from England, much about the lands through which he would travel.

When Richard and John Lander found in 1830 that the Niger entered the sea in the series of rivers between Warri and Bonny, they were discovering something that Europeans did not know, but which many Africans were fully aware of. After all Aboh and Onitsha were great markets on the Niger which dealt in goods coming upstream from the coast and downstream from Bussa, Jebba and Yola.

Similarly when René Caillié, the French explorer, reached Timbuktu, he 'discovered' a city for the French but not for West Africans or even Arabs who had long known it as an important centre of trade and scholarship.

The European explorers were only making discoveries for other Europeans. They were not telling Africans in the lands they 'discovered' anything they did not already know. What is significant about the work of the explorers is that they gave their own governments information about the interior of West Africa, in particular about its trading possibilities. Immediately after Richard and John Lander 'discovered' that the Niger emptied into the sea at Brass the British Government backed an expedition up the river by the Liverpool trader, MacGregor Laird. At first the information the explorers brought back served peaceful ends; the promotion of trade and the opening up of the continent to Christian Missionary enterprise. But when the European powers undertook the Scramble for Africa, they had already obtained a considerable amount of the geographical information they needed to conduct their invasions.

Additional information was supplied to the European governments by missionaries and traders who moved into the interior. The missionaries, often unintentionally, were of great importance to the eventual occupation of West Africa by Europe. Apart from venturing into hitherto unknown parts and supplying information to their home countries about the possibilities of trade, they also sent home reports of practices such as human sacrifice and domestic slavery or twin murder which the colonial powers used as justification for occupying Africa for its own good. Often these reports were exaggerated, and in fact the real motive of the colonial powers for occupying Africa was economic, not moral. By and large the missionaries operated near the coast, within reach of the coastal colonial establishments so that in times of trouble they could seek refuge in them. But some missionaries ventured far into the interior, and were in their own right explorers. Such a missionary was Samuel Ajayi Crowther, a freed slave who had been educated in Sierra Leone. He helped explore the lands on the lower reaches of the Niger and became Anglican Bishop of West Africa in the days when the Anglican Church Missionary Society still had the policy of using African missionaries to open up Africa.

Missionaries served the cause of imperialism further by providing a small elite of Africans with Christian Western Education. They and their child-

17.2   *European Missionaries, like the Reverend Townsend and the Reverend Wood in Abeokuta, also did much to encourage European interest in Africa and pave the way for occupation.*

ren were to prove invaluable to the colonial rulers in establishing their administrations: they provided government clerks, junior officials in the commercial houses and interpreters in the very early days of colonial rule.

As a result of the work of explorers, traders and missionaries, by the time the European powers began to compete with each other for control of African territory in the 1880s, they knew a very great deal more about the interior of Africa than they did in 1800 and were in a position to occupy it.

2 *Background to the Scramble*

Between 1850 and 1880 the only new territories acquired in West Africa by the Europeans were the Gold Coast Colony, Lagos Island and a small part of the mainland, and a stretch of land up the River Senegal (see Map 18.1). The attitude of governments in France and Britain was that Tropical African

colonies were a burden. Sir Frederic Rogers of the British Foreign Office described them as 'expensive and troublesome'. But this did not mean that these governments did not want to support their traders in West Africa; they just did not want to involve themselves in the costly business of administering West African colonies.

While the French and British Governments felt that expansion into the African hinterland was undesirable, the administrators of their tiny colonies on the spot thought otherwise. We have seen how Faidherbe conquered parts of Senegal because of hold-ups of trade on the rivers by the Moors and Al-Hajj Umar. We have seen how Commander Glover in Lagos intervened in the Yoruba civil wars when these held up the free flow of trade to Lagos. Whatever home policy may have been, the Governor on the spot often felt it necessary to occupy African territory in order to maintain the revenues of his colony. Others had ambitions to make the colonies they administered larger. But whatever the ambitions of these men, the amount of territory controlled by France and Britain on the west coast of Africa on the eve of the European Scramble was very small.

Britain possessed Bathurst (Banjul) at the mouth of the Gambia; the peninsula of Freetown; the Gold Coast Colony; and the island of Lagos and a tiny part of the mainland. Despite the small amount of land the British controlled at that time, they had considerable influence up-river in the Gambia and in the hinterland of Freetown. On the Gold Coast, as we have seen, the British were deeply involved in the long-standing hostility between the Fante and Asante and fought the Asante on several occasions. In Lagos the British were similarly deeply involved in the disturbed internal affairs of Yorubaland. Further down the coast in the Niger Delta, though there was no formal British administration there, Britain had long been involved in the internal affairs of its states. What is more, a British trader, George Taubman Goldie, was trying to create a company with a monopoly of trade there which would have governmental powers.

French policy with regard to the establishment of colonies on the west coast was not so consistent as that of the British. Frequent changes of government were partly responsible for this. However, the French military, who had suffered a humiliating defeat by the Prussians in 1870–71, were anxious to re-establish French prestige by expanding France's Empire. So there were important pressures on the governments in France to undertake expansion in Africa. But before 1880, France had made major inroads only into the hinterland of the colony of Senegal. Elsewhere on the coast, it had no official possessions, though it did have major trading interests on the Guinea coast, the Ivory coast and the Dahomeyan coast.

In 1880, then, we can see that France and Britain controlled very small portions of West African territory. Lord Salisbury, the British Foreign Minister, later remarked 'When I left the Foreign Office in 1880, nobody cared about Africa. When I returned to it in 1885 the nations of Europe were almost quarrelling with each other as to the various portions of Africa they could obtain'. What changed the situation so that within twenty-five years all of

Africa, with the exception of Liberia and Ethiopia, had come under European control? The answer to this question is as much tied up with the history of Europe as with that of Africa, and it has been the subject of many debates by historians. We will try here to outline the reasons for the Scramble which most historians accept.

3 The causes of the Scramble

The industrial states of Europe in 1880 were seeking further markets for their products and competing with each other for raw materials, some of which, like palm-oil and groundnut oil, were principally supplied by West Africa. These powers were also looking for new places to invest the profits they made from their factories, and they looked at Africa as a possible place to invest these profits and make further profits. Now all of these powers would have preferred to trade with and invest in Africa without the necessity of conquering African states and administering them. Conquest was expensive in terms of men and materials while the costs of administration would have to be deducted from the profits made by traders. But at the end of the nineteenth century a number of European powers practised protectionism: that is they placed taxes on foreign goods coming into their countries to make them more expensive than similar goods made in their own factories. They thus protected their own products from competition by cheaper foreign goods. Other powers practised free trade which allowed foreigners the same trading privileges as nationals of the territory in which they traded. While no European power really wanted to occupy African territory, they were all frightened that one power which practised protectionism would occupy an area in which their nationals traded and thus exclude them by imposing taxes on the goods they imported. In particular they were terrified that the Congo and Niger, which, in the absence of railways, were the main trading highways into Africa, might be controlled by a protectionist power. In 1879 France, which was protectionist, made treaties with chiefs on the Congo. About the same time the British trader, Goldie, as we saw earlier, drove his French rivals out of business by a ruthless price war. Britain practised free trade, but what Goldie was doing on the Niger was the same as if it were protectionist: creating a monopoly of trade for the British company.

Suspicion of each others' intentions in Africa played a major role in persuading European powers to occupy African territory. If they could not be sure of freedom of trade for their nationals, the best course for them was to make sure they got their share of African trade by occupying the areas that most interested them. Moreover, as more countries became industrialised competition for raw materials and markets increased greatly.

There were other important considerations in the European occupation of Africa. Nationalism was a very important force in Europe in the 1880s. Many Europeans felt that their nations could not be great without an empire. King Leopold of the Belgians tried to make his tiny country more important by acquiring colonies. Hence his interest in the Congo. Many people in France, after their defeat by the Prussians in 1871, sought to restore their national self-respect by extending their empire in Africa. This was preferable to costly European wars to extend their territories in Europe as they had done in the past. At this time the population of Europe was increasing rapidly and there were many poor people who might find better lives abroad: in the Americas, North Africa, and now possibly in Tropical Africa. While climate and disease made European settlement impossible in West Africa, it was an important factor in East, Central and Southern Africa where large numbers of Europeans settled.

The Scramble was also stimulated by colonial administrators, soldiers, traders and missionaries on the spot. Even if the metropolitan power was against further colonial expansion because of the costs, the local administrator could argue that events made it necessary for him to extend his frontiers. While traders preferred to work outside the control of colonial administrations so that they did not have to pay taxes, immediately they came up against trouble, they appealed for the assistance of the local colonial administration. Thus French traders on the Senegal appealed to the Governor of Senegal, Faidherbe, to conquer the Moors of Trarza on the River Senegal who were interfering with their trade. Missionaries

were happy to work outside colonial control if they were well treated by their African hosts. Once they found themselves in trouble with them they called on the colonial administrators for help.

Soldiers, too, pushed forward the frontiers of colonies without permission from their governments and for their own ends. Despite the fact that the French Chamber of Deputies had forbidden further colonial expansion in the Western Sudan, the soldiers pushed ahead regardless. War meant recruitment of more soldiers, and the promotion of officers to control them. War meant that senior officers who died had to be replaced by the promotion of junior officers. The newly acquired territories had to be administered and this usually meant further opportunities for promotion. The conquest of the Western Sudan was of little advantage to France. It is one of the poorest stretches of African territory, and much of it is desert. But it suited not only soldiers who gained promotion but also business interests. Materials had to be supplied to build the new colonial administrative posts. Telegraph lines had to be constructed to link the territories with the capitals. Railways had to be built. All this meant profits for businessmen who supported such ventures.

Many Europeans tried to justify the conquest of West Africa by saying that they were trying to suppress the internal slave trade and restore order to a part of the continent that they alleged was in anarchy. Yet no mention was made of the slave trade at the Berlin Conference which was called to settle the rules for the European occupation of Africa. Nor too, with the possible exception of Yorubaland, could West Africa in any way be described as in a state of anarchy that made trade difficult. As we have seen, the greater part of the continent was under the rule of strong, and often dynamic powers: Samori's Empire, the Tukolor Empire, Asante, which was reforming itself despite British attacks, and the Sokoto Caliphate.

4 The Berlin Conference 1884–5

Basically the Scramble for Africa was sparked off by the mutual suspicions of European powers. By the time of the Berlin Conference of 1884 it was well under way. That Conference was not the start of the race for African territory: rather it tried to lay down rules so that European powers would not clash in Africa and as a consequence trigger off wars between them in Europe.

The Berlin Conference, under the chairmanship of Chancellor Bismarck of Germany, required that each European power claiming a piece of African territory should inform all the other European powers who signed the Act produced by the conference. This would enable any of these other powers to make their claims to this territory if they had any. Once a European power had claimed a

territory it should make good its claim by occupation. The Berlin Act also ruled that there should be freedom of navigation on the Niger and Congo whichever powers controlled their banks.

Claims to territories were based on treaties signed by African chiefs. These treaties, actually giving or claiming to give European rights over African territories, were often signed without African rulers realising what they meant. When the Europeans came to take over these territories, they were not able to do so peacefully but had to undertake expensive military operations which met with fierce opposition.

18 African resistance to the European conquest

1 *African and European armies in West Africa*

In the twenty-five years between 1880 and 1905 nearly all of West Africa was conquered by the British and the French. How was it that small French and British armies, operating in lands which were largely unknown to their commanders, were able to overcome African armies many times their size?

The European armies were always better equipped with guns than the African armies. Since the guns were manufactured in Europe, the European armies had direct access to the latest models, whereas African armies could usually only get hold of models that were long out of date in Europe and then only in small quantities. Most important of all, when machine guns were invented in Europe, these became available to the European armies invading West Africa but not to the African armies. Now while African armies often outnumbered the European armies as much as five-to-one, sometimes even ten-to-one, not only did the European armies have more rifles than them, they also had machine guns. The Maxim gun which was used, for instance, in the conquest of Sokoto, could fire eleven shots every second, that is 660 a minute! Many of the guns used by the Africans might only fire once a minute. With guns like the Maxim, the Gatling and heavy artillery before it, European invaders did not have to worry that they were outnumbered.

Not only did they have greater fire-power, they also had well disciplined, well-drilled armies. It was no use possessing a gun if you did not know the best way to use it. For instance the Ijebu never took advantage of the fact that breech-loading rifles permitted you to fire lying down thus presenting a smaller target to the enemy. Instead they continued to fire them standing up as though they were the old fashioned muzzle-loading guns. Few African generals tried to find out how best the new arms they managed to get hold of could be used.

The European armies were well drilled because they were permanently employed or standing armies. Most African states did not employ standing armies but just called up farmers, who had some training in war, when they were needed. It was not true to say that the European armies were necessarily better than African armies, but because the European armies, which consisted largely of African troops, were standing armies, war was their full-time occupation. It is significant that two of the hardest battles fought by European armies were against African standing armies: those of Samori and Bai Bureh of Sierra Leone, who had a standing army of 'war-boys'.

Even though the European armies had these advantages, the conquest was no easy task. It took twenty-five years, and even after 1905 some parts of Mauritania and Ivory Coast were not subdued. The African armies and their generals were much more familiar with the land they were fighting in. They usually had the support of the local population. Cannons and Maxim guns may have given Euro-

peans an advantage in fire power, but they were
heavy and had to be carried through the bush,
making the European columns easy targets, particularly for guerilla groups.

African resistance was often more effective when
leaders adopted guerilla tactics, as Bai Bureh did:
that is never attacking the invader head on, but in
surprise attacks. The invader had a much easier task
dealing with the massed armies of Sokoto than with
the small forces of Bai Bureh which surprised them
on the march, using his best marksmen to pick off
the European officers. Indeed the Europeans found
some of their most difficult conquests were those of
people, like the Igbo and Tiv, who did not live in
states and where each village had to be dealt with
separately.

Finally, the African states fell more easily prey to
the European armies because they took them on
separately, rather than united in alliances. Indeed,
some African states aided the Europeans against
their African enemies only to find that the same fate
later befell them.

2 *The conquest*

It would take a whole book to describe the European
conquest of West Africa and African resistance. If
we look at Map 19.1 (p. 144) of colonial West Africa
we can see that most of it was French. Does this
mean that the French were more successful than the
British? Only if we consider that the quantity of land
is the measure of success. In West Africa France
occupied 4,700,000 square kilometres compared
with 1,200,000 occupied by the British, but when we
consider the quality of the land and its human and
mineral resources, we can see the British did much
better. Much of French West Africa was desert, a
great deal more of it was poor sahel and savannah.
The only rich territories France conquered were
Ivory Coast with its cocoa and coffee, Guinea with
its banana and timber and Senegal with its
groundnut crop. Britain, on the other hand, not only
had rich cocoa land in Ghana but also the gold
mines; in Nigeria she had palm-oil, cocoa, timber,
cotton and groundnuts as well as tin; Sierra Leone

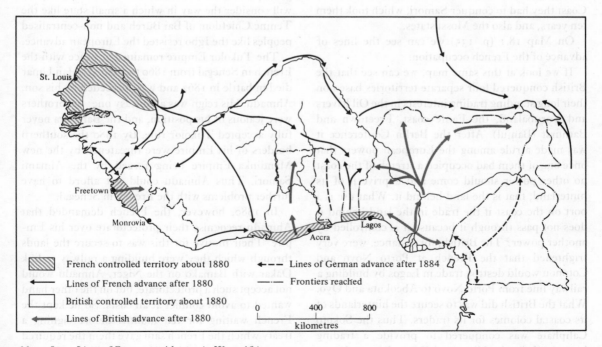

Key:

French controlled territory about 1880

Lines of French advance after 1880

British controlled territory about 1880

Lines of British advance after 1880

Lines of German advance after 1884

Frontiers reached

0   400   800
kilometres

Map 18.1   Lines of European Advance in West Africa.

and the Gambia were never very rich, but they were never as poor as Niger and Upper Volta, and of course, diamonds were discovered in Sierra Leone.

What explains this? Essentially the British conquest was based on occupying land in which her traders had interests. The French conquest of the Western Sudan, as distinct from the coastal colonies of Guinea, Ivory Coast and Dahomey, was largely the work of soldiers. The French push into the Western Sudan and its conquest of the Tukolor Empire of Ahmadu was inspired by the desire of the military to extend their conquests. It was not inspired by trading concern as was the conquest of the Kingdom of Dahomey in 1892 after it had made French trade on the coast almost impossible, or in Futa Djallon where the French feared the British might deprive them of the trading hinterland for their stations on the Guinea coast.

The French also had the ambition to link their North African, West African and Equatorial African territories. This meant occupying a lot of territory that had no economic value to them. They also wanted to link their interior colonies with the sea. Thus to link Sudan with Guinea and the Ivory Coast they had to conquer Samori, which took them ten years, and also the Mossi states.

On Map 18.1 (p. 135) we can see the lines of advance of the French occupation.

If we look at this same map, we can see that the British conquered four separate territories based on their long standing trading interests in the Oil Rivers and Yorubaland, the Fante coast, Freetown and Bathurst (Banjul). After the Berlin Conference it was made a rule among the European powers that once one of them had occupied a stretch of the coast no other power should come and deprive it of its hinterland, that is the land behind it. What use is a port on the coast if the trade in the land behind it does not pass through it because it is controlled by another power? The British, for instance, were very frightened that the French at Porto Novo and Cotonou would destroy trade in Lagos by building a railway line from Porto Novo to Abeokuta and Oyo. What the British did was to secure the hinterlands of its coastal colonies for its traders. Thus the Sokoto Caliphate was conquered to provide a trading hinterland for the Niger and Benue Rivers. If you look at Nigeria it forms a natural hinterland for those parts the British had already occupied before 1880. The same is true for the Gold Coast, Sierra Leone and the Gambia.

3 Resistance by the great Muslim states: the Tukolor Empire, the Mandinka Empire of Samori and the Sokoto Caliphate

We cannot, of course, look at all the many cases of resistance by West Africans to the European invasion in a book such as this: the vast majority of African states tried to resist their take-over by the Europeans. We can only look at a number of instances to see how successful they were in their resistance, and why it failed in the end. We cannot even look at the course of the battles between the European and African armies because of limitation of space. First, we will consider how the great Muslim states – the Tukolor Empire, the Mandinka Empire of Samori and the Sokoto Caliphate – tried to resist the Europeans. Then we will look at two great past states: Dahomey and Asante. Finally we will consider the way in which a small state like the Temne Chiefdom of Bai Bureh and non-centralised peoples like the Igbo resisted the European advance.

The Tukolor Empire remained at peace with the French in Senegal from 1860 to 1880. Al-Hajj Umar died in battle in 1862 and was succeeded by his son, Ahmadu. His reign was an uneasy one: his brothers were jealous of his position, and the Bambara never fully accepted Tukolor rule. By 1880 the southern borders of his Empire were threatened by the new Mandinka Empire being forged by the Almami Samori. Thus Ahmadu could not afford to have further problems with the French in Senegal.

In 1880, however, the French demanded that Ahmadu recognise their protectorate over his Empire. Their motive for this was to secure the lands through which they were building a railway to link Dakar with Bamako on the Niger. Ahmadu would not accept such a protectorate, but on the other hand wanted to avoid conflict at all costs. So he kept the French waiting for ten months before signing a treaty which the French said gave them the required protectorate, but which Ahmadu said merely gave them the position of most favoured trading nation. Despite these differences of interpretation, the French did not immediately invade Ahmadu's Empire to take the land through which the railway would pass. They had too many troubles elsewhere in their colonial Empire. However, three years later in 1883 they took Bamako, the town on the Niger which would be the railway's first destination. They also assembled and floated a gun-boat on the Niger which could then menace Ahmadu's capital at Segu. Ahmadu did not retaliate, though between 1880 and 1893 he was to come into frequent conflict with the French particularly after the Berlin Act made it necessary for the French to make good their claims to the Tukolor Empire before another power took it.

18.1 *Ahmadu, Caliph of the Tukolor Caliphate.*

We have no space to look at the course of the long and complex wars between the French and the Tukolor. The latter fought very bravely in the face of superior weapons. At the French siege of Oussebougou even women took up swords against them and the Chief, Bandiougou Diara, blew himself up inside his stronghold rather than surrender. We only have space to consider the reasons for the ultimate failure of Ahmadu to stave off the French. The main problem was that he was not solidly in control of his Empire. His brother, Aguibou, Emir of Dinguiray, eventually joined the French and fought with them against him. Another brother, Muntaga, Emir of Nioro, was in revolt against him at the time of the French capture of Bamako and Ahmadu's troops were diverted to dealing with him rather than the French. Apart from disloyalty among his subordinate rulers, Ahmadu had to deal with the problem of the Bambara, who had never really accepted Tukolor rule. The French played on the divisions amongst the provincial rulers, offering alliances with one against the other. They also supported the Bambara with arms against their Tukolor overlords. Given this complex situation, Ahmadu tried to avoid confrontation with the French by using diplomatic delaying tactics. But in the end the French were determined to take over his Empire if not by treaty by force. Their task was made easier by the divisions in Ahmadu's Empire and the superiority of their weapons. Ahmadu was not close to the coast so he had difficulty in obtaining arms to match the French ones.

This was not the case with Samori who had easier access to European arms. After earlier clashes with the French, between 1881 and 1884, Samori had signed the Treaty of Bisandugu whereby the zones of expansion of both the French and his own Empire were delimited. It suited Samori not to have to take on the French at this particular stage in the building of his Empire. Likewise, the French had enough troubles with the Senegalese states and the Tukolor Empire and so peace with Samori at that time was an advantage.

In 1891 war broke out between the French and Samori: each accused the other of breaking the Treaty of Bisandugu. But whether or not one of the parties to the Treaty had broken it, it was of little consequence. The French were now determined to conquer Samori's territory for fear a rival European power might take it. They could have had little idea how difficult this conquest would be when in April 1891 they occupied Kankan and sent an expedition to burn Bisandugu. It was to take them seven years to defeat Samori, who proved to be by far the most successful leader of resistance against the Europeans in West Africa.

How was Samori able to hold off the French for so long? In the first place Samori had a standing army of Sofas, well-disciplined and constantly drilled. Secondly, he had an efficient system for calling up reserves who themselves underwent annual military training. Thirdly, he had an efficient trade network for getting firearms from the coast, even from French traders. He established his own armouries which not only repaired his weapons but manufactured effective copies of them. Fourthly, as we have seen, one of the secrets of the success of the European armies was that they were well drilled to make maximum use of their weapons. Samori made

his own soldiers enlist in the French colonial armies to learn their drill and come back and teach it to their fellow soldiers. Thus he was better able to fight the French on their own terms than any other African resistance leader. Fifthly, Samori had a very efficient administration for his Empire so that when he was defeated in battle he could move headquarters without too much disruption. In fact as you can see on Map 16.2 (p. 126) he moved his whole Empire eastwards to a completely new area in the face of French successes. He held off French advances, while he rebuilt his Empire, by following a scorched earth policy. That is as his army retreated they burnt all the crops in the path of the French so they would have no food for their troops.

Finally he used guerilla tactics, not only taking on the French in open battle, but harassing their columns from the bush which his troops knew much better than theirs. Ultimately he was unable to deal with the superiority of French weapons, but his tactics staved off the French for seven full years.

By contrast the great Sokoto Caliphate fell an easy

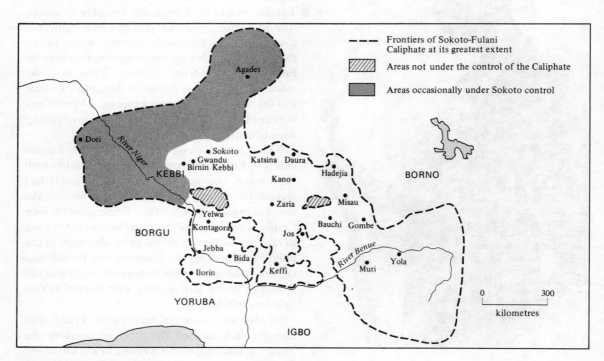

Map 18.2   The Sokoto Caliphate.

prey to the British. By the time of the conquest the Caliphate had been in existence for nearly a century. Its military aims were to defend itself from attack by its neighbours and to suppress rebellions against its authority by those who had never really accepted their conquest by the forces of the jihad. The chief feature of its armies was its cavalry. It did not have a single united army, but rather a series of armies based on each of its emirates. Thus in times of attack each emirate was supposed to defend itself though it could call on neighbouring emirates for support.

When the British invaded the Sokoto Caliphate they did not do so at one point only. Thus the armies of the Caliphate could not join as one to oppose the British. Indeed, it would not have been safe to do so, for it would have left many of the emirates undefended against their other enemies. But the real reason for the failure of the Caliphate armies against the British can be put down to the superiority of the tactics and weapons of the latter. The great defensive walls of the towns and cities which were impregnable to African enemies were easily breached by cannon. The massed cavalry of the armies of the Caliphate were easily mowed down as at Kano in 1902, and Sokoto in 1903 when they charged the small squares formed by Lugard's troops. These squares consisted

18.2 *Many of the defeated Caliph of Sokoto's subjects fled to the east rather than submit to British rule. They settled in the present day Republic of Sudan under the leadership of the son of Caliph Atahiru I, who was killed by the British as he led the* hijra *or flight from the infidel. His son, Mai Worno, was photographed in 1928 in the Sudan with his Wazir (left).*

of rapid firing maxim-guns at each corner, with rapid firing rifles along each side. Though the Caliphate cavalry charged bravely they could not get near the British troops. The armies of the emirate thus failed to devise tactics to deal with the British and so fell quickly to them. As Hilaire Belloc, the well-known English poet, put it concisely:

> 'what a pity we had got
> The Maxim gun and they had not'.

4 Resistance by Dahomey and Asante

The four major wars between the Asante and the British in 1824, 1826, 1863 and 1874 did not result in British occupation. In 1897 the British finally decided to place a Protectorate over Asante, but as we shall see, their rule, imposed by force, had to be confirmed by a further war in 1900. Asante was not the only great forest state to offer fierce resistance to the European conquerors. The Kingdom of Dahomey was only taken by the French in 1892 with great difficulty. Before looking at the way the Asante finally fell under British rule let us look at the case of Dahomey.

The French considered the coast of Dahomey their own sphere of influence and were determined that neither the British in Lagos nor the Germans in Lomé, who had shown interest in neighbouring Dahomey and its hinterland, should take that part of the coast. In the early 1880s they obtained a Treaty of Protection over the Dahomey tributary Kingdom of Porto Novo, which by 1888 felt secure enough, with its French allies, to throw off Dahomey's suzerainty. In 1890 the French occupied Cotonou and repulsed all attempts by the Dahomeyans to re-take it. The French thus controlled Dahomey's two major outlets to the coast. Because of commitments elsewhere the French did not attempt to take over any more territory, and eventually made peace with Behanzin, the King of Dahomey in October 1890.

The Dahomeans had been surprised at the French successes: they had thought of Europeans as traders not soldiers. The French, by the terms of the peace treaty, had agreed to pay 20,000 francs annually to Dahomey for Cotonou and allow Dahomeyan ad-

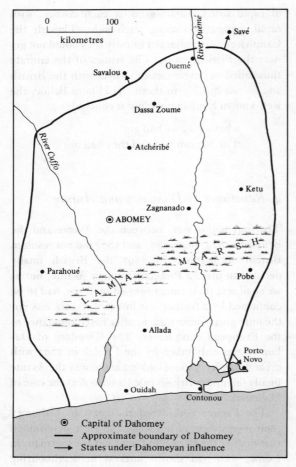

0   100
kilometres

River Ouémé

Savé

Oueme

Savalou

River Cuffo

Dassa Zoume

Atchéribé

Ketu

Zagnanado

⊙ ABOMEY

M A R S H

Parahoué

Pobe

L A M A

Allada

Porto
Novo

Ouidah

Contonou

⊙ Capital of Dahomey
── Approximate boundary of Dahomey
──▶ States under Dahomeyan influence

Map 18.3   The Dahomey heartland.

ministrators to look after the Dahomeyan inhabitants. Dahomey could claim that Cotonou still formed part of the state even though the French flag flew over the town and it was garrisoned by French troops.

But it was only a matter of time before France would occupy the hinterland of her ports. In April 1892 the French Parliament, which had hitherto been opposed to occupation of Dahomey, now voted funds for its conquest as a result of an attack by the Dahomeyans on the French residents of Porto Novo. An expeditionary force was placed under a Senegalese, Colonel Dodds. The Dahomeyans, despite the peace treaty with the French, had recognised the long-term threat and had bought up arms from German traders. When the French force set out to conquer Dahomey its standing army of 4,000 troops, half of whom were the famous Amazon women, and 8,000 levies were well equipped. 1,700 rapid firing rifles, five machine guns, six krupp cannon and 400,000 cartridges plus shell for the cannon had been purchased through German traders at Ouidah.

Dodds led a 2,000 strong force consisting mainly of Senegalese. It set out on its invasion on 4th October 1892. Within just over a month Dahomey had been conquered. The Dahomeyans fought with great bravery during that month. But their tactics, especially in using their newly acquired weapons, were no use against the better equipped, though smaller, French force. The French estimated 2,000 Dahomeyan soldiers had been killed and 3,000 wounded. The French themselves lost only ten officers and sixty-seven men.

The French forces had superior fire-power, were well-drilled, had better lines of supply and were aided by Yoruba who had been conquered by Dahomey and saw the occupation of Dahomey by the French as a chance of obtaining their liberty. They rose in savage vengeance against their masters.

Where Dahomey had resisted the French invasion fiercely, the Asante offered no resistance when Britain finally decided to occupy their state. Britain was becoming fearful of the revival of Asante's power under Prempe. The Empire had been left in disarray after the British invasion of 1874, but it

18.3 *Prempé forced to submit to the British after the defeat of his army in 1896.*

now looked as though it might once more be a threat to British interests. Prempe tried to sue for peace but the British marched on Asante and sacked Kumasi which had been deserted. As a result of bitter experiences in the past the Asante war-leaders refused to fight the British, knowing they could not deal with their superior fire-power. Prempe was exiled and a British Protectorate was established.

Asante seemed at first to be peaceful under British rule. In truth the Asante felt they had been deceived into submission. They had deserted Kumasi in the hopes that an honourable settlement, not including a British Protectorate, might be negotiated. In 1900 the discontent of the Asante flared into open war with the British. It was caused by the Governor of the Gold Coast, Sir Frederick Hodgson, who demanded that the Asante hand over the Golden Stool to him. The Asante feared that Governor Hodgson intended to sit on the Golden Stool, a thing no Asante, not even the Asantehene, had ever done. This provocation led to open war.

When the Governor went to Kumasi to obtain the Stool, the Asante, led by the Queen Mother of Edweso, besieged him in the British fort. A relief column from Lagos came up to relieve the fort but could not break through the Asante armies. With great difficulty and severe losses the Governor broke out of the Fort and made his way to the coast. From April to September the Asante kept the British pinned down. The British had to call up reserves from Sierra Leone and Nigeria, thus delaying Lugard's conquest of the Sokoto Caliphate. So fierce was the Asante resistance that in one case a British force of 4,000 levies was driven back by 250 Asante warriors. Eventually, as a result of superior firepower the British broke through to Kumasi and after a final battle the Asante armies were at last conquered at Aboaso. Asante was then finally annexed as a British possession as distinct from protectorate.

5 Resistance by smaller African states and non-centralised states

So far we have only considered resistance by the great African states. Many smaller states resisted the European occupation just as fiercely as the larger ones: notable examples are provided by the resistance of Ali Bouri, the Bourba Djollof and Lat Dior, the Damel of Cayor in Senegal, Bai Bureh in Sierra Leone and Nana of Ebrohime in Nigeria. Non-centralised peoples like the Tiv and Igbo in Nigeria and various groups in southern Ivory Coast also bitterly opposed the European conquerors.

Where both small states or non-centralised peoples had any measure of success against the invading European armies it was because they adopted guerilla tactics, using their knowledge of the land to compensate for the small size of their armies.

Bai Bureh, ruler of the small Temne state of Kasseh in northern Sierra Leone, is perhaps the most outstanding example of a leader who used guerilla tactics successfully against the Europeans. From January to November 1898 he fought the British and for the first four months he held them back.

The war in which he fought the British was part of the Hut Tax wars of 1898. These wars were in protest against the Hut Tax levied by the British Colonial Government in Freetown. Actually Bai Bureh had initially accepted British protection, but when he and his people saw its full implication, as demonstrated by the levying of the 5/- Hut Tax, they tried to drive the British out.

Bai Bureh had already established himself as a brilliant general in wars in northern Sierra Leone and Guinea before the European occupation. With his regular force of 'war-boys', he turned his experience of war with neighbouring African States to dealing with the British.

In the thickly wooded country of Temne land, the British columns, followed by their carriers, could only advance through the bush in single file. Instead of attacking the British in positions where they could form their deadly squares, Bai Bureh's troops harassed them from the bush where they were in single file. They picked off carriers and their best marksmen were reserved for killing the officers thus depriving the rank and file of leadership. Bai Bureh kept up an efficient spy system so he always knew when the British forces were planning to attack.

He removed all canoes on the rivers they would cross. Paths they could follow were barricaded. His

18.4 *Bai Bureh, ruler of Kasseh, who gave the British some of the stiffest resistance by any African leader during their occupation.*

towns and villages were surrounded by huge stockades which could not be penetrated by the shells of the British cannon. Furthermore Bai Bureh, like Samori, was very efficient at obtaining supplies of rifles and ammunition from the European traders at the coast – including one British trader.

It took the British four months before they were able to occupy Kasseh, and another five months before they were able finally to track down Bai Bureh. This ruler of a chiefdom which would be lost in the Tukolor Empire tied down the whole complement of British forces in Sierra Leone. Eventually the British had to bring in troops from Britain and Nigeria to defeat him.

The guerilla tactics devised by Bai Bureh were the only tactics for a decentralised people like the Igbo

to adopt. Lacking any central authority beyond the village group, and having no standing armies, each village took on its own defence. All adult males became soldiers in time of war. Despite the small size of the forces raised by each village group, they had a considerable advantage over the British. They knew the thickly forested terrain like the back of their hands. The many streams and rivers that crossed their homelands provided added obstacles. Most important of all, the British could not defeat them in one major engagement as with the armies of the emirates of the Sokoto Caliphate. They had to take on each village in turn. Thus some of the stiffest resistance they met with in their conquest of Nigeria came from peoples organised at the level of the village group.

6 Anglo–French rivalry

What is remarkable about the Scramble is that the Europeans only came into serious conflict on one occasion, and that was in 1896–1898 around Bussa. Then, the French, who wanted to gain a port on the stretch of the Niger navigable to the sea so that they could connect the trade of northern Dahomey, Upper Volta, eastern Haut-Senegal-Niger and Niger with the sea, were opposed by the British who claimed that Bussa was theirs. Above Bussa the Niger is not navigable, below it large boats can go direct to the sea. At one time armed Frenchmen faced armed British soldiers but finally the matter, like so much of the Scramble, was settled in Europe, and France did not gain a port on the Niger giving her access to the sea.

The great pity for Africa was that Europe which was so often at war was not divided at this time, so that France, Britain and Germany at peace at home, could concentrate on their imperial conquests. Even though African states were divided and fell to the Europeans, the heroism of leaders like Bai Bureh, Samori, Behanzin and Nana Olomu, in the face of great odds, remains an inspiration for succeeding generations.

19 The establishment of colonial rule

1 The situation after the partition

By 1900 the partition of West Africa was virtually over. All of West Africa, except Liberia, had been divided between the European colonial powers – Britain, France, Germany and Portugal. In the last chapters we have studied the causes for this sudden expansion of European rule and the reasons why the European powers were able so rapidly to conquer such large areas; now we must begin to examine some of the final stages and consequences of the partition.

The actual partition was really only the first step in the establishment of effective European rule. The last two decades of the nineteenth century (1880–1900) witnessed the partition of West Africa. The first two decades of the twentieth century (1900–1920) can be regarded as the period of the gradual establishment of colonial rule. During this period both the British and the French had to complete the military side of the partition. Large areas remained to be subdued for the first time and other areas had to be reconquered after rebelling against the imposition of colonial rule. For example it took the French from 1908 to 1915 to establish any effective control over the forested interior of the Ivory Coast and it proved even more difficult to conquer the desert chiefs of Niger and Mauretania, many of whom were not finally subdued until well into the 1920s. Similarly the British had to invade Asante in 1900, occupy the Sokoto Caliphate between 1901 and 1903, and send many small military expeditions to establish control over the Igbo of Eastern Nigeria between 1901 and 1919. At the same time as the final stages of the military conquest of West Africa were taking place, the colonial powers were also occupied in defining the exact boundaries between their various territories.

However, the main task facing the colonial powers in the period 1900–1920 was the creation of some form of administration by which their vast, new colonial possessions could be ruled peacefully and cheaply. Shortages of manpower and money and the great size and ethnic complexity of the newly acquired territories made this a long and difficult process. In many respects the military conquest of the African states proved to be a simpler job for the technologically more advanced Europeans than the actual organisation and consolidation of effective colonial rule.

As we saw in Chapter 17 France had occupied by far the largest part of West Africa during the partition. Its colonies comprised more than three-quarters of the total area of West Africa, though it must be remembered that much of this was sparsely populated, economically unproductive desert or semi-desert. The total population of French West Africa at the beginning of the twentieth century has been estimated at as low as approximately 12 million. The British territories, though much smaller in area, had a much larger population; the population of Nigeria alone was about 17 million in 1912, and also they were economically much more valuable. Compared to the large French and British Empires in West

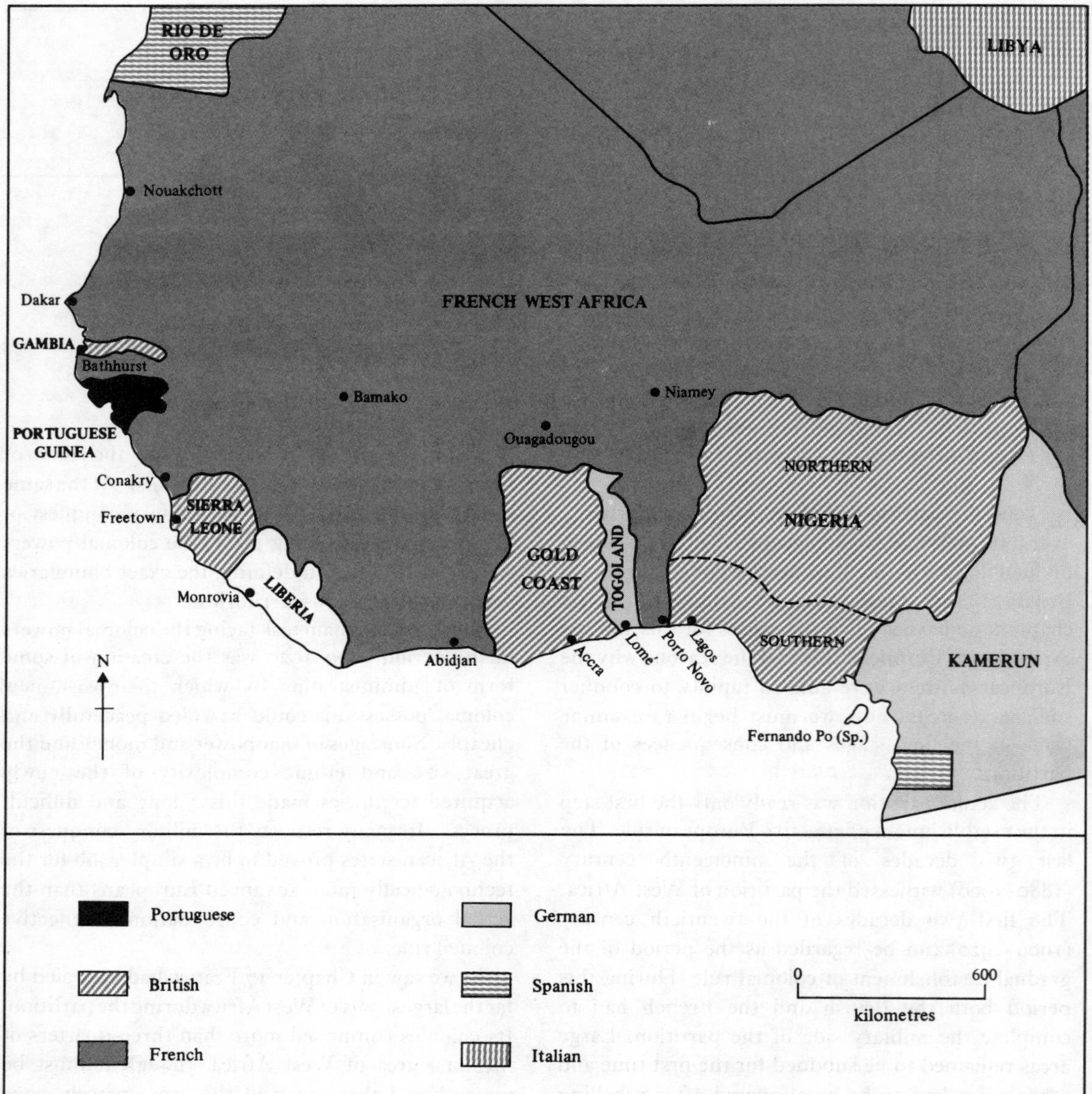

RIO DE
ORO

LIBYA

Nouakchott

FRENCH WEST AFRICA

Dakar

GAMBIA

Bathhurst

Bamako

Niamey

Ouagadougou

PORTUGUESE
GUINEA

NORTHERN

Conakry

SIERRA
LEONE

Freetown

GOLD
COAST

NIGERIA

TOGOLAND

Monrovia

LIBERIA

Lagos

Porto Novo

Abidjan

Accra

Lomé

SOUTHERN

KAMERUN

N

Fernando Po (Sp.)

	Portuguese		German
	British		Spanish
	French		Italian

0   600

kilometres

Map 19.1   West Africa in 1914.

Africa, Germany and Portugal controlled very small areas; this explains why little attention need be paid here to German and Portuguese methods of colonial rule.

2 *Main types of colonial rule*

Before examining how the European powers ruled West Africa and how West Africa was influenced by colonial rule, a few important introductory points should be clearly understood. Firstly, the tendency to exaggerate the length of the period under colonial rule must be avoided. Most of West Africa experienced colonial rule for only fifty or sixty years – about half a century. Secondly, the difference between the old, coastal colonies – Bathurst, Freetown, Lagos, the Gold Coast and the *Four Communes* of Senegal – which were under European control for a century or more, and the interior conquered during the partition must always be remembered and will frequently be referred to. Thirdly, the reader should appreciate that broad generalisations are used here because the complexity of different types of colonial administration cannot be explained in an introductory survey such as this.

In the first decades of the twentieth century the British and the French had very little knowledge of the areas they had conquered or were still conquering. Consequently many different methods of rule developed to suit different circumstances and different individuals. When colonial rule became more firmly established in the 1920s it is possible to distinguish three main types of rule at least in theory, though in practice the distinctions were less obvious and the differences between British and French methods much more blurred.

Firstly, the term *assimilation* is used to refer to one type of colonial rule, usually associated with the French. As we have already explained in Chapter 15 the French tried to make the people of their colonies as like French people as possible. Being proud of their civilisation, the French assumed that what was good for them was good for all people. Thus their colonies, collectively called *France Outre-Mer* (Overseas France), should be ruled in all respects, politically, administratively and economically, in exactly the same way as parts of France. Personal or cultural assimilation meant making colonial subjects into imitations of Frenchmen, linguistically, socially, educationally and culturally. By the beginning of the twentieth century this policy had already been in operation for more than a hundred years in the town of St Louis and the island of Gorée, and had been extended to Dakar when it was founded in 1857

and to neighbouring Rufisque. Together these four formed the *Four Communes* of Senegal. The very rapid expansion of the French Empire at the end of the nineteenth century made full-scale personal assimilation no longer possible and the Four Communes, and to a very small extent other parts of Senegal, were the only areas in West Africa where assimilationist policies were in any meaningful sense used. In the rest of French West Africa the policy of assimilation was almost wholly abandoned as we shall see.

The second main type of colonial rule is usually called *indirect rule*. This is not a general term like assimilation but simply the name given to a method of local government. Various types of indirect rule have been used throughout history. In the early years of British occupation many different methods of rule were tried but by the 1920s the British tended wherever possible to move towards indirect rule methods of local government. This was largely because of its success as used by Lugard in Northern Nigeria and the influence of Lugard's ideas on colonial administration. The basic idea behind indirect rule was that the methods of government most suitable to Africans were those which African societies had themselves developed, therefore Europeans should rule through the traditional rulers and the existing institutions.

A third main type of colonial rule is sometimes referred to as *paternalism* or *association*. Both of these are vague, general terms covering all the various half-way methods between the extremes of pure assimilation and pure indirect rule. The policy of association was used by the French wherever full-scale assimilation proved impossible and similar methods were employed by the British where local circumstances made indirect rule difficult to operate. The policy of association held that Africa should be developed for the mutual benefit of French rulers and African subjects in association with each other. But the association was like that of a horse and rider with the French in the saddle!

It must be remembered that all these are very generalised categories of colonial rule. They reflect certain basic differences of approach between the

British and the French which will become more apparent in the next chapter. Recent research has, however, shown that over large areas British and French methods were in practice much more similar than has often been thought.

3 *The beginnings of French administration*

It was one thing for the Europeans to conquer Africa, quite another for them to administer it. The French, for example, took over an area of West Africa nearly as large as the United States of America. Its sparse population of twelve million ranged from the nomadic Tuaregs of the desert to the Europeanised *habitants* of St Louis. Before the partition the French had only colonised the coastal area of Senegal. There, as we have seen, they had administered the inhabitants of the 'Four Communes' as though they were Frenchmen. Once they began to take over large areas in the interior they had to adapt their methods to the new circumstances. One of the early problems facing both the British and the French was the question of whether to join their colonies into one federation or to allow them to develop separately. The French eventually decided in favour of federation joining all their West African territories into a single federation of French West Africa – the AOF (*Afrique Occidentale Française*).

Before the 1890s the French favoured separate development, partly to allow for freedom of initiative by local military commanders, partly to allow for economic initiative by the different coastal territories, and partly because the French colonial department (which until 1894 was merely part of the Ministry for the Navy) was too busy to undertake any full-scale organisation of the separate French West African territories. Increasingly in the 1890s arguments in favour of some form of federation were put forward. French conquests during the partition had linked all France's territories in West Africa together into a continuous bloc of land. There were frequent unnecessary conflicts between governors of different territories over the exact boundaries between them and the difficulties of defeating Samori Toure emphasised the need for a united military command.

The Federation of French West Africa was created in several stages between 1895 and 1904. In 1895 the four colonies of Senegal, Soudan, Guinea and Ivory Coast were placed under the authority of a Governor-General in St Louis who was also the Governor of Senegal. The Governor-General had little real power because the separate territories retained control of their own budgets and it soon became apparent that the federation was not sufficiently centralised to solve the problems which had led to its creation. Slight changes were made in 1899 and 1902, increasing the powers of the Governor-General and including Dahomey in the federation.

It was not until 1904 that the federation took its final form and the Governor-General acquired real power. Then the Governor-Generalship was separated from the office of Governor of Senegal and Dakar was made the capital of the Federation. The federation was given a source of revenue from customs duties and its own staff to carry out its policies. As we shall see in the next chapter, the central government of the French West African territories was to remain a highly centralised federation until the 1950s.

4 *The beginnings of British administration*

Whereas the French colonies in West Africa formed one unit, the four British colonies were separated from each other by colonies belonging to other powers. This made it much more difficult for the British to consider administering them as a group. Some attempt was made at linking the British territories in the nineteenth century, but this was later abandoned in favour of separate development. In 1900 there were in fact more than four British colonies in West Africa: the Gambia, Sierra Leone, the Gold Coast (called Ghana after independence), the Lagos Colony and Protectorate, the Protectorate of Southern Nigeria, and the Protectorate of Northern Nigeria. In 1906 Lagos and the Protectorate of Southern Nigeria were united, but the Protectorate of Northern Nigeria continued to be separately administered until 1914. From 1900 onwards there was little contact between the administrations of

19.1 *Sir Frederick, later Lord Lugard, who as Governor for Northern Nigeria developed the theory of indirect rule which he later applied to Southern Nigeria when in 1912 he was given the responsibility of amalgamating the two British colonies.*

Britain's West African territories. Once the two Nigerias had been amalgamated each of the four British territories was divided into a colony and a protectorate. The colony represented the lands acquired by the British before the partition. Throughout the colonial period there were considerable differences between the two. For example the Africans living in the 'colonies' were British subjects entitled to British passports. The inhabitants of the protectorates were British 'protected persons' with no right of entry into Britain without special permission.

In 1912 Sir Frederick Lugard, who had been

High Commissioner for the Protectorate of Northern Nigeria from 1900 to 1906, was appointed Governor of the Colony and Protectorate of Southern Nigeria and Governor of the Protectorate of Northern Nigeria. The purpose of his holding both offices at once was so that he could join the two territories together under one administration. He himself was based in Lagos, the capital of the Colony and Protectorate of Southern Nigeria. In Zungeru, the capital of the Protectorate of Northern Nigeria before it was moved to Kaduna, he was represented by a deputy who was called the Lieutenant-Governor. He accomplished his task in 1914 when the two territories were amalgamated.

The reason for joining the two territories together was not the fact that they were next to each other. In East Africa the British ruled Uganda and Kenya separately even though they shared a common frontier. The fact was that the Protectorate of Northern Nigeria was so poor that it had to be given grants-in-aid by the Government of the Colony and Protectorate of Southern Nigeria. Now the British Government believed that all of its colonies should pay for their own administration and development from their own taxes and customs duties. They did not believe they should be given financial aid either by Britain or by another colony. Since Southern Nigeria earned more than it spent from taxes and customs duties, when the two were joined together the southern surplus would make up for the northern deficit. Furthermore, some of the Southern Nigerian surplus came from goods exported from Northern Nigeria through southern ports. The duties levied on these goods would have been Northern Nigeria's if they had been able to pass through a port under its control.

Another reason for the amalgamation was to unite the railway systems of the two protectorates. While one railway was being built to link Southern Nigeria with Northern Nigeria, the Northern Nigeria Government was also building a railway to link its major cities with Baro, which was a port on the Niger where it could charge customs duties. There were thus two competing systems being built: the southern line which left Lagos via Jebba to Minna, and a northern line linking Minna with Baro on the Niger (see Map 21.1, p. 160).

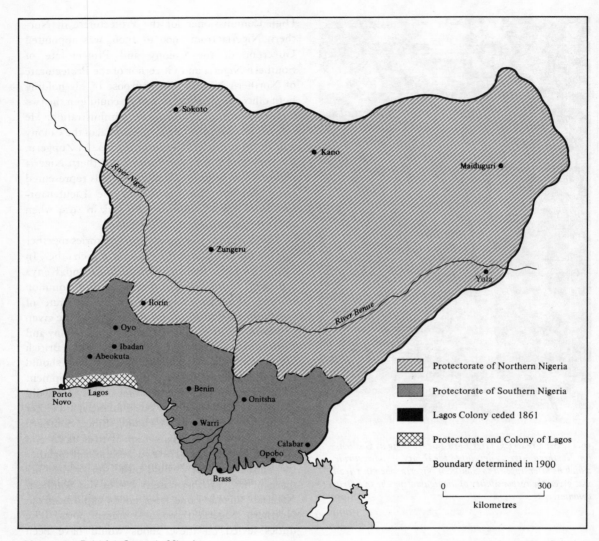

Map 19.2   British influence in Nigeria.

In amalgamating Northern and Southern Nigeria, Lugard did not fully unite the country. He retained the division between the two Nigeria's installing a Lieutenant-Governor in Kaduna to run Northern Nigeria and a Lieutenant-Governor in Enugu to run Southern Nigeria. The Governor-General, who was Lugard himself, coordinated the two governments in Lagos. Others had suggested that the new Nigerian Colony and Protectorate should be differently organised. One suggestion was that it should be divided into four provinces (see Map 19.3). If this suggestion had been followed, the distinction between North and South that has bedevilled Nigerian politics might have been avoided. As it was the administrations of the Northern and Southern Provinces continued to exercise most of the functions they had under the old Protectorate days. Only the Treasury, Railways, Survey, Judiciary, Military, Posts and Telegraphs and Audit were centralised under the Governor-General.

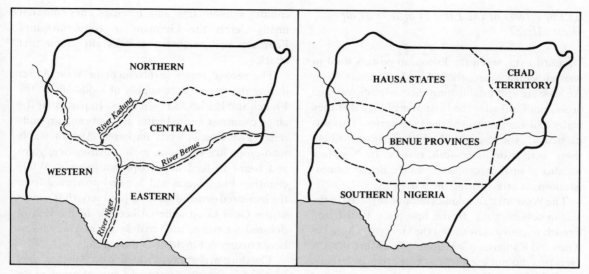

Map 19.3   The proposed administrative reorganisation in Nigeria.

5 *Togo and Portuguese Guinea*

Apart from the British and the French two other powers had West African colonies. Until its occupation by British and French forces at the outbreak of the First World War in 1914, Togo was administered by Germany. The Portuguese ruled the small colony of Portuguese Guinea (now called Guinea-Bissau) and what must have been the smallest colony in the world: the fort of Sao João Batista da Ajuda, which was a small fortified house in the middle of the town of Ouidah in Dahomey. It remained a Portuguese possession until the Dahomeyan Government occupied it in 1963.

Like the British and the French, the Portuguese ruled Guinea with the help of African chiefs. But, unlike the British, they treated their West African colony as part of Portugal itself. They considered their colonies as overseas provinces. Portuguese Guinea was poor, and with one of the poorest nations in Europe as its colonial master, little development took place.

By contrast, the Germans during their short period of rule in Togo did a great deal to develop its agricultural and mineral resources. They called Togo their model colony. A British writer, Albert F. Calvert, wrote admiringly of Togo in 1918:

In the thirty years that the country had been under German administration, a stable government had been established, the hinterland had been opened up, a railway and many excellent roads had been built, slavery had been abolished and intertribal warfare discouraged, and a number of experimental plantations had been farmed. The Government, by its energetic policy, had developed the resources of the country, established trade and commerce on sound lines, and made considerable progress towards the betterment and prosperity of the people.

After the end of the First World War, however, the Germans were not allowed to return to Togo. Instead, it was divided between the British and the French who administered it on behalf of the League of Nations under what was called a *Mandate*. This meant that they were supposed to rule their sections of the territory on behalf of the people without forced labour or the enlistment of troops. The British administered their section of Togo as part of the Gold Coast, while the French administered their share as a separate colony until the World Depression of the 1930s when, for economic reasons, they administered it jointly with Dahomey.

6 The effects of the First World War on West Africa

Up until 1914, when the European powers went to war with each other, the colonial powers in West Africa were still establishing their administrations. It was not until after the First World War that they really took firm control of their territories. This was particularly the case with the French, against whom there were many large-scale revolts. In Nigeria a number of smaller revolts against the British administration occurred during the war.

The West African colonies became involved in the war in several ways. In the first place British and French territory surrounded the German colonies of Togo and Kamerun (Cameroun). To ensure that the Germans did not use these as bases to attack them, the British and French invaded them, occupying Togo after a brief campaign in August 1914. Kamerun, where the British and French were helped by Belgian forces from the Congo, proved more difficult to conquer, partly because of the

19.2 *A mounted orderly of the Gold Coast Regiment photographed at the time of the Anglo-French conquest of German Togoland in 1914.*

country's mountains and forests. They did not finally defeat the Germans in Kamerun until February 1916, eighteen months after their first attack.

The second major involvement of West Africa during the war was the supply of foodstuffs to the French and British and their allies. In particular the allied countries wanted palm products and groundnuts. The French even imported African staple food-crops like sorghum, millet, maize, rice, yams and beans to feed her troops and people. While countries like Nigeria and Senegal prospered from the increased demand for their products, the farmers of the Gold Coast suffered because of the lack of demand for cocoa, used mainly for making chocolate, a luxury not in demand during the war.

The third major way in which West Africans were involved in the war presented a special problem for the French. Both the British and the French recruited Africans to serve in their armies, but the French demands were much higher than the British. In the French colonies Africans rose in revolt because of excessive recruitment. Furthermore, at the same time as the French were trying to recruit every available, able-bodied man, they were also asking the African farmers to supply them with more food crops. In British West Africa about 30,000 troops were recruited for service in the Togo and Kamerun campaigns, and then for the war against the Germans in East Africa. Many fought bravely and greatly helped the British in winning these campaigns. In French West Africa, where the population was smaller than that of Nigeria, nearly 200,000 men were taken into the army; that is more than six times as many as from the much more heavily populated British West Africa. These troops were used not only in France's African campaigns, but also in Europe where they had to fight in terrible conditions against the Germans. Many men, rather than leave their homes for the war, fled to the bush or across the border into British territory or even deliberately wounded themselves so that they would be considered unfit for service. In Upper Volta, Soudan, Dahomey, Ivory Coast and Niger large areas revolted against the French because they did not want their men taken away. In revolting they were encouraged by the fact that so many French administrators and traders had left for France to

19.3 *French African conscripts on their way to the front in the European war between the French and British allies and the Germans.*

19.4 *Blaise Diagne, High Commissioner for the Recruitment of African Troops and Deputy for Senegal talking to a Mauretanian notable.*

fight the Germans: it seemed as though the French were becoming weak.

In Nigeria a number of revolts, not provoked by recruitment but equally disturbing to the British, broke out largely in protest against the imposition of taxation. The most serious of these were in Iseyin and Abeokuta in Yorubaland, and, like the French revolts, these were fiercely put down. The British and the French could ill afford to use soldiers against their colonial subjects when they were so short of troops to use against the Germans. Despite the widespread revolts, the French Government continued to demand more men and more food. The Governor-General of French West Africa, Van Vollenhoven, wrote in July 1917: 'To extract from this country yet another few thousand men will set it aflame, drench it in blood and ruin it completely'.

The French, however, were determined to recruit more troops. In 1918 they appointed Blaise Diagne, the African Deputy for Senegal, as High Commissioner for the Recruitment of Troops in West Africa. In return for his assistance in recruiting, the French promised a relaxation of the *indigénat*, or summary administrative justice (see page 154), improved medical facilities, jobs for demobilised soldiers and the general development of West Africa. The Governor-General, who wanted no more recruitment, resigned. Diagne toured West Africa as a man equal in status to the Governor-General. He managed to get even those areas that had been in revolt to supply troops and succeeded in recruiting

over 60,000 men. Few of these actually fought because the war ended in November 1918. Diagne has been accused of being a traitor to his race in supplying troops for the European war. But he genuinely believed that the French would honour their promises. As we shall see, they did not.

The revolts in French West Africa and Nigeria during the war were the last major revolts to worry the British and French before their colonies became independent. Between 1918 and 1939, when the Second World War broke out, West Africa remained remarkably quiet and the colonial powers got down to the business of running their colonies without fear of revolt.

19.5 *After the end of the war, French African troops were used as part of the peace time occupation force in the former German controlled Ruhr.*

20 British and French colonial rule

1 General comments

The First World War had seen widespread revolts against the colonial regime in West Africa. Thereafter law and order reigned supreme with only a few isolated outbreaks of resistance or rebellion. Right up to the time of the outbreak of the Second World War in 1939, the French and British seemed securely

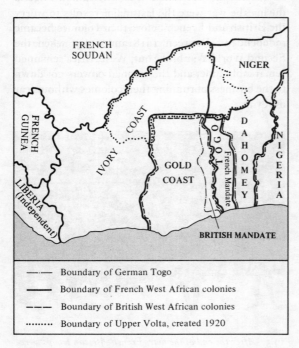

Map 20.1   West Africa in 1920.

FRENCH SOUDAN

NIGER

FRENCH GUINEA

IVORY COAST

GOLD COAST

DAHOMEY

TOGO

French Mandate

NIGERIA

LIBERIA (Independent)

BRITISH MANDATE

———— Boundary of German Togo

———— Boundary of French West African colonies

– – – Boundary of British West African colonies

········ Boundary of Upper Volta, created 1920

in control of their West African territories. This situation was greatly changed by the Second World War: France was defeated by Germany in 1940 and Britain was only saved from defeat because Germany attacked Russia and America entered the war on Britain's side. West Africa, as we shall see, was to become vital to the Allied victory and many concessions were made to Africans to secure their support in the war. New ideas about the rights of colonial peoples spread widely as a result of the participation of Russia and America in the war. For the first time the European occupation of Africa was called openly into question by both Europeans and Africans. The twenty year period between 1918 and 1939 marks, therefore, the heyday of colonial rule in West Africa when France and Britain were fully in control of their subjects and few – either African or European – questioned their right to be there.

During this period the chief concern of the colonial administrations was the maintenance of law and order so that the African farmers could produce the export crops which Europe required. To secure peace the two colonial powers developed different systems of administration, but their goal was the same: the economic exploitation of Africa's resources. In the past much emphasis has been laid on the differences between French and British administration and certainly these differences have left important marks on the independent French-speaking and English-speaking West African territories. However, the differences between British and French methods of government should not be exaggerated: the maintenance of peace to facilitate economic exploitation was the main aim of both colonial powers. Although each of the two main colonial powers developed different theories of colonial rule, in practice, especially in the earlier years, the differences were not so marked. To simplify our study of colonial rule, however, we will deal with French and British methods separately, looking first at central government and then at local government.

2 French central government

By 1904 the general shape of French West Africa's administration had been laid down as it was to continue until 1956. There were seven colonies: Senegal, French Soudan (Mali), French Guinea, Ivory Coast, Niger, Mauritania and Dahomey. In 1920 a new colony, Upper Volta, was created from parts of Niger, French Soudan and Ivory Coast, but it was broken up in 1932, only to be recreated in 1947. Most of German Togo came under French control under a League of Nations Mandate after the First World War, but was always administered rather differently from the rest of French West Africa because of the Mandate.

We have already examined in the last chapter the creation at the beginning of the twentieth century of a highly centralised federation including the whole of French West Africa. The whole federation was governed uniformly from Dakar, the only exception being the Four Communes of Senegal: St Louis, Dakar, Rufisque and Gorée. They elected a Deputy to the French National Assembly and elected their own municipal councils. Only in the Four Communes was full-scale personal assimilation practised with all the inhabitants having the full rights of French citizens and using the French legal, administrative and educational systems.

One of the main features of French rule was a high degree of centralisation and thus little local initiative. The whole federation was controlled by a Governor-General in Dakar and each of the component colonies of the federation was supervised by a Lieutenant-Governor. During the early years of the twentieth century the relationship between the Governor-General and the different Lieutenant-Governors was uncertain and flexible. By the 1920s, however, there was no doubt as to the dominant position of the Governor-General. The fact that the governors of the various colonies were not allowed to correspond directly with the Ministry of Colonies in Paris was an important feature in establishing this position of supremacy. If they had any request or complaint to make they had to do it through the Governor-General. If he disapproved of the request or thought the complaint not justified, he could refuse to pass it on. He also appointed all civil servants in the colonies except the Lieutenant-Governors and their Secretaries-General and Magistrates. He controlled Posts and Telegraphs, Public Works, Communications, Higher Education, Agriculture and Health Services throughout the federation. Only he could raise loans for development, and it was he who prepared the Federal Budget derived from customs revenue and independent of, and larger than, the budgets of the constituent colonies.

Nevertheless, although his powers within West Africa were very great, the Governor-General had to take his orders from Paris and he possessed very little freedom of action. He had no legislative authority of his own; that is he could not make laws. Only the Chamber of Deputies or the Minister of Colonies in Paris could do that. This contrasts with British West Africa where even the Governor of the tiny Gambia could, through his Legislative Council, make certain laws. The important decisions were taken in Paris and passed through the Governor-General to the Lieutenant-Governors of the various colonies, thus clearly showing the uniform, highly centralised nature of French administration.

In his administration of French West Africa the Governor-General was advised by a Council of Government which included all the Governors of the colonies under his control. But this met only once a year and was therefore not very effective. Although some attempts were made in the 1930s to decentralise the federation, it retained its basic structure until it was dissolved by the *Loi Cadre*, or Outline Law, of 1956 which resulted in the constituent colonies gaining their separate independence.

20.1   *Forced labour or* corvée: *Africans compulsorily conscripted for porterage carry French officials in hammocks in the era before the introduction of the motor car.*

3 French local government

The local government system of the whole of the federation of French West Africa, except the Four Communes, was similar to and modelled on that of France. Traditional boundaries were ignored and the whole area was divided into *cercles* each with approximately the same size and/or population and each administered by a *commandant de cercle*. Each

20.2   *In British West Africa forced labour was also used, though not on so large a scale, or on a regular basis after 1918 as by the French. Here, a wooden panel from the palace door of the Ogogo of Ikere Ekiti in Yorubaland commemorates the arrival of the first British District Commissioner, Captain Ambrose, in 1898 carried by porters in a hammock.*

cercle was in turn divided into *subdivisions* under the control of a *chef de subdivision*. This 'administrative assimilation' involved the use of a much larger number of political officers than the British ever used.

Africans outside the Four Communes were not regarded as French citizens but as subjects. They were given no political rights, no freedom of association or movement and no appeal against the decisions of the French administration. They could be arbitrarily arrested by a French administrator and sentenced to up to fourteen days in prison and had no right of legal defence: this system of imprisonment without proper trial was known as the *indigénat* and was one of the most hated features of French rule. Moreover, subjects were made to do forced labour (*corvée*) on roads and other projects.

Because of the shortage of Europeans to govern the huge area of French West Africa, the French used African chiefs to assist them. At first the French, for the most part, used those chiefs who would normally have governed before the conquest. They did, however, break up the large African states like Dahomey, the Tukolor Empire and Futa Djallon, and use their provinces as the basis of their administration. As time went on the French became more interested in choosing men as chiefs who spoke French and carried out their orders effectively. They did not mind if they had no traditional claim to the chieftancy they occupied. In any case chiefs under the French lost most of their traditional powers and no longer had judicial authority over their people or powers of punishment and imprisonment. They were only given such unpleasant jobs as collecting taxes and raising forced labour and became by and large junior civil servants in the French administration. The chiefs had no control over revenue and thus there was no real local self-government in the British sense. Moreover, the chiefs were often roughly treated by the French, and were even thrown into prison without trial. In 1902 the King of Nikki in Dahomey was imprisoned and committed suicide in shame. Differences in the attitude to and role of the chiefs is one of the main distinctions between British and French colonial rule.

The French introduced taxation throughout their West African territories before the 1914–18 war. Taxation in French West Africa was higher than in British West Africa. Even children were taxed, and often villagers had to pay the taxes of those who had died or who had left the village because the French did not take them off the roll. Tax was seen by the French as a means to make the African farmers work on the export crops they required. If a farmer had to pay tax he had to produce something to sell to make the money to pay the tax: if he could not grow a cash crop on his own land, then he had to migrate to other areas. In order to be able to pay their taxes thousands of men from Soudan, Niger and Upper Volta migrated to Senegal, Ivory Coast and the Gold Coast. This was deliberate policy on the part of the French who even forced people in some areas to cultivate the crops the French needed. In Upper Volta the compulsory cultivation of cotton was responsible for nearly 100,000 Mossi people leaving for the Gold Coast to work on the cocoa plantations or gold mines where they were comparatively well paid. Thus, we can see that in many respects French rule produced much suffering and hardship.

4 British central government

After the amalgamation of Nigeria in 1914 Britain possessed four territories in West Africa: the Gambia, Sierra Leone, the Gold Coast and Nigeria. These were separated from each other by French territory and were administered as four distinct units. Each territory was controlled by a Governor who possessed legislative or law-making powers. In contrast to French methods, the British colonial office in London allowed its Governors considerable freedom of action.

Each colony had a Legislative Council and an Executive Council. The Legislative Councils were composed of British Government officials, who were, until after the Second World War, always in the majority, as well as some European businessmen and sometimes some leading Africans who were nominated by the Governor. Even if they did not like a law being passed by the Council there was little the nominated members could do because the Governor could always rely on his majority of officials to vote in favour of it. The Executive Councils were made up entirely of British officials. The Legislative Councils of the Gambia and Sierra Leone legislated for both the Colony and Protectorate. In the Gold Coast only the Colony came under its control. Asante and the Northern Territories were ruled by proclamation: that is the Governor proclaimed laws on his own authority. In Nigeria the 1923 Clifford constitution allowed the Legislative Council to make laws for Southern Nigeria while the Governor issued laws by proclamation for the Northern Provinces.

20.3 *The Nigerian Legislative Council in session. Note the vast majority of British official members. The Governor presides under the British Royal Coat of Arms.*

5 British local government

To begin with the British had no overall policy of local government and a great variety of methods developed. Later, the success (as far as the British were concerned) of Lugard's system of indirect rule in Northern Nigeria made British administrators increasingly believe that indirect rule was the only possible method of local government and led them to try and impose this system even where it was obviously unsuitable.

Like the French, the British ruled through chiefs because there were not enough European administrators. But they used chiefs somewhat differently from the French. First of all the British were more concerned to rule through chiefs whom the people considered to be their own. They did not mind if chiefs did not speak English, but if they were very inefficient or corrupt they would replace them with someone else from the ruling family. They tried not to appoint people as chiefs who had no traditional claim to be so. However, where they found people who had no chiefs, they appointed men who seemed to them to be strong enough to rule, for example the Warrant Chiefs in Eastern Nigeria. Similarly, when they found chiefs ruling over small numbers of people they grouped them together under a paramount chief (or super-chief) who usually had no claim traditionally to such a position. Like the French, they broke up the great empires of, for example Sokoto and Asante, into their constituent parts though later they restored the unity of central Asante.

Under the British the chiefs headed local government organisations responsible for such things as roads, markets and agriculture. They were also responsible for justice and prisons, though the British did place limits on the crimes which they could try and the penalties they could impose. Cases of murder, for instance, were tried by the British administrators except in the courts of some major chiefs like the Emir of Kano. All in all, the chiefs under the British had much more power than those under the French. In the last analysis, however, like their French counterparts, they formed part of the British administrative system and had to fall in line with British desires.

The British, like the French, used the chiefs to collect taxes, though taxation was not introduced everywhere at first; for example the people of the Gold Coast were not directly taxed until after 1936. Taxation was the foundation of the Native Authority system developed first in Northern Nigeria and then introduced at different stages throughout British West Africa. Lugard, who first introduced the Native Authority system, like the French, believed in taxation as a means of forcing Africans to work. He also believed that African chiefs should run their own local governments under the supervision of the British administrators. To do this they would keep part of the tax, giving sometimes only as little as 30 percent to the British administration. Taxation did not lead to widespread migration in British West Africa because the people in each Native Authority had their taxes realistically assessed. No chief wished his people to migrate, since he would thus lose his taxpayers, so if a tax was assessed at too high a rate leading to migration, it would usually be lowered when the District Officer assessed the area.

While French administration was uniform in West Africa that of the British differed from territory to territory. Even titles of administrators differed. Where the French under the colonial Governors were all called Commandants de Cercles and under them Chefs de Subdivision, those in British West Africa were called variously *Residents* (Nigeria) or *Chief Commissioners* (Gold Coast) and under them *District Officers* or *District Commissioners*. It is therefore necessary to look briefly at the operation of indirect rule methods of local government in various parts of British West Africa.

The best example of the use of indirect rule is provided by Northern Nigeria. When Lugard conquered the Sokoto Caliphate at the beginning of the twentieth century there was no possibility of ruling it in any other way. Direct rule methods were ruled out because of Lugard's very limited supplies of manpower and money. Moreover the Sokoto Caliphate already possessed a highly developed and efficient system of government headed by the emirs and was therefore ideally suited to indirect rule. If the British controlled the emirs, the emirs could continue controlling and administering their people as before. The main reason for the smooth running of indirect rule in the far north of Nigeria was the fact that the area possessed strong, respected traditional rulers each ruling over a large area. Once the British convinced the people that they would not interfere with their customs or religion, it was reasonably easy for them to take over Sokoto's role of supervising the emirs. A Resident, or District Officer, was sent to each of the larger emirate headquarters to supervise the emir. Although it was originally intended that the District Officers should be constantly improving and modernising the emir's administration, they increasingly came to regard their role as one of preserving rather than modifying. As a result little change took place and Northern Nigeria was allowed to stagnate. The emirs continued to appoint officials responsible to them (for example district heads), control the legal system, collect taxes (part of which went to the local treasury) and control the local administration. As far as the British were concerned the system worked well because it enabled them to

rule a large, densely populated area cheaply and peacefully. For Nigeria, however, the success of indirect rule in the north meant little development there and helped to increase the differences between the north and the south.

It is not surprising that, when he was the first Governor-General of a united Nigeria from 1914 to 1919, Lugard tried to introduce indirect rule methods in Southern Nigeria. In Yorubaland indirect rule worked less smoothly than in the north, partly because there existed a small, but growing Western-educated elite for whom there was no place under indirect rule, and partly because the Yoruba chiefs or obas did not possess the same centralised powers of the northern emirs. Thus when the Alafin of Oyo was required to collect taxes in Iseyin under the newly introduced system of indirect rule, the people rioted. Moreover, the British tried to recreate Oyo's position of supremacy over Yorubaland, although Oyo had been greatly weakened by the civil wars of

20.4 *Paramount Chief Auyama, a British appointed Warrant chief in Enugu in Eastern Nigeria, with some of his sub-chiefs.*

the nineteenth century. This was bitterly resented by Ibadan, which, as we have seen (page 88), had superseded Oyo in power in the nineteenth century and did not now wish to be placed under its authority. In Eastern Nigeria the attempt to introduce indirect rule faced even greater difficulties and was eventually abandoned as impractical. Most of the Igbo people lived in segmentary societies with no chiefs and so the British had to create artificial chiefs, known as warrant chiefs with no traditional claim to power. These chiefs proved to be very unpopular as was shown by the Womens' Riots against the collection of taxes which took place in Aba and other Igbo towns and villages in 1929. Though these riots were provoked by resentment of taxation at a time of economic depression, they were also directed at the rule of the warrant chiefs who had no place in traditional society. As a result, the British changed the structure of local government in south-eastern Nigeria to correspond more closely with the political systems of its societies in pre-colonial times. During the 1930s the British moved away from attempts to rule the east through chiefs and gradually established a more democratic system of local government based on different levels of councils.

In the early years Benin and Asante were ruled directly because their traditional systems of government had been destroyed by British conquest. Later, however, the British carefully re-built the traditional systems of government so that they could rule indirectly through them. In the case of Asante this was largely the work of Governor Guggisberg who did much to introduce indirect rule methods in the Gold Coast. In 1924 the exiled Asantehene, Prempe II, was allowed to return to Kumasi as plain Mr Prempe. In 1926 he was installed as Kum-asihene, that is as ruler of Kumasi alone. In 1935 he was recognised as Asantehene once more and the Ashanti (Asante) Confederacy Council was made the supreme native authority for Asante. The British thus partially restored the integrity of the ancient Empire as they had done in Benin in 1914 when they appointed Eweka II as Oba in succession to Oven-ramwen who had died in exile. Indirect rule was also used in Sierra Leone and the Gambia as a method of controlling the Protectorates.

The attempt by the British to introduce indirect rule methods throughout their West African territories was based on the false idea that all Africans were ruled by powerful chiefs. In reality many African societies (for example the Igbo and the Tiv of Nigeria) possessed no real chiefs and many others possessed chiefs with limited powers (for example the Yoruba). Therefore, in many areas indirect rule never worked very smoothly because it was not suitable to the existing circumstances. Moreover, for indirect rule to work well it was necessary to increase the powers of the chiefs wherever possible, thus producing greater opportunities for tyranny and misrule.

The British administrators remained aloof from the people they were governing and did little to prepare the way for eventual independence. Their attitude to the Western-educated elite was one of the worst features of British rule. This group, which was rapidly increasing in the coastal areas as a result of missionary education, were completely excluded by the indirect rule system, which emphasised the role of the traditional rulers. They were given few employment opportunities and were often treated by the British administrators with suspicion or even contempt.

21 Economic and social developments during the colonial period

1 General policy

The colonial economic policies of the British and French, unlike their methods of government, were basically similar. Both powers thought that their colonies should be financially self-supporting and both regarded their colonies primarily as suppliers of raw materials for home industries and as consumers of European manufactured goods. This economic policy, usually referred to by the French as the *Colonial Pact*, was generally applied more strictly by the French than by the British. Everywhere, African interests were subordinated to those of Europe: communications were improved only to benefit external rather than internal trade; the production of cash crops was encouraged while little was done about local food crops; virtually no industrialisation was allowed since that would compete with European industries. It would perhaps be more correct to talk of economic exploitation rather than economic development during the colonial period.

For the ordinary African farmer the most important feature of colonial rule was undoubtedly tax collection. It is significant that the great majority of Africans during the height of colonial rule had no other form of contact with the colonial government, and that this form of contact should be essentially economic. For basically that was what colonial rule was largely concerned with: exploiting Africa's resources to Europe's advantage. The reason why taxation was introduced so late into the Gold Coast is that the British administration there was making

enough from export duties on the valuable export crop to support itself. Taxation was not needed to force the farmers to produce cocoa: they did this on their own initiative because cocoa brought them in good returns for their labour. This is in strong contrast to cotton which produced so low a return that many of the Mossi from Upper Volta, as we have seen, preferred to migrate rather than grow cotton.

By and large the colonial governments in both British and French West Africa did not want to interfere very much in economic matters. This policy is known as *laissez-faire* and was followed by both the colonial powers except when, for short periods, socialists came to power. Socialists believe that the people should own the means of production rather than companies belonging to small groups of rich men. Thus they want the governments elected by the people to run industries and shops. In West Africa, though of course the governments were not elected by the people, they did run some major industries which in France and Britain at that time were privately owned, for example electricity supplies, water supplies, ports and railways. This was not because the governments believed in socialism but because no private companies were interested in providing the money to finance these essential services.

One basic principle of colonial economic policy was that all colonies should be financially self-sufficient. This meant that all public works, for example roads, railways, schools and hospitals, had to be paid for out of locally raised revenue, usually taxes or customs duties. These facilities, however, which were paid for by Africans, were built largely to benefit the trade of the European powers and the interests of the large European trading companies. Generally governments in West Africa did little to develop the countries they controlled during the period 1918–1939. This was partly because it was a time of depression in the world economy when there was little money for development even at home. Thus both the French and the British supplied funds only for what was essential to keep the countries they controlled going. Throughout the period before the Second World War very little money was invested by the colonial powers in the economic development of West Africa. It was only after the Second World War with the creation of the Colonial Development and Welfare Fund and the French FIDES ('Fonds d'Investissement pour le Développement Economique et Social') that large-scale aid was provided by the colonial powers to assist economic development.

2 *Improvements in communications*

In order to get raw materials from the interior to the coast and to get European manufactured goods from the coast to the markets of the interior communications had to be improved. All other aspects of the colonial economy were dependent on improved communications and it was this communications revolution, especially the building of railways, which brought the greatest changes to West Africa.

Since the colonial powers were concerned primarily with the import and export trade of their colonies, the first essential was good harbour facilities. The only good natural harbour in West Africa is Freetown and so elsewhere large sums of money had to be spent in order to create man-made harbours. During the 1920s a large proportion of the taxes collected in Nigeria were spent on creating a harbour at Lagos-Apapa, while at the same time the resources of French West Africa went into creating the port of Dakar. Later, Takoradi in the Gold Coast and Abidjan in the Ivory Coast were developed, but

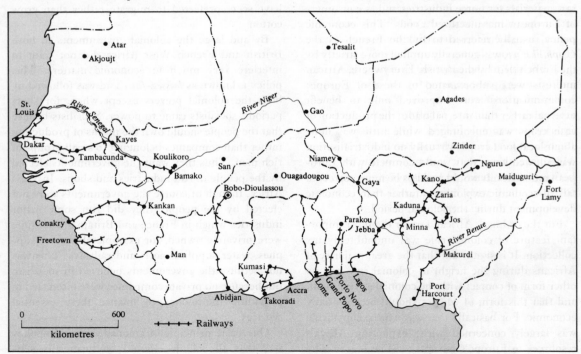

Map 21.1   The colonial railway system in the 1930s. Other major towns shown not connected with the railway system, were reached by a very poor, laterite road system, often impassable in the rainy seasons.

many areas (for example Dahomey) had to wait until after independence before they acquired reasonable harbour facilities.

Right from the beginning of colonial rule much emphasis was placed on the construction of railways. Most colonies tried to finance at least one railway line from the coast to the interior, for example railways into the interior were begun from Dakar in 1880, from Lagos and Freetown in 1896 and from Sekondi, Conakry, Cotonou and Abidjan later. Between 1880 and 1930 approximately 6,000 kilometres of railway were built in West Africa and only a few hundred kilometres have been added since. Nigeria, however, was the only colony with sufficient revenue to develop a railway system consisting of several lines; most colonies had to be content with a single line, or, in the case of Niger, none at all.

A study of the railway map of West Africa will show that all the railways possessed certain common features and that all were built primarily to benefit the European colonial rulers rather than the Africans. Railways were built to facilitate external rather than internal trade, the colonial powers being primarily concerned with getting raw materials (cash crops like groundnuts, cotton and cocoa and minerals like tin) to the coast for shipment to Europe and opening up the interior for the sale of surplus European manufactured goods. This explains why almost all the railways ran from the coast to the interior, for example linking Northern Nigeria with Lagos and Port Harcourt and Bamako with Dakar. Moreover, there were virtually no railway links between the colonies and railways were built only to where there were raw materials needed by the Europeans, for example tin around Jos and

groundnuts around Kano.

After the First World War cars and lorries began to be used in large numbers in West Africa and some road development took place. The emphasis, however, was on the construction of 'feeder' roads rather than trunk roads. Roads were built merely to 'feed' the railways, that is new areas were opened up for cash crop production and they could send their produce by lorry to the nearest point on the railway. Colonial governments were very reluctant to build trunk roads which would provide competition for the railways. Trunk roads would be to the benefit of lorry owners, who were mostly Africans, and take traffic away from the government-owned railways. Thus no attempt was made to bridge the River Niger so that goods could go by road from Lagos to Enugu and until after independence there were no tarred road links between southern and northern Nigeria. As with the railways, there were virtually no inter-territorial road links. All these improvements in communications were paid for with money raised in the colonies and forced labour was frequently used for their construction.

These improvements in communications, especially the building of railways, produced such far-reaching results that they deserve to be called a revolution. Firstly, they made possible a great increase in the production of cash crops for export; only where there were adequate transport facilities was the large-scale production of cash crops economically possible. Secondly, improved communications greatly facilitated the import and spread of European manufactured goods. This often meant severe competition for the local African manufacturers and in many areas of West Africa traditional manufacturing crafts almost completely disappeared.

Moreover mobility of population was greatly increased and large-scale migration made much easier (for example the movement of many Mossi people from Upper Volta to the cocoa and coffee areas of the Ivory Coast and Gold Coast). With this mobility of population went rapid urbanisation (growth of towns) especially at the coastal termini of the railways. The population of Lagos increased from under 50,000 at the beginning of the twentieth century to over 200,000 by the 1950s, while that of

21.1 *The railway station at Ibadan.*

Dakar increased during the same period from about 10,000 to a quarter of a million. This rapid, unplanned urbanisation produced a great mixing of peoples, unemployment, poor living conditions and an ideal environment for the development of various types of organisation all seeking change and reform.

Improved communications also helped to create greater unity within individual territories. The building of the railways provided virtually the only link between the east, the west and the north in Nigeria. Lastly, and most importantly, the better communications developed during the colonial period provided the means for the introduction of new ideas and for changes in every aspect of life. A novelist, Joyce Cary, writing about the effects of the building of a new road in West Africa, imagines the new road saying: 'I shall change everything and everybody. I'm abolishing the old ways, the old ideas, the old law; I am bringing wealth and opportunity for good as well as vice, new powers to men and therefore new conflicts. I am the re-volution'.

3 Raw materials

Once the railways had been built the colonial governments did everything possible to encourage the production of cash crops. The main products the colonial powers wanted from West Africa were palm produce, groundnuts, cotton, rubber, cocoa, coffee and timber. In exchange for these they sent cheap manufactured goods to West Africa like cotton print cloth, enamel bowls, matches and soap.

Eastern Nigeria and Dahomey remained the largest exporters of palm products especially palm-oil. Ivory Coast became the largest coffee producer and Liberia concentrated on rubber. Groundnuts were important in two main areas: in Senegal where their production spread inland along the railway and in Northern Nigeria, once the railway from Lagos reached Kano in 1911. Cocoa, introduced into the Gold Coast in 1879, soon spread into western Nigeria and the Ivory Coast. It soon became West Africa's most important export crop and the Gold Coast became the world's largest producer. The

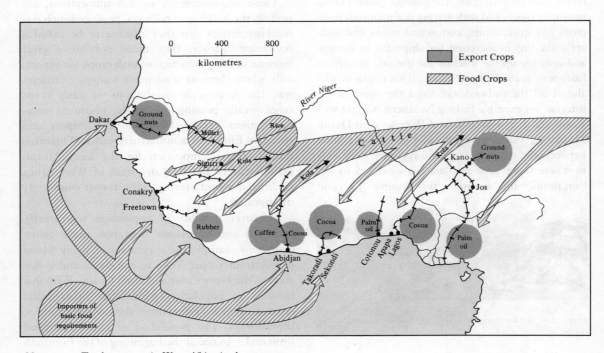

Map 21.2   Trade patterns in West Africa in the 1930s.

following statistics give some indication of the extent of the changeover to cash crop production: between 1910 and 1930 the production of groundnuts in Nigeria increased from 8,000 to 250,000 tonnes and in Senegal from 25,000 to 450,000 tonnes; during the same period the Gold Coast's production of cocoa increased from 5,000 to 240,000 tonnes while Nigeria's increased from 1,000 to 80,000 tonnes.

Those colonies which exported valuable cash crops (Nigeria, Gold Coast, Senegal and Ivory Coast) experienced an increase both in government revenue and in living standards. However, the areas unsuitable for the production of the raw materials Europe required, for example Niger and Upper Volta, were largely neglected by the colonial governments. Apart from groundnuts and cotton, almost all the valuable cash crops came from the coastal areas and these areas consequently developed at a faster rate than the interior.

Little money was invested in agricultural research and the production of cash crops was left almost entirely in African hands. No attempt was made to diversify the economy, the Gold Coast for example relied almost entirely on cocoa and gold, and so each territory was at the mercy of fluctuations in the world market price for their particular product. Much suffering was caused when prices fell, especially during the great world depression of the early 1930s.

Colonial governments took little interest in the encouragement or increase in the production of staple food crops. Almost everywhere in West Africa, except Nigeria, the great increase in cash crop production resulted in a decline in the production of food crops. This produced an increase in food prices, frequent food shortages and the need to import large quantities of basic foodstuffs, for example most of French West Africa had to import rice. This emphasis on cash crop production at the expense of food crops is another example of the extent to which colonial economic policy was designed to suit European rather than African needs.

Great development also took place in mining. Gold from Asante had always been important to West Africa, but during the colonial period large-scale mining of other minerals began such as

21.2 *Africans working on a cocoa plantation in the Gold Coast.*

21.3 *Working a tin 'paddock' on the Jos Plateau. Labourers in the background are seen removing the overburden, while those in the foreground are removing the 'pay dirt' for washing.*

coal, manganese, tin and bauxite. Unlike the production of cash crops, mining was completely controlled by a few large European companies; for example the United Africa Company owned all the mineral rights in Northern Nigeria. The profits of these companies went to their shareholders in Europe and were almost completely untaxed by the colonial governments. Consequently Africans benefited hardly at all from the great increase in the production of minerals during the colonial period.

4 Other economic developments

The trade of both British and French West Africa during the colonial period was dominated by large European trading companies. In British West Africa the most important were the UAC (United Africa Company) and John Holt's; in French West Africa SCOA ('Societé Commerciale de l'Afrique Occidentale') and CFAO (Compagnie Française de l'Afrique Occidentale'). Before the 1914–18 war there had been quite a number of Africans trading in imports and exports but these were driven out of business by their stronger rivals mainly as a result of the economic depression that followed the war in the 1920s and 1930s. European banks would not lend them money to finance their businesses or to help in times of difficulty. The large European companies preferred to use European and Lebanese traders to act as their agents. The Lebanese and Syrians first arrived in West Africa at the very end of the nineteenth century. They came from the very poor regions of their countries and found West Africa could provide them with a much better way of life. They proved to be very shrewd businessmen and were prepared, at first, to live at a much lower standard of living than their African rivals who had extensive families to maintain from the profits they made from their trade. Used to extreme poverty, the Lebanese and Syrians were content with very small profits so they undercut the prices charged by Africans, and soon took much of their trade from them. They were also very adventurous and shrewd. For example they would find out the direction a new railway line or road would be taking and open up shops at the towns and villages through which the

railway would eventually pass, thus profiting from the new trade the railway brought before anyone else. Finally European companies owned the shipping lines and charged higher rates to the African merchants for shipping exports than they did to themselves. This meant that by the 1930s there were very few large-scale African traders left in West Africa. There were, of course, a few exceptions such as Sanusi Dantata in Kano, who built up a flourishing business as a groundnut agent. But for the most part it was the Lebanese who took over the African's role as middleman between the farmers and the European import-export firms.

When two people wish to sell you the same cloth you will buy from the one who will let you have it cheapest. There is competition for your custom and you benefit. If only one person has the type of cloth you want, he can charge whatever price he wishes. This person has a monopoly or sole control of the sale of cloth. In this situation you have no alternative but to accept the prices he fixes because you cannot get your cloth from anywhere else.

Now in West Africa, as we have seen, in each colony there were at least two or three large European companies controlling the purchase of cash crops and the sale of imported goods. In principle this should have suited the Africans; different companies competing against each other for his custom, his produce or his labour. In practice the large companies agreed with each other what prices to charge for goods and what prices to pay for crops and labour. Thus they acted as though they were a single company and created a monopoly situation. Even in the Gold Coast where nine European companies were purchasing cocoa, they all came together to fix the price they would pay the farmer. They made it low so that when they sold the cocoa in Britain they would make most of the profit, not the farmer. This was known as the *Cocoa Pool* and operated in Nigeria as well as in the Gold Coast. Eventually this made the Gold Coast farmers stop supplying cocoa to the European companies: this was known as the Gold Coast Cocoa Hold-Up. The farmers preferred not to make any money at all than to be cheated.

The British Government was so worried that a Commission of Enquiry was appointed in 1938 on the marketing of West African cocoa. As a result of the criticisms of the large European companies made by the Commission, the governments in the British West African territories took over the purchase of cocoa and other crops. The profits they made were kept to help raise the price paid to the farmer when the world price fell low. This was one of the first instances of strong government intervention in the economy.

Other economic developments need to be mentioned. Portable currencies, first coins and later notes, were introduced by the colonial powers to replace earlier forms of currency, such as cowrie shells and manilla bars, and trade by barter. The large-scale alienation of land to European settlers which took place in East and South Africa did not occur in West Africa. The French gave a little land to settlers, especially in the Ivory Coast and Guinea, but in British West Africa there was no alienation of land at all. An attempt to introduce a Land Bill in the Gold Coast in the last years of the nineteenth century produced such strong opposition, led by the Aborigines Rights Protection Society (ARPS), that the British never dared to try and alienate land again. This was a great advantage at the time of independence because the West African countries did not have a white settler problem like Kenya and Rhodesia (Zimbabwe).

Forced labour was frequently used especially in French West Africa. Even where wages were paid, for example in the Enugu coal-mines and the Asante gold fields, they were often so low and conditions were so bad that compulsion had to be used to provide a sufficiently large work force. Although the right to form trade unions and to strike for better conditions was not recognised until the 1930s, strikes among miners and railway workers often occurred and were always brutally suppressed by the colonial governments.

Very few industries were established in West Africa during the period between the wars. If there was a choice between siting an industry in a colony or in the ruler's country the latter nearly always won. This was because the companies that exported Africa's raw materials invariably owned the factories that would process them in Europe. Thus UAC exported palm-oil for processing into soap to the soap factories in England which were owned by its parent company, Unilever. This soap was then exported to West Africa for purchase by Africans. Indeed, during this period West Africa was seen as a source of raw materials for the industries of Europe. There was little attempt to invest capital in manufacturing industries in West Africa. In 1938 French oil contractors became alarmed by competition from Senegalese oil mills which had been allowed to send oil to France duty free. To protect French interests from this competition, the French Government placed a limit on the amount of Senegalese oil that could be imported to France free of duty.

The bulk of the industries established during the inter-war period were ones that could only be effectively carried out on the spot. The mining industries – gold in Asante, diamonds in Sierra Leone, tin in Jos – are examples, so too are groundnuts and cotton because they are too bulky if they are not processed on the spot and take up a great deal of shipping space. As a result European firms invested in groundnut decorticating mills to shell groundnuts, and cotton ginneries to gin raw cotton. Apart from these, a few minor industries like soft-drink bottling companies and breweries were established. But West Africa had to wait till independence for a really significant growth in her industrial infrastructure.

What is surprising about the lack of industrial development during this period is that few Europeans were prepared to take advantage of the cheap labour supply available in West Africa. For instance in the Enugu coal mines, miners were paid only 7d – 1/6d per day in 1929 while in 1930 in the Asante gold mines they were paid only 1/– a day for unskilled surface labourers. 1/6d a day was paid to labourers in the Jos tin mines. Conditions of work were generally poor throughout West Africa and led to strikes. In 1926 the Sierra Leone Railway Workers Union which was not recognised by the Government went on strike for improved conditions of service but the Government took a strong line against them and they had to return to work on the Government's terms. The year before, Bambara, conscripted for work on the Thiès-Kayes line, went on strike after the arrest of three of their leaders who expressed their general discontent with conditions. Trade

Unions and strikes were illegal at that time but the French were unable to deal with the strike, which became general, because their troops, many of whom were Bambara, refused to be involved in any action against the strikers. The French gave in to the strikers and released their leaders.

5 Social developments

The European governments provided social services for the Africans only in so much as they benefited their system of government. Schools were built in just sufficient number to produce the clerks and technical assistants necessary for running government and commerce. There were few government run secondary schools because there was little demand for clerks trained beyond the primary school level. In 1934 there were less than six hundred pupils in the whole of French West Africa in secondary or post secondary schools. At the time of self-government in Northern Nigeria there were only five graduates in a population of over twenty million.

In French West Africa education was strictly controlled by the government and there were few mission schools. In British West Africa, by contrast, the majority of schools were run by missionaries and in non-Muslim areas children had a much better chance of getting to school than in French West Africa. In Muslim areas, however, where missionary schools were not allowed, little was done by the British to provide alternative government sponsored education. In many areas Africans quickly saw the value of education and some even financed their children's education abroad in France, Britain or America, but they received little encouragement from the colonial governments. In Ghana and Nigeria some educated people even pooled their resources to found schools of their own to which they could send their children. They saw that the only way in which their children could better themselves, and one day take part in the government and administration of their countries, was by obtaining the same knowledge that was at the disposal of their rulers. For the most part they did not care that the curricula their children studied was modelled on those used in the schools of France and Britain. The

21.4 *Western education was perhaps the most revolutionary change introduced by the colonial rulers. Here Nigerians of all ages attend a school at Enugu.*

main thing was to get their children to school. It was only with the approach of independence that Africans began to demand curricula relevant to West Africa; for example the study of the Ghanaian constitution rather than the British constitution.

In the countryside, parents were much more reluctant to send children to school, for it took them off the farms and often taught them to be discontent with their way of life. Not surprisingly then, it was in towns that the nationalist movements developed for as we have seen education gave those who wanted to take over government from the Europeans the skills, arguments and understanding to press their claims. Very few of the leaders of nationalist movements had not been to school; and many of them, like Kwame Nkrumah of Ghana, Nnamdi Azikiwe of Nigeria and Léopold Sédar Senghor of Senegal, had been to university.

Health services in British West Africa during this period were largely concerned with the health of the European community, even to the extent of building separate hospitals for Europeans. In 1936 in the whole of Nigeria only 3,503 hospital beds were available for African patients and only 995 in the Gold Coast. The record of the Government of French West Africa was much more impressive. Its medical services made a concerted effort to eradicate basic diseases such as smallpox and sleeping sickness. Doctors, assisted by African auxiliary doctors, went out into the rural areas to track down sick

21.5 *Under colonial rule Islamic educational institutions also spread. Here children attend a Koranic school, where instruction is in Arabic, at Abeokuta.*

people. In 1936 over three million people were treated in this way.

One of the most striking developments that took place during the colonial period was the wide scale conversion of Africans to Christianity and Islam, particularly the latter. While the traditional religions of Africa could explain the world in which particular ethnic groups lived, once their members left their homelands for towns inhabited by other ethnic groups whose religions were alien to them, they found that the Christian and Muslim religions gave a more satisfactory explanation of the new world in which they lived. In the multi-ethnic towns of the colonial rulers, for instance, there were no priests of the traditional religions of the immigrants. Islam and Christianity, which treated all men alike and ignored ethnic, regional and national frontiers, provided for them spiritual needs as well as serving as a common bond between them.

But why did Islam spread more rapidly than Christianity, which after all was the official religion of the colonial rulers? While Christianity was the religion of the white man and was thus considered prestigious by many Africans, and whilst it provided education through missionary schools in which, at the same time, children were indoctrinated it had certain drawbacks as compared with Islam.

In the first place Islam had become an indigenous religion over the centuries, and its message was carried by Africans, not white men. Though at first the European churches had used Africans as missionaries, in the twentieth century they increasingly relied on Europeans. It is significant that African-run churches were more successful in gaining adherents when competing with Islam than were the white-run churches. Islam permitted polygamy, whereas Christian missionaries forbade it. Some churches founded by Africans, however, permitted polygamy and were as a result more tolerant of African traditional religious practices than the white missionary churches. Also, in response to the fact that many Africans wished to convert to Christianity but were unwilling totally to abandon their ancestral religions, certain churches developed which mixed Christianity with some local practices not normally permitted by the Church. These churches, like the Aladura churches in Yorubaland, permitted traditional African music in their churches and made a great feature of possession.

While Islam and Christianity made tremendous progress in the colonial period, the traditional religions proved remarkably resilient. Those people who were not directly affected by the colonial presence continued to practice the religion of their ancestors. Furthermore, many converts to both Islam and Christianity continued to fall back on their old religion and their priests in times of trouble.

The inter-war period, when the European powers seemed fully in control of their West African territories, was thus one in which great changes were taking place. These were not always very obvious given the colonial governments lack of concern about development, but European administration had led to many changes in the African way of life. The boundaries of the colonial territories grouped people into new political units and made movement easy within them. Large cities grew up and acted like magnets to the rural population. Increasingly farmers became involved in a cash as distinct from a barter economy. Indigenous religions lost ground to the world religions of Islam and Christianity. Most important of all, through education, a small number of Africans gained an understanding of the way of life and thought, and in particular the technology of their European masters. As we shall see in the next chapter they were to use this knowledge to secure their freedom.

22 The growth of African nationalism

1 General background

By 1920 there had grown up a group of educated Africans (for example Blaise Diagne in Senegal and Casely-Hayford in the Gold Coast) who had begun to think of themselves not just as Fante or Yoruba or Wollof but as Gold Coasters, Nigerians and Senegalese as well. While the people of Dahomeyan Borgu who revolted against the French in 1915–16 had wanted to regain Borgu's independence, this group of educated Africans did not think in terms of the independence of the states the Europeans had conquered but rather in terms of gaining more control over the affairs of the states which the Europeans had created. They accepted that such countries as Nigeria, the Gold Coast and Senegal were there to stay. They did not as yet want independence but rather constitutional reforms which would give them some say in the conduct of their own affairs. It was not really until after the Second World War that independence movements as such developed.

There were many long-term reasons for the development of nationalist feeling. Many of the economic changes studied in the last chapter, such as the migration and the domination of trade by the Europeans and Lebanese, produced much hardship and suffering especially during the great depression of the 1930s. Unemployment, economic exploitation and racial prejudice all helped to increase opposition to colonial rule. Urbanisation weakened family and tribal ties and improved communications helped to develop national feeling and increase unity within countries. The growth of western education produced leaders for the nationalist movements and provided them with a common language and new ideas. They had learnt about the practice of democracy in Britain and France and therefore advocated that the peoples of the colonies should have a say in their own government. Wherever education was most developed nationalism was strongest (for example most of the nationalists in the Gold Coast came from the Fante coastal area where education was well developed). Christian missionary activity also helped to strengthen nationalism; partly as a reaction against missionary attempts to destroy African culture and partly because of the Christian emphasis on the equality of all men. Moreover, common language, trade, law and administration during the colonial period gave the states created by the partition a growing feeling of unity and nationhood.

Nationalism is a vague term: in its African context it can perhaps be defined as a feeling of national consciousness, an awareness by people that they are members of a nation-state and a desire for freedom from colonial rule. Some of the more immediate causes for the rise of nationalism will be examined in the next two chapters. Here we must study some of the external influences on African nationalism and the growth of political activity in British and French West Africa between the two world wars.

2 *Pan-Africanism*

In the rise of nationalism in West Africa, that is of a group of men interested in taking some part in the government of the European colonies, the influence of West Indians and Black Americans was important. In 1900 a West Indian lawyer, H. Sylvester Williams, called the first Pan-African Congress in London. Only three West Africans attended it and it was mainly concerned with the problems of discrimination against the coloured educated elite in America. One of the participants at the Congress was a then unknown coloured American, W.E.B. Dubois, who was to become the acknowledged father of Pan-Africanism. At the Congress he made his famous prophesy: 'The problem of the twentieth century is the problem of the colour-line'.

No further Congresses were held until 1919 when more West Africans took part. The Congresses held in 1919, 1921, 1923 and 1927 all called for black solidarity and the removal of the inferior status imposed on black people both in Africa and America. At the 1919 Congress a resolution was passed that 'The natives of Africa must have the right to participate in the government as fast as their development permits, in conformity with the principle that government exists for the natives and not the natives for the government'. At none of these congresses was any demand for independence made, nor indeed, despite their title, did they put forward any ideas on the eventual establishment of a Pan-African government. This was done by a different negro organisation, the Universal Negro Improvement Association (UNIA), founded and led by a Jamaican, Marcus Garvey. Garvey told his followers in New York in 1920: 'If Europe is for the Europeans then Africa shall be for the black peoples of the world. . . . The other races have countries of their own and it is time for the 400,000,000 Negroes to claim Africa for themselves'. Later he told another audience: 'The Negroes of this world are striking homeward towards Africa to make her a big black Republic'.

'Africa for the Africans' was Garvey's main idea. He also wished to develop black commerce and trade. He founded the Black Star Line to carry goods and passengers between Africa and America. Garvey's ideas were to have a great influence on later nationalists such as Kwame Nkrumah. At the time many of West Africa's politically conscious men like Casely-Hayford of the Gold Coast were inspired by his message. Though Garvey's movement failed and he was imprisoned on a charge of fraud, he did as much as anyone to draw the attention of the world, and in particular Africans, to the problems of Africa.

There were also other external influences encouraging the growth of nationalism in West Africa. The existence of the independent African states of Liberia and Ethiopia proved that Africans could rule themselves and influenced West Africans to try and

22.1 *Dr W. E. B. Du Bois, addresses a Pan-African Conference.*

22.2 *Marcus Garvey, the Jamaican founder of the Universal Negro improvement Association wearing his uniform as 'President of the Republic of Africa'.*

free themselves from colonial rule. Communist and socialist ideas which attacked colonialism also influenced many members of the growing Western-educated elite. Moreover, the success of nationalists in Asia, where India gained her independence in 1947, provided an example for Africans to follow.

3 The Senegal election of 1914

In Senegal, as we have seen, the inhabitants of the Four Communes had the right to send a deputy to the National Assembly in Paris. Until the 1914 elections they had always sent either a white or a mulatto deputy, even though African voters were in the majority. In 1914 Blaise Diagne, a French-educated African, stood for election and defeated the existing deputy, the mulatto François Carpot, and six European rivals. There were several reasons for his success. He was a good orator with a magnetic personality and played on forces of discontent. The Young Senegalese Party, for instance, was upset because all scholarships for further education in France seemed to go to mulattoes while Frenchmen enjoyed better benefits for the same jobs as Africans. There had been attempts by the French authorities to deprive the inhabitants of the Four Communes of their rights as citizens. Diagne promised to secure these rights once and for all provided the voters would accept the obligation of military service which went with citizenship. This they gladly agreed to by voting him into office because they did not want to be subject to the indigénat like the people in the interior. In 1916, when France was desperately short of soldiers, Diagne succeeded in getting a law passed that 'the natives of the *communes de pleine exercice* of Senegal are and remain French citizens subject to military service'.

In 1919, after the First World War, Diagne was re-elected as deputy but gradually he gave up his radicalism and began to cooperate more and more with the colonial administration, Diagne continued as deputy until his death in the early 1930s but was increasingly opposed by the younger, more radical elements of the educated elite.

4 Politics in French West Africa

Up until 1940 when northern France was occupied by Germany and a neutral government was established at Vichy in southern France, the only part of French West Africa where politics flourished was in the Four Communes. In the hinterland of Senegal and in the rest of French West Africa the vast majority of the population were subject to the indigénat. This meant that as soon as they made any kind of protest against the French colonial government they could be imprisoned without trial. Outside the Four Communes there were only 2,136 Africans who had the rights of French citizens and these had been very carefully selected before being made French citizens. No form of political activity was allowed and therefore no political parties were formed. This did not mean that French West Africans were not politically aware. They made their protests in other ways: some people migrated into British West Africa; in Porto Novo in Dahomey in 1923 there were violent riots against an increase in the head-tax; despite the indigénat there were strikes by workers in Guinea, Senegal, Soudan and Dahomey; and the Harrisite Movement in the Ivory Coast was an attempt to assert African independence in the church.

From the point of view of understanding the development of politics in French West Africa between the two world wars we have to consider three main factors. Firstly, in Paris, those Africans who had gone there to obtain further education and to work were not subject to the indigénat and were politically active. There they could freely discuss among themselves the policies of their colonial masters. It was in Paris that Léopold Sédar Senghor developed his theories on *négritude* which rejected French assimilation and insisted that Africans had a valuable culture of their own. These ideas became very popular among the educated elite of French West Africa.

A second important factor in the development of politics in French West Africa was the *Ecole Normale William Ponty* in Dakar. This was a teacher training school where the very best students from the whole of French West Africa were sent. There they found themselves in a place where politics were openly discussed and where newspapers were comparatively free from censorship. This one school had as its students in the inter-war years many of the men who were to dominate the politics of French West Africa after the Second World War: for example Modibo Keita, who became President of the Republic of Mali; Mamadou Dia who became Prime Minister of Senegal; Hubert Maga, who became President of Dahomey; and Ouezzin-Coulibaly who became Prime Minister of Upper Volta.

The third important factor was the voluntary associations. Groups of young educated men got together to discuss 'culture', 'sport' or 'theatre' or else formed old boys associations. Very often, however, they talked about politics. Whenever the colonial administration suspected that politics were being discussed, they broke up the association. A change came in 1937 when the Popular Front Government in France, made up of Socialists and Communists who were more liberal in their policies towards Africans, began to encourage these voluntary associations. They used them to spread the socialist ideas of their government. In Bamako, the capital of French Soudan, they founded an Association of the Friends of the Popular Government (ARP) for which they provided a building known as the *Maison du Peuple* (House of the People) which was used by other voluntary associations as well. Modibo Keita was a member of the ARP and when after the war he founded the *Union Soudanaise*, which was to become the main political party in the Soudan, most of its leading members were associated with either the Maison du Peuple or the ARP.

In 1940, however, when France fell to Germany, French West Africa came under the control of the neutral Vichy Government. The Vichy Government banned all politics in French West Africa and even the citizens were deprived of their rights. French West Africa had to wait until after the Second World War before full political activity was allowed for the first time. As we shall see in the next chapter, the Second World War marked a vital turning point in

the development of political activity and nationalism in French West Africa.

5 The National Congress of British West Africa

In the coastal cities of British West Africa – Bathurst, Freetown, Cape Coast, Accra, Lagos and Calabar – there was a small group of well-educated men who were prepared to protest against government measures they did not like. In the Gold Coast, for instance, they had formed the Aborigines Rights Protection Society (ARPS) in 1897 to protest against the government's land policy. In Lagos the People's Union was founded in 1908 to protest against the levy of a water rate. In addition there were several newspapers that frequently criticised the colonial governments, for instance *The Gold Coast Leader*, the *Lagos Weekly Record* and the *Sierra Leone Weekly News*. These protest movements and their associated press brought forward leaders who were

22.3 *The delegation of the National Congress of British West Africa sent to London in 1920. From left to right seated: Dr H. C. Bankole-Bright (Sierra Leone), T. Hutton Mills (President of the Congress), Chief Oluwa (Nigeria), J. E. Casely-Hayford (Ghana), H. Van Hein (Ghana). Standing: J. Egerton Shyngle (Nigeria), H. M. Jones (Gambia), Herbert Macaulay (Chief Oluwa's Secretary), T. M. Oluwa (son of the chief), F. W. Dove (Sierra Leone), E. F. Small (Gambia).*

22.4 *J. E. Casely-Hayford (seated right) was the leading politician in the Gold Coast until his death in 1930.*

to dominate politics in British West Africa until the 1930s. In Lagos Herbert Macaulay, who led the protest against the water rate, was to become the most important political figure until 1937. In the Gold Coast, J. Mensah Sarbah and J. F. Casely-Hayford were similarly to dominate politics until the late 1930s.

Another important factor in the development of nationalist protest movements was the independent African churches. Some of these were modelled on the European churches, but had broken away from them because the former were run by white priests. Others mixed African religion with European Christianity. Whatever the case, they asserted the idea of African independence and initiative.

In 1913 the political elite of British West Africa founded the National Congress of British West Africa, and in 1920 the Congress held its first meeting in Accra with six delegates from Nigeria, forty from the Gold Coast, three from Sierra Leone and one from the Gambia. They proposed that half the seats in the colonial legislative councils should be reserved for African members elected by the people. They also asked that the budgets be subject to debate and called for the establishment of town

councils. In commerce, education and the medical and legal services they called for greater opportunities for Africans.

The National Congress of British West Africa was not asking for independence: rather it was requesting greater participation by Africans in the administration of their own affairs. This was to set the pattern for politics in British West Africa over the next twenty years.

6 Politics in British West Africa in the inter-war years

British policy in the inter-war years, as we have seen, relied on the chiefs as the leaders of the people. The educated elite, however, felt that they, not the chiefs, should be the leaders. While the elite was better equipped to deal with the problems of modern government than the chiefs, they had little contact with the ordinary people outside the towns. This was a major criticism made by the British Governments against them. Nevertheless, in new constitutions introduced in Nigeria in 1922, Sierra Leone in 1924 and the Gold Coast in 1927 provision was made for the election of a few African representatives to the Legislative Councils. But these elected representatives were carefully balanced with traditional rulers. Though the elected members were in a very small minority, at least they could make their voices heard. However, in the Executive Councils, where policy was actually carried out, there were no African members, either elected or nominated. There, as in the Legislative Councils, the government officials were in the majority. Thus real power during this period lay with the colonial governors.

Nevertheless, important political developments that helped to prepare the way for the rise of nationalist parties after the Second World War did take place. In Nigeria, Herbert Macaulay, a grandson of Bishop Crowther, founded the Nigerian National Democratic Party (NNDP) which was to dominate Nigerian politics until the late 1930s. While the NNDP claimed it was a national party, it was really only a Lagos party. The important point was that a political party aimed at securing reforms for the people that it represented had been formed.

22.5 *Dr Nnamdi Azikwe, one of the most important political figures in Nigeria in the inter-war years and after.*

In the Gold Coast, rivalry between the leading political personalities delayed the formation of an effective political party. In Sierra Leone the local branch of the NCBWA transformed itself into a political party for the purpose of fighting elections, but it was essentially a Freetown party interested only in the affairs of its Creole electors. All of these parties were essentially elite parties expressing the grievances of the elite at their exclusion from the government, administration and commerce of their countries.

Organisations which tried to look beyond the needs and grievances of the elite did however emerge during the inter-war years. The West African Students Union (WASU), founded in London in 1925, criticised British policy on many issues and demanded radical reforms in the colonial administration. By the 1930s there was quite a large group of students who had returned to their capital cities full of ideas of colonial reforms. In 1934 such students formed the Nigerian Youth Movement (NYM) in Lagos. It included in its leadership H.O. Davies, who had shared rooms in London with Jomo Kenyatta, Obafemi Awolowo and Ernest Ikoli, a journalist. In 1937 Nnamdi Azikiwe, an Igbo, joined

the Movement thus ensuring broader support for what had seemed to be largely a Yoruba organisation. The NYM could therefore claim to be the first truly national political party. It gained considerable popular support through its criticism of the invasion of Abbysinia (Ethiopia) by the Italians and of the Cocoa Pool. Macaulay and his NNDP supporters did not favour the hands-off Abyssinia campaign and in 1938 the NYM won all three Lagos seats on the Legislative Council. It was greatly helped by support in the newspapers, especially Ernest Ikoli's *Daily Service* and Azikiwe's *West African Pilot*. The *Pilot* declared:

> . . . the era of submission, without constitutional opposition . . . is gone . . . the Nigeria of today and tomorrow must realise that it is part of a Sleeping African Giant who must be awakened from its deep sleep, in order to harness its energy and usher in a new Nigeria.

In the Gold Coast no such political party developed though the Gold Coast Youth Conference, founded in 1930 by J.B. Danquah, did provide an opportunity for the elected representatives to express their grievances. It brought together a number of voluntary organisations like literary and debating societies and encouraged them to think about national issues.

Much more active was the West African Youth League founded in Freetown in 1938 by I.T.A. Wallace-Johnson. It had as its aims the mobilisation of African labour and the bringing together of the peoples of the Colony and Protectorate. Wallace-Johnson's organisation proved to be a great success: an English observer wrote that:

> Night after night the Wilberforce Hall has been crowded to the doors and windows by those assembled to consider and foment grievances, and though the subjects of protests and demonstration have by no means always been well chosen or well founded, the ventilation of constitutional or labour grievances has begun to bridge the old deep cleavage between the Creoles and the peoples of the Protectorate.

The Sierra Leone Government became so frightened

of Wallace-Johnson that they imprisoned him and banned his party.

By and large though, politics in the inter-war years were restricted to the educated elite in the coastal towns. Little attempt was made to recruit members from other walks of life or to concentrate on national rather than local issues. The Youth Movements,

however, were beginning to show the way politics would develop after the Second World War. Then, political leaders tried to gain the support of the masses and concern themselves with national issues. Those leaders who continued to practise the type of elitist politics of the inter-war years were soon forgotten.

23 The effects of the Second World War on West Africa

1 General importance

Most of West Africa stagnated under colonial rule in the period between the First World War of 1914–18 and the Second World War of 1939–45. There was little economic development; both the revenue and the trade of Nigeria was less in 1938–9 than it had been in 1925–6, and even less political development; no African members were appointed to the Executive Councils of the British colonies. Large areas of West Africa remained virtually untouched by colonial rule. This situation was greatly changed by the outbreak of the Second World War in 1939.

The Second World War marked a turning point in West African history. From a position of relative insignificance West Africa was suddenly transformed into an area of vital strategic and economic importance to the great powers. The war brought the long economic depression of the 1920s and 1930s to an end. West Africa became very closely involved in the world struggle between the Allied powers (Britain, France and later America and Russia) and the so-called Axis powers (Germany, Italy and Japan). Political and social reforms were introduced that set both the British and the French West African territories on the road to independence.

The Second World War affected West Africa in many ways, all of which tended greatly to increase and strengthen the forces of African nationalism. For the first time colonial governments accepted their obligation to develop their colonies in the interests of the inhabitants and agreed to let these inhabitants have a say in their own future. The Second World War marked the change from the period of colonial rule proper to the period of decolonisation, which turned out to be a much shorter process than either the British or the French realised at the time.

2 Course of events

The Second World War began in September 1939 and as early as June 1940 France was forced to surrender to the Germans. The northern half of France was occupied by the Germans, while the southern half, known as Vichy France, was neutralised and became almost a German tributary state under the leadership of Marshal Pétain, a hero of the First World War. Some Frenchmen refused to accept this surrender and a Free French Government, headed by de Gaulle, was formed in exile to continue the struggle against Germany. French West Africa, under the leadership of Governor-General Boisson, supported the Vichy Government and was therefore neutralised.

French West Africa was strategically important for many reasons: firstly because of its large resources in both manpower and raw materials; secondly because of its long, strategic coastline, especially the port of Dakar, the third largest port in the French Empire; and thirdly because both Niger and Chad, Nigeria's northern neighbours, possessed common borders with the Italian colony of Libya.

23.1 *Dakar was well defended for the Vichy Government by Pierre Boisson against the Anglo-Free French invasion force of September 1940 which was successfully held back.*

23.2 *Before the Anglo-Free French force retreated it did severe damage to parts of Dakar including the mainly African residential area of the Medina.*

Nigeria also gave access through Chad to the Anglo–Egyptian Sudan and to East Africa where a war was being fought against the Italians in Ethiopia and Somalia.

Chad's governor, Felix Eboué, handed his territory over to de Gaulle and the Free French and soon all of French Equatorial Africa (the present day countries of Chad, Gabon, Central African Republic and Congo-Brazzaville) and Cameroun recognised de Gaulle's Free French Government. While French West Africa remained under Vichy control the British West African territories watched it nervously for any sign of German activity. British submarines blockaded its coast preventing shipping entering or leaving ports like Dakar and large British forces were stationed in West Africa. In September 1940, the British and the Free French even launched an unsuccessful attack on Dakar in the hope of bringing French West Africa over to the allied side.

In November 1942, after the allied landings in French North Africa, French West Africa joined the Free French side and re-entered the war against Germany. This allowed the British to send the troops stationed in West Africa to the Far East to fight against the Japanese. Except for the attempted attack on Dakar, there was no actual fighting in West Africa during the war.

Large numbers of African troops, however, were used to help the allies in other parts of the world. Even before the surrender of France in 1940, 80,000 French West African troops had been sent to fight in France. While French West Africa was under Vichy

control it took no part in the war, but from 1943–5 over 100,000 troops left French West Africa to fight on the side of the Free French. In British West Africa at the start of the war the Royal West African Frontier Force was increased in size from 8,000 to 146,000 men. In the early stages of the war most of these troops were used in the East African campaign against the Italians in Ethiopia. Later most of them were sent to fight against the Japanese in the jungles of Burma in south-east Asia where they proved to be extremely good soldiers and made an important contribution to the eventual victory of the allies.

3 Economic and social results of the war

The most important immediate impact of the war was to revive the West African economy after the long depression of the 1920s and 1930s. The factories of Europe became busy once more supplying their armies with equipment and food. Consequently the demand for West African products, such as groundnuts, cotton, palm-oil and tin increased considerably. After the conquest of British Malaya and the Dutch East Indies (Indonesia) by the Japanese, West Africa became even more vital to the allied war effort. Previously Malaya had been the allies main source of supply of tin and rubber and Indonesia of palm-oil. Now these important items had to be obtained principally from West Africa.

At the beginning of the war French West Africa immediately became important to France as a

23.3 *British West African troops took part in the East African campaign against the Italians in Abyssinia (Ethiopia) and were responsible for the restoration of Emperor Haile Selassie to his throne. Here he is being welcomed to Addis Ababa by his British Commander-in-chief while a West African rifleman presents arms.*

supplier of raw materials, especially foodstuffs. During the period of Vichy control (1940–42) trade was very greatly reduced because of the British naval blockade and therefore the production of cash crops declined; for example groundnut production in Senegal decreased from 419,000 tonnes in 1940 to only 114,000 tonnes in 1942. After French West Africa rejoined the allies in 1942, however, it again became an important supplier of raw materials. Every effort was made to increase the production of the much-needed cash crops. Frequently the ordinary African farmer suffered greatly by being forced to grow certain crops and to produce more than could reasonably be expected. In the cities considerable development took place aimed at helping the war effort; for example ports were improved and airports were built. Moreover many small-scale industries were begun because of the difficulty of importing goods; all shipping being used for war purposes and being vulnerable to German attack. Another important economic consequence of the war on French West Africa was a great increase in government participation and planning in all aspects of the economy, a trend that was to be continued after the war.

The economic benefits of the war were felt even more consistently and strongly in the British West African territories. The economic activities of all four colonies were co-ordinated for the first time and government control and intervention was greatly increased; for example the establishment of marketing boards. The war greatly increased demand for the basic export crops and consequently production of them increased. This led to an economic boom for Nigeria and the Gold Coast in particular. Communication facilities were improved and a wide range of secondary manufacturing industries were begun for the first time.

The revival of the economy in British West Africa in 1941 and in French West Africa after 1942 led to a rapid growth of major towns like Accra, Dakar, Lagos and Port Harcourt. The factories set up to manufacture goods that could not be imported offered new opportunities for employment as did the air-bases, army transit camps and busy ports. Large numbers of people flocked to the towns in search of work and lived in makeshift houses which soon became overcrowded slums. While many were fortunate in gaining jobs, there were at least as many again who did not. The many new jobs meant that there was plenty of money, but there was little to spend it on. Because of German submarine activity along the West African coast only essential goods were imported. With too much money chasing too few things to buy, there was a great rise in prices. There was therefore a lot of discontent among the employed as well as the unemployed.

Many of the newly arrived people in the towns grouped together in associations to help look after each other in the difficult world of the city. Usually these associations were based on ethnic origin, but trade unions were also organised. These associations and unions were to be one of the main sources of support for nationalist leaders like Nkrumah, Azikiwe, Modibo Keita and Sekou Toure in their struggle for independence.

Nationalist feeling was further strengthened by the influence of the returning soldiers at the end of the war. While in the First World War few troops had returned with new ideas about the future of their countries, many of those who fought in the Second World War did. First of all many of the soldiers were taught to read and write or learnt trades. Secondly, they saw that the white man was not invincible, for example the conquest of the British Empire in the Far East by the Japanese. Thirdly, in India they came into contact with strong nationalist feeling. There they saw people about to be given their independence who were much worse off than they were. It is therefore not surprising that so many of the soldiers returned to West Africa with ideas of reform.

Basically the war had brought into question the whole nature of colonial authority and destroyed for ever any mistaken idea of white superiority. Conflicts between supporters of the Vichy Government and the Free French greatly weakened French prestige and unity, and British defeats, especially by the Japanese, weakened the colonial powers' image of invincibility. All these factors helped to strengthen nationalist feeling against colonial rule and weaken the colonial powers' hold over their African territories.

4 Reforms

While neither the French nor the British Government considered the prospect of independence for their African territories during the war, they both agreed to social, economic and political reforms that, in retrospect, we can see prepared the way for independence. Both the British and the Free French were under great pressure from their powerful American and Russian allies to reform their colonial governments. Neither America nor Russia approved of colonies, nor too did some of the socialists in the British war-time government. Reform was also necessary to encourage African support for the Allied cause. While German radio was accusing the British of all sorts of atrocities in their African colonies, one way of countering this was to offer Africans a brighter future and to contrast the relatively liberal policies of the Allied powers with the racist policies of Nazi Germany. For example the Atlantic Charter signed by Britain and America declared 'the right of all people to choose the form of government under which they live'. Promises of reform had been made during the First World War and not kept after it; the circumstances of the Second World War, however, forced the colonial powers to put into effect many long-awaited reforms.

The first important reform in British West Africa was the Colonial Development and Welfare Act of 1939 which firmly committed the British Government to a policy of development of its West African colonies. Relatively large sums of money were voted for the building of schools, roads and hospitals, and for the first time this money was to be supplied by the British tax-payer. Previously any development that had taken place had been financed almost entirely by African taxpayers.

During, and shortly after the war, reforms were made which gave the Africans a much greater say in their government. In 1942 Africans were appointed for the first time to the Executive Councils of the Gold Coast and Nigeria. In 1943 Accra's new Town Council was given an elected majority. Shortly after the war Nigeria was given a new constitution, the Richards Constitution, which created an unofficial majority in the Legislative Council. It was not, however, an elected majority, since many of the unofficials were chiefs nominated by the Governor. About the same time a new constitution was issued for the Gold Coast which provided for an elected majority on the Legislative Council. In Sierra Leone the only concession made to constitutional advance was in 1943 when two nominated Africans were given seats on the Executive Council. Africans quite rightly regarded these changes as far too slight: after all, real power lay in the Executive Councils where

23.4   *General de Gaulle, leader of the Free French Government, addresses the Brazzaville Conference of 1944 which recommended sweeping reforms in the administration of France's colonies.*

African members now formed a small minority. However, it is significant that Britain had at last accepted its obligation to help develop its colonies and to give Africans a greater say in the administration of these colonies.

The same sort of reforms were accepted by the French in 1944 at the Brazzaville Conference. Here General de Gaulle, the Free French leader, agreed to the abolition of the status of *sujet* (subject), the end of the hated *corvée* (forced labour) and the indigénat.

The basic freedoms were at last granted and the formation of political parties allowed. The colonies would be represented in the National Assembly which would draw up the constitution for France and her overseas territories. Furthermore all colonies would have representative assemblies like Senegal. General de Gaulle also promised a major investment fund for social and economic development (FIDES). Roads, schools and hospitals would be built at the expense of the French taxpayer.

24 The path to independence

1 The situation after the Second World War

By the time the Second World War finished in 1945, there was a considerable demand throughout West Africa for both constitutional change and an able leadership ready to spearhead the movement towards independence from colonial rule. It had taken the Europeans only about twenty years to partition West Africa (1880–1900) and it was to take most of West Africa even less than twenty years to win back its independence. The Gold Coast was the first country to become independent in 1957 and most of the rest of West Africa gained its independence in 1960. In the absence of a common language, culture or history, the nationalist leaders, who for the most part were made up of members of the educated elite, had to rely largely on anti-colonial feeling for their support. As we have seen in the last chapter, the Second World War greatly accelerated the growth of nationalist movements and further progress was made by the constitutional reforms carried out by both Britain and France immediately after the war. Nationalist parties were formed (for example the NCNC in Nigeria and the CPP in the Gold Coast) which used modern political methods to appeal to the mass of the people and these parties rapidly took the place of the old western-orientated elite parties.

2 Gold Coast to Ghana

It was only during the Second World War that the idea of obtaining independence from colonial rule began to become a goal which political leaders in West Africa thought they realistically could achieve. And they achieved it in a remarkably short time. The Gold Coast became the independent country of Ghana only twelve years after the end of the war. Ghana immediately became a symbol of African freedom for other African countries still subjected to colonial rule.

As we have seen the new constitution introduced for the Gold Coast in 1946 provided for an elected African majority in the Legislative Council. Most of the leading nationalists, however, did not consider this sufficient: not only were most of the elected members chiefs, but also real power still lay with the Executive Council, where the British remained in a large majority. Dr J. B. Danquah and other nationalists organised a political party in 1947 known as the United Gold Coast Convention (UGCC) to protest against the constitution. They invited back from abroad Kwame Nkrumah to be its secretary. Nkrumah, who had been educated in America, came to prominence as a dedicated nationalist as a result of his prominent role in the Fifth Pan-African Congress in Manchester in 1945. Several factors helped to gain the UGCC wide popular support. One was the disease which had affected the cocoa trees that provided the Gold Coast with most of its wealth. The only known way to deal with this disease was to cut down affected trees. This understandably angered the farmers who did not understand why their trees had to be destroyed and so they gave strong support

24.1 *On 18th September 1956 Prime Minister Dr Kwame Nkrumah announced to the Gold Coast Legislature Assembly that Britain had agreed that the colony should become independent as Ghana.*

to the leaders of the UGCC. To add to this discontent a group of leading expatriate businessmen made agreements to fix prices to the disadvantage of the African customers. This led to violent demonstrations and rioting, headed by ex-servicemen, and involved wide-scale destruction of expatriate property. The British colonial authorities reacted by imprisoning Danquah, Nkrumah and other leaders of the UGCC in 1948; this immediately made them heroes in the eyes of most Ghanaians.

The British colonial Government, however, then appointed a Commission of Enquiry to examine the causes of the rioting. It was significant that this Commission was composed entirely of Africans. It suggested several radical changes in the constitution of the Gold Coast, recommending that in the Legislative Council the number of members elected by the people, as distinct from by the chiefs, should be increased and that an Executive Council should be formed in which eight out of the eleven ministers would be Ghanaians. The British agreed to these proposals and put them into effect and they were accepted by Danquah and most of the UGCC leadership.

For Nkrumah, however, it was not enough and he grouped together a large number of voluntary associations into a new political party, the Convention People's Party (CPP) to demand 'self-government now'. At the beginning of 1950 he called for 'Positive Action' and there were further riots and demonstrations and a national strike. Nkrumah and several others were imprisoned, but the CPP won the elections held in 1951 under the new constitution and Nkrumah was released from prison to become the first African head of a government in colonial Africa.

From then on the pace of constitutional change was rapid. Peaceful political and constitutional bargaining took the place of violent action. Nkrumah immediately asked for a greater degree of self-government and the British gave way, granting a new constitution in 1954 which gave full internal self-government and ministerial responsibility. There was growing concern among many Ghanaians about what they considered to be the dictatorial methods of Nkrumah and the CPP. Other political parties were formed representing regional interests (for example the National Liberation Party in Asante) and so violent were the clashes between them and the CPP that the British decided that they must have an election to see whether Nkrumah really had the support of the country before they handed it over to him. In the general election held in July 1956 the CPP won seventy-two out of the one hundred and four seats in the Legislature and on 6th March 1957 Nkrumah became the head of the independent state of Ghana, the first tropical African colony to free itself from colonial rule.

Several factors help to explain why Ghana achieved its independence earlier than the other colonies. It was greatly assisted by the rapid economic and social change caused especially by the large-scale cultivation of cocoa. Moreover Ghana, especially the coastal Fante area, had for a long time possessed a large educated elite. The CPP under Nkrumah had managed to preserve a reasonable unity throughout the struggle for independence and, as the 1956 election showed, the party was supported by public opinion. Lastly, it was an advantage that Ghana was comparatively small and possessed a reasonably good system of communications to link it together.

3 Nigeria

Nigeria's struggle for independence took longer because of the size and diversity of the country and its peoples. Nigeria possessed no nationalist leaders as radical as Nkrumah and, apart from some disturbances in 1948–50, progress towards independence was largely non-violent. One of the main problems was that, until 1946, the north and the south had effectively been administered as separate colonies. The three constitutions introduced before independence (The Richards Constitution of 1946, Macpherson Constitution of 1951 and Lyttelton Constitution of 1954) were attempts to find a way in which the north and the south could be united and ruled together under one stable government.

The 1946 constitution introduced by Governor Richards brought the north and the south together for the first time in a central legislature. There would now be a majority of members in the Legislative Council who were not members of the Government, that is an 'unofficial majority'. The Legislative

Council could, for the first time, make laws for the whole country, and Nigeria was divided into three regions (the North, the West and the East) each of which was to have a Regional House of Assembly with limited powers. Most of the unofficial members of the Legislative Council were not to be elected directly, but indirectly by the Regional Assemblies. This constitution in no way satisfied the nationalists. Dr Azikiwe, who had founded a political party called the National Council of Nigeria and the Cameroons (NCNC) with Herbert Macaulay, led a strong protest against it. Supported by the trade unions, he complained that the Richards Constitution had been imposed on Nigeria without consultation.

The British Government agreed to consult with Nigerians over future constitutional changes and the next Governor, Macpherson, began a series of discussions which were to lead to another new constitution in 1951. During these discussions there was an unfortunate development: the emergence of ethnically based political parties. While the NCNC had started off as a party with wide support from both Yoruba and Igbo, the two main ethnic groups of Southern Nigeria, the Igbo and Yoruba leaders soon began to quarrel with each other. The northerners, who were educationally more backward than the southerners, began to fear southern domination. Thus, while the new constitution was being negotiated, three regional and ethnically dominated parties emerged: the Northern Peoples Congress (NPC) representing the Northern Region and dominated by the Hausa-Fulani; the Action Group (AG) representing the Western Region and dominated by the Yoruba; and the NCNC which, having lost most of its non-Igbo support, became primarily the party of Eastern Nigeria and the Igbo. From then on regional politics dominated national politics. The strength of the ill-feeling between the north and the south showed itself in the Kano riots of 1953 between northerners and southerners when many people were killed.

The only hope of keeping the country together was a constitution that gave strong powers to the regions so that no group had to fear domination by another. The Macpherson Constitution of 1951 replaced the Executive Council by a Council of Ministers with an unofficial majority and containing four representatives from each region. It also made the Regional Houses of Assembly (complemented in the North and the West by a House of Chiefs) into real legislatures able to make laws dealing with a certain range of topics. The three regional parties soon established their control over the regional legislatures, and then kept it throughout. During the 1950s there were a series of constitutional conferences, some in London and some in Lagos, aimed at moving gradually towards independence. The 1954 Lyttelton Constitution greatly increased the powers of the regional legislatures and also made the Federal House of Representatives directly elected, with the north being given half the total number of seats. In 1954 the first Federal General Election was held and a coalition government of the NPC and the NCNC was formed. Later the NPC leader in the House of Representatives, Alhaji Sir Abubakar Tafawa Balewa, became the first Federal Prime Minister.

Internal self-government at the regional level was achieved by the Western and Eastern regions in 1957 and by the Northern region in 1959, before self-government was achieved at the national level. Because of the strength of regional feeling, the final constitution for Nigeria was a federal one, allowing the regions a great deal of control over their own affairs. The British insisted on holding a general election in 1959 before they granted independence in 1960. The NPC won in the North despite successes by the AG in some of the non-Muslim areas, and the AG and NCNC won in the West and the East respectively. The NPC had been so offended by the activities of the AG in what they considered their territory that Tafawa Balewa formed an independence government which excluded the Action Group and was thus composed of the NPC, and NCNC. Nigeria became independent on 1st October 1960, but with a legacy of regional and ethnic hostility which was to lead to violent political disturbances and a bitter civil war in the decade after independence.

4 Sierra Leone

It was the educated elite in Sierra Leone, as in Nigeria, which led the struggle for independence. Until the end of the 1940s the leading nationalists were Creoles from Freetown belonging to the moderate Sierra Leone National Congress. From the late 1940s onwards, however, the leadership of the nationalist movement was mainly in the hands of the educated elite of the Protectorate, mostly Mende by tribe (for example Dr Milton Margai and his brother Albert Margai). These men formed the Sierra Leone Organisation Society (SLOS) in 1946 and strongly opposed attempts by the Creoles of the Colony to keep their dominant position.

In 1947 Sierra Leone was given a new constitution which established a Legislative Council with an unofficial majority, but one which greatly favoured the chiefs rather than the educated elite; the entire Protectorate area for example was represented only by chiefs. The chiefs and traditional elite also dominated the Protectorate Assembly, a kind of legislature set up in 1945. The SLOS was largely aimed at gaining some say for the educated commoners of the Protectorate in these bodies, and

24.2 *Sir Abubakar Tafawa Balewa, first Prime Minister of Nigeria.*

therefore strongly attacked the 1947 constitution. There was serious rioting in the Protectorate in the late 1940s and in 1951 the Governor, Beresford-Stooke, introduced a new constitution which provided for representative government similar to that in the Gold Coast. A new political party, the Sierra Leone People's Party (SLPP) was formed by the Protectorate chiefs and the SLOS to resist the attempts by the Creoles of the Colony area to retain their dominance. The SLPP, under the leadership of Dr Milton Margai, won the 1951 election and formed Sierra Leone's first representative government. From then on the path towards independence was largely smooth and peaceful with a series of constitutional amendments throughout the 1950s. New constitutions were introduced in 1956 and 1958, allowing for ministerial responsibility and the office of Premier, first held by Dr Milton Margai.

At a constitutional conference in London in 1960, it was decided that Sierra Leone should gain full independence in 1961. Margai's SLPP united with several other groups to form a coalition party, the United Progress Party (UPP). During the year before independence there was considerable conflict between the UPP and the All People's Congress

24.3 *Sir Milton Margai, first Prime Minister of Sierra Leone.*

(APC) which was led by Siaka Stevens, a Temne trade union leader, who wanted an election to be held before independence. There was some violence and Siaka Stevens and other APC leaders were arrested. Nevertheless, Sierra Leone became independent in April 1961 with Dr Milton Margai and his party firmly in control.

5 The Gambia

The Gambia did not become independent until 1965 partly because of its very small size and population (only about three hundred thousand), partly because of its economic weakness and partly because of the question of the relationship of an independent Gambia with Senegal, which completely surrounded it. As in Sierra Leone, the first nationalist leaders came from the Colony area of Bathurst, one of them was the lawyer P. S. N'Jie, but later, leaders from the much larger Protectorate area took over control, people like David Jawara, a veterinary doctor. There were no organised political parties until the early 1950s and very often it was the British Government that initiated constitutional reform with little pressure from the Gambians.

In 1946 the Gambia got its first elected members of the Legislative Council and their number was greatly increased in 1951. A new constitution in 1954 created an unofficial majority on both the Legislative and Executive Councils, but was extensively criticised, especially by the United Party led by P. S. N'Jie. Further constitutional advances were made in 1960 and 1962, including the extension of universal adult suffrage to the Protectorate. This led to the formation of a political party based on the Protectorate, the Progressive People's Party (PPP) led by Dauda Jawara. The PPP won a majority of seats in the 1962 election and Jawara became Chief Minister. Several constitutional conferences took place in the early 1960s with much discussion of the question of possible union with Senegal which came to nothing because of Gambian fears of being submerged by the much larger and better developed Senegal. However, the Gambia became fully independent in 1965 under Jawara's leadership.

6 French West Africa

Nationalism developed more slowly in French West Africa than in British West Africa for several reasons. The western-educated elite was much smaller and was anyway generally better treated than in British West Africa. Little activity of any political nature could take place until after the Second World War because there was no freedom of the press, and political associations were barred until then. The French territories were represented in the National Assembly in Paris and the French were generally more eager to keep control of their colonies than the British were.

Unlike their British counterparts, French-speaking African leaders after the Second World War did not at first talk in terms of independence. Rather they were aiming at a French-African community in which African states would share power with France on an equal basis. It was only when leaders like Sekou Toure in Guinea and Djibo Bakary in Niger saw that France was not really prepared to treat her African territories as equal partners in such a venture that they demanded independence.

Under the new constitution which France introduced in 1946, the indigénat, the corvée and the status of sujet were all abolished. Each territory was given an assembly for which a limited number of Africans could vote and each territory could send representatives to the French National Assembly and Senate. The position of Europeans was safeguarded by giving them separate status as electors: this ensured that although they were a very small minority they would have representatives in the assemblies. Thus, though all Africans in the French dependencies were now French citizens, they were second-class citizens, since only some of them had votes, and their votes in any case did not count as much as those of metropolitan Frenchmen.

The main result of the establishment of assemblies and the right of each territory to elect deputies was the formation of political parties. By far the most important party was the *Rassemblement Democratique Africain* (RDA) led by Félix Houphouët-Boigny of the Ivory Coast and with branches throughout French West Africa. But real power did not lie in the territorial assemblies or in the Federal Great Council in Dakar; it lay in the National Assembly in Paris. There, African deputies could make their criticisms of colonial policy heard. Since there was no one party dominating the French National Assembly French governments were all formed from coalitions. Thus each French party, in

24.4 *Sekou Toure, first Prime Minister and later President of Guinea.*

24.5 *Félix Houphouët-Boigny, first Prime Minister and later President of Ivory Coast.*

an attempt to increase its strength, sought the support of the African deputies. To begin with the RDA allied with the Communists who formed part of the Popular Front government of France until 1947. When that government fell, its more conservative successor persecuted the RDA in West Africa and so in 1948 Houphouët-Boigny broke all connections with the communists. In return, the administration gave the RDA its support.

In the middle 1950s France suffered from both political instability at home and military defeat abroad (for example in Indo-China) and so was prepared to make concessions in West Africa in order to avoid trouble there. The *Loi Cadre* (Outline Law) reforms of 1956–7, largely the work of Houphouët-Boigny, introduced new constitutions for the African territories. The idea of centralisation and federation was abandoned and each territory was given a degree of internal self-government. The assemblies would be elected by direct universal suffrage and executive councils would be formed presided over by the territorial governor but with the leader of the majority party as its Vice-President. In

the 1957 elections to the new territorial assemblies the RDA won control of the Ivory Coast, Guinea, Upper Volta and Soudan (Mali).

While executive councils with African majorities were established in each of the territories, one was not established at the level of the Federation. Many members of the RDA as well as Léopold Sedar Senghor, the most powerful leader in Senegal, wanted the eight territories to remain united in a federation and so demanded the creation of a Federal Executive Council.

The political situation changed greatly when the French political leader, General de Gaulle, overthrew the Fourth French Republic and held a public vote on a new constitution for France and her overseas territories in 1958. De Gaulle was in favour of a Franco-African community in which the partners would be the individual territories, not the former federation. In this he was supported by Houphouët-Boigny, who, as leader of the rich Ivory Coast, did not want his budget used to support the poorer territories like Soudan (Mali) and Niger. De Gaulle told African leaders that they could vote

24.6 *Léopold Sedar Senghor, first Prime Minister and later President of Senegal.*

24.7 *Africans opposed to De Gaulle's new constitution of 1958 stuck up posters saying 'no' to the official government posters which urged them to vote 'yes' to France. A 'no' vote implied a demand for independence.*

24.8 *Freedom fighters in Guinea-Bissau on their way to do battle with the Portuguese colonialists.*

either 'yes' or 'no' to his constitution. If they voted 'no' then they could have immediate independence 'with all its consequences' which meant the withdrawal of all French aid and officials. Only Guinea, under the leadership of Sekou Toure, voted 'no'. Sekou Toure declared that it was better to have freedom in poverty than slavery in riches. Thus in 1958 Guinea became independent without preparation and with the immediate withdrawal of all French assistance.

During the next two years there were several attempts to recreate a Federation of French West Africa, but these came to nothing mainly because of the opposition of de Gaulle and Houphouët-Boigny. More and more, the other territories wished to follow Guinea's example and become independent. De Gaulle came to the conclusion that it would be easier to keep the territories linked closely to France by granting independence than by refusing it. In 1960, therefore, independence was granted to all the French West African territories.

7 Guinea-Bissau

The last country in West Africa to gain its independence was Portuguese Guinea, sandwiched between Senegal and Guinea, in 1974. The Portuguese had done very little to develop the territory and on the eve of independence it was one of the most backward countries in Africa. For many years before Portugal recognised its independence, guerillas had harassed the Portuguese under the leadership of Amilcar Cabral. A year before independence Cabral, who was a great political thinker as well as nationalist leader, was assassinated by men in the pay of the Portuguese. But this was not before he had seen much of the country come under his control. Indeed, it was the success of guerilla armies in Portuguese Guinea, which Cabral named Guinea-Bissau, and in Angola and Mozambique, Portugal's other African territories, that brought about the downfall of Caetano, the Portuguese dictator, in 1973.

The Portuguese army which overthrew Caetano was tired of the losses they sustained in a war with Africans whose cause many Portuguese soldiers considered a just one. Guinea-Bissau was the only state in West Africa which had to conduct a full-scale war against the colonialists to secure independence. Indeed, such was the success of Cabral's guerilla army in taking over control of the interior of Guinea-Bissau from the Portuguese that a majority of member states of the United Nations recognised it as a sovereign member state of that organisation in 1973, a year before the Portuguese finally left and recognised its independence.

25 West Africa since independence

1 General background

It is difficult to treat this topic as history rather than as current affairs because the nearer one gets to the present-day the more difficult it is to avoid taking sides. We have a mass of detailed knowledge of this period, yet it is often not easy to sort out the important from the unimportant developments, because we only know the beginning of a story which is still unfolding. It is not possible in this book to

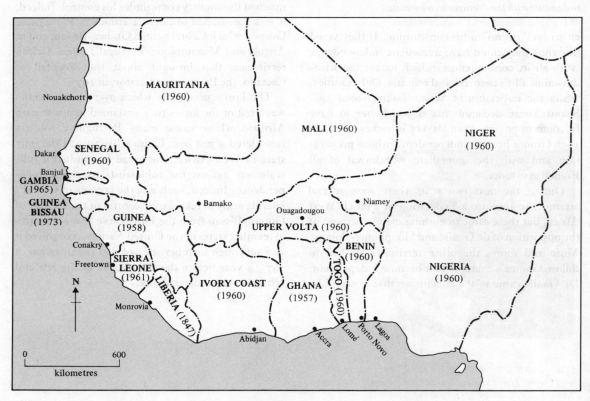

Map 25.1   Independent West Africa showing dates of independence and capital cities.

study in detail the current problems of West Africa, but, in order to bring the story of West Africa's development as near as possible to the present-day, it is necessary to indicate a few major trends. After that we will look at the problems four West African countries – Ghana, Guinea, Senegal and Nigeria – experienced in the first decade of independence.

In the short period since independence the states of West Africa have faced many problems – social, economic, educational and especially political. Added to the many problems inherited from the period of colonial rule have been many new problems. By far the most important of these difficulties have been those of maintaining and strengthening internal unity and bringing about economic development as quickly as possible in order to raise the living standards of the people. To some extent the newly-independent West African nations have attempted to solve these problems in similar ways and so it is possible to examine general trends rather than give a detailed account of the development of each West African country since independence.

In each country at the time of independence, the former colonial rulers were replaced by a new, Western-educated political elite. The exact composition of this new elite is difficult to define because its members belonged to different social classes, but certain common factors can be seen. Most were the

products of Western education. In many cases the early elite of the coast was challenged and replaced by an elite from the interior before the attainment of independence (for example in Sierra Leone and in Senegal). In some countries (for example Sierra Leone and parts of Nigeria) the chiefs and other traditional rulers kept considerable influence, while in others (for example Guinea, Mali and Ghana) their power was attacked and weakened by the Western-educated elite. All the new elites were concerned with the consolidation of their own political power.

25.2 *West African states began to play an important role on the world stage. Here Sir Abubakar Tafawa Balewa, Prime Minister of Nigeria, inspects the Nigerian contingent of the UN Peace-Keeping Force in the Congo.*

25.1 *Independent West Africa quickly emerged on the world scene. Here the President of the Gambia, Sir Dauda Jawara, is welcomed by the leader of the world's most populous nation, the late Chairman Mao Tsetung of China.*

2 Political developments

Most West African states have experienced considerable political instability since the time of independence. Today only five of the leaders of the fourteen West African states who led their countries to independence are still in power: Sekou Toure in Guinea; Mokhtar Ould Daddah in Mauritania; Houphouët-Boigny in the Ivory Coast; Léopold Senghor in Senegal; and Sir Dauda Jawara in the Gambia. By 1973 three out of the four ex-British states (Nigeria, Ghana and Sierra Leone) and five out of the nine ex-French states (Dahomey, Niger, Upper Volta, Mali and Togo) had experienced coups leading to the establishment of military governments. In the cases of Upper Volta, Ghana and Dahomey return to civilian rule was followed by further military take-over.

It must be remembered that the leaders of the newly-independent states inherited from the last years of colonial rule central and local government institutions, as well as educational and legal systems. During the first years of independence they tried to gain full control of these established systems, but in the process the structure of the government was often drastically changed. During this period the main political problem was that of the unity of the nation and the role of opposition groups.

The boundaries of the West African states were largely arbitrary creations of the colonial powers. Most of the states possessed little ethnic, religious, linguistic or cultural unity and the experience of just over half a century of colonial rule had done little to encourage real unity. However, the borders inherited from the period of colonial rule were accepted largely without question by the new leaders. Only the Ewe people (split between Ghana and Togo) exerted any strong pressure in favour of boundary changes. The troubled history of the short-lived Mali Federation revealed the difficulties of trying to govern political units other than already existing states. This federation comprised Mali and Senegal but it only lasted eighteen months, from April 1959 to August 1960 (see page 196).

In the years immediately after independence there was great emphasis placed on unity and several different methods were used to strengthen national unity. Many leaders have done everything possible to stress the separate identity of their own nation, even at the expense of making neighbouring African states hostile. During the colonial period many people worked in countries other than their own; for example, a great number of the civil servants throughout French West Africa came from Senegal or Dahomey (now Benin) and in British West Africa Creoles from Freetown were active in all four territories. Since independence, however, Africans from other states have usually been discriminated against or, in many cases, even expelled (for example the expulsion of Dahomeans from Senegal in 1959 and Nigerians from Ghana in 1969). In Nigeria this practise was even, at one stage, enforced at a regional level.

A second method frequently used to try to maintain unity has been the creation of a kind of united party of all groups and peoples within the state. This trend has been particularly strong in French-speaking West Africa where often trade unions, youth organisations and others have all been joined together into the dominant political party (for example Senghor's 'Bloc Populaire Sénégalaise' in Senegal and the 'Union Soudanaise' in Mali). In most West African countries the effort has been so successful that it has led to the creation of a one-party state.

Where these methods have failed to produce sufficient unity, the governing party has used various kinds of force to destroy all opposition. The first, and one of the best examples of this is the activities of the Convention People's Party (CPP) in Ghana in the years following independence. Foreigners involved in politics were deported; religious, tribal and regional parties were made illegal and chiefs who did not fully support the government were deposed. Moreover the government gave itself the power to imprison anybody without trial for up to five years. The only important (if secret) opponents of Nkrumah's Government who remained were some of the army officers and it was they who overthrew him in February 1966. Some French-speaking territories, such as Guinea, Mali and the Ivory Coast, were already virtually one-party states at the time of independence, but in others, such as Upper Volta, Niger, Dahomey and Togo, government power had to be used to ban opposition parties and imprison rival leaders. In Dahomey, for example, in 1961 President Hubert Maga banned the leading opposition party and many opposition leaders were arrested and sentenced by a special court.

There were similar, though more complicated, developments in Nigeria. With three main regional parties, it seemed possible that a real opposition party could exist at least at the federal level, but the Action Group never really filled this role. The Action Group split in May 1962, and the federal government took responsibility for the government of the Western Region (see p. 197). This began a long series of ever-worsening crises culminating in the civil war of 1967–70. Malpractices in the 1964 elections led to a boycott and a constitutional crisis; and similar activities during the regional elections in the West in October 1965 produced a virtual rebellion in the Western Region by supporters of the Action Group and the NCNC. This political crisis was still continuing when the Nigerian army stepped in and seized power in January 1966.

Everywhere, open opposition to the government rapidly disappeared and at the same time the powers of the executive, especially those of the president, rapidly increased. By the end of the 1960s there was no effective legal opposition anywhere in West Africa with the exception of the Gambia. Faced as they were with great political and economic problems, it is hardly surprising that the ruling parties dealt harshly with any forces which they considered likely to foster disunity. The concentration of all power in the hands of the dominant party left the opposition no alternative but to use unconstitutional, and often violent, methods. This concentration of power often gave rein to the greed, corruption and incompetence of many of the political leaders; and this, together with their failure to solve the serious social and economic problems, helped to create situations favourable to military take-overs.

The emergence of one dominant party generally occurred more speedily in the French-speaking states and these states experienced fewer violent changes of government. This is largely because the British, before independence, had tried to impose their own institutions of government, in particular the concept of an official opposition recognised by the ruling party, on their colonies much more strongly than the French, who had concentrated on centralisation and strong executive

power. The military coups of Colonel Lamizana in Upper Volta, Colonel Soglo in Dahomey, Colonel Eyadema in Togo, General Ironsi in Nigeria and the National Reformation Council in Sierra Leone were largely attempts by the various armies to preserve political stability and protect the institutions of government. Military rule has generally been conservative, with little change in the existing institutions of government and with reliance on civilians to run the government because of the relatively small number of army officers. In general, the soldiers have found their job far from easy because they have been faced with the same social and economic problems which their civilian predecessors had failed to solve.

The causes of political instability in West Africa since independence are complex, but a few general factors can be seen: the fear of domination by any one ethnic group; the failure of democracy to work smoothly; the lack of any tradition of organised opposition; failure to solve economic problems; rivalries within the ruling elite. Two main solutions to this problem of instability have emerged: one-party states and military rule. The states with a one-party system (for example Guinea and the Ivory Coast) have the advantages of leadership, unity and continuity. However, the very nature of the one-party state makes it vulnerable to several possible dangers: an increase in inefficiency and corruption; oppression and lack of freedom; violent revolution as the only way to change the government. In other countries (for example Benin, Togo and Nigeria) military rule has been established. This possesses advantages similar to those of the one-party state but also certain possible disadvantages (for example an uneconomically large army, oppressive rule and inexperience in political and economic affairs among the small officer class).

The pattern of West African political development continues to change rapidly as old problems are solved and new ones arise. Some progress has already been made in the short period since independence in developing political institutions more suitable to the needs of West Africa than those left by the colonial rulers, but much still remains to be done.

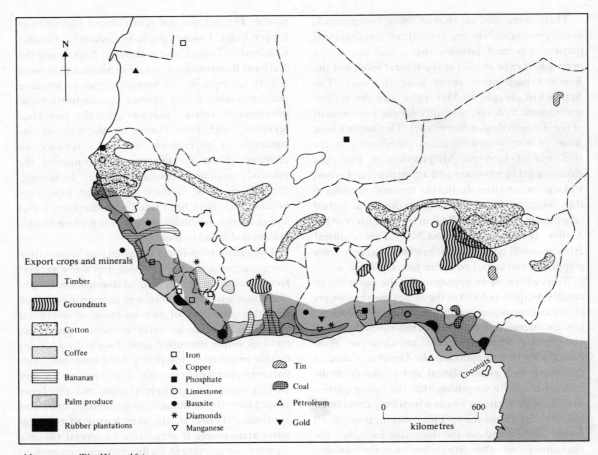

Map 25.2   The West Africa economy

3 Economic and social development

As we have seen in a previous chapter, the colonial period was one of economic exploitation rather than economic development. The independent West African states faced many serious economic and social problems inherited from the period of colonial rule: for example communications facilities only to suit the needs of external trade; lack of industrialisation; trade closely tied to the colonial powers; domination of the economy by a few monopolistic expatriate trading companies; uneven social and economic development; poor educational and health facilities. Some slight attempts were made to try and solve some of these problems during the last decade of colonial rule, but most West

African states were to find that it was easier to obtain political freedom than economic freedom and development. Despite these enormous difficulties and despite the political problems mentioned in the previous section, the states of West Africa have succeeded in making impressive social and economic progress since independence. A few examples out of the many available to illustrate this rapid progress are the Volta River Project in Ghana, the Kainji Dam in Nigeria, and the very great increase in transport, educational and health facilities throughout West Africa. When compared with the industrialised nations of the Western world, the states of West Africa are still poor and underdeveloped (for example the average per capita income of Guinea is only about £30 per annum). However, many West

25.3 *The great hydro-electric dam over the River Volta in Ghana.*

African countries, especially those with valuable economic resources, are developing rapidly.

The leaders of West Africa's governments have understood the economic problems of their countries and have stressed the need for everyone in the country to make a contribution to the much needed economic revolution. They have regarded their efforts to develop economically and socially as a continuation of their struggle against colonial rule and have therefore tried to free their economies as quickly as possible from foreign control. This has, of course, been easier for the countries rich in resources, like Nigeria, Ghana and the Ivory Coast, than for those with few valuable resources, like Niger and Upper Volta. Most of the development plans of the West African governments have been aimed at weakening foreign influence on their economies as much and as quickly as possible.

The first major problem was to convince the mass of the people of the need for widespread change, a difficult task when the majority of the population were illiterate peasant farmers. Some countries such as Ivory Coast and Upper Volta have passed laws establishing a form of compulsory service to the state, a mild form of which has been introduced into Nigeria in the form of the National Youth Service Corps, whereby all post-secondary graduates spend one year in state service. In some countries, such as Senegal, sections of the army have been used to carry out development projects and everywhere leaders have stressed the need for hard work to facilitate economic development and nation-building.

Throughout the colonial period the economies of all the West African countries remained primarily agricultural. A major problem after independence has been to encourage the growth of industries in order to free West Africa from her colonial role as a supplier of raw materials and an importer of manufactured goods. Most governments have accepted that West Africa will, for many years, remain primarily an agricultural area, but West African governments have made great efforts to diversify their economies by establishing a wide range of industries.

Most West African economic development has been controlled by the state rather than by private individuals, that is it has been socialistic rather than capitalistic. This has been particularly true of some countries, especially Mali and Guinea, but even in countries like Ghana and Senegal state control of the economy is considerable. Several reasons help to explain this socialist approach to economic problems adopted by most West African leaders. Most of the leaders of French-speaking West Africa were influenced by communist or socialist ideas. Moreover, for most of them, private enterprise meant domination by the large European trading companies, whose control over the economies of West Africa they wished to destroy. In any case few private individuals or indigenous companies possessed the necessary capital and resources for large-scale economic activities and so most economic development depended on the state. Despite all this, the large European trading companies still play an important part in the economies of West Africa, but measures have been taken to prevent them exploiting West Africa in the way they did during the period of colonial rule.

Three main difficulties have prevented development being as rapid as the national development plans of the various countries had hoped for. Firstly shortage of trained manpower has caused many problems. The educational systems inherited from the period of colonial rule were not suited to provide the manpower requirements for the rapid economic development attempted since independence. Although the independent states of West Africa have achieved a very great advance in education, this has still failed to keep pace with the requirements of

25.4 *Mining bauxite in Ghana.*

rapid economic development. Another problem has been a shortage of capital to finance economic projects. The world prices for many of West Africa's basic export crops has been disappointingly low since independence and the amount of foreign aid received has not been as much as had been hoped for. Moreover some leaders have failed to show the abilities necessary to implement large-scale development projects: political instability has scared away foreign investment; important jobs have often not been occupied according to merit; and vital industries have often been built in the wrong places or not built at all because of rivalries between different sections of the political elite.

Much more economic and social development has taken place in West Africa since independence than during the period of colonial rule, but much remains to be done. Many fundamental economic problems cannot be fully dealt with until the independent states of West Africa achieve greater political stability.

4 Ghana: from Nkrumah to military rule

We have examined the common political, economic and social problems that have faced West African states since independence. Now let us look briefly at how these problems have affected the course of independence in four West African countries.

As the first state in sub-saharan Africa to gain its independence from colonial rule, Ghana was watched closely by other African states as well as by the world at large.

In 1957 when Ghana became independent under the leadership of Kwame Nkrumah it had a two-party system, and it was very wealthy compared with other African countries as a result of its earnings from cocoa, much of which were held in reserves. The election immediately prior to independence had given Nkrumah's Convention Peoples Party a large majority of seats over his opponents, who gained 32 seats to his 72. Unfortunately, most of the opposition to the CPP came from two regions: Asante and the Northern Territories. By 1960 when Nkrumah held a referendum on the new Republican Constitution for Ghana much of the opposition had come over to the CPP voluntarily. But it became clear that Nkrumah was not prepared to tolerate any opposition and he set about the creation of a one-party state. In the years that followed the introduction of the Republican constitution, an-all-out attack was launched against the opposition parties. Nkrumah became known as *Osagyefo* (he who is successful in war) and he became President in place of the

25.5 *Dr Kwame Nkrumah is proclaimed first president of the Republic of Ghana in 1960.*

Governor-General, nominated by the British Queen.

Press censorship was introduced, a Preventative Detention Act was passed whereby opponents of the regime were imprisoned without trial. Furthermore chiefs hostile to the government were deposed. In 1964 the CPP was recognised as the only legal party in Ghana. Ghana was now a one-party state.

Opposition still continued. It was based partly on regional hostility to Nkrumah's rule, particularly in Asante and the Northern Territories, and partly on discontent with his methods. Corruption was widespread among Government ministers and officials, though Ghana was meant to be a socialist state. Many educated people resented the dictatorial methods of, and suppression of freedoms by their ruler. Furthermore the Government had been extravagant in its spending on major projects, while its revenue from cocoa whose price declined disastrously from £400 a ton in the 1950s to £100 a ton in 1965/6. One project of the government which was of lasting benefit to the nation was the great Volta River project which created the largest artificial lake in Africa and provided for all Ghana's electricity needs. This project was jointly financed by the Americans and the British but Nkrumah, in an attempt to lessen his country's dependence on the western world, also sought aid from the Russians and East Europeans which made the Americans and British more cautious about investments in Ghana.

In 1966, when Nkrumah was in Peking on a state visit the military and police took over the government of the country. The coup was generally welcomed because so many people resented the oppressive nature of the later years of Nkrumah's rule, and because many people had suffered as a result of the economic depression caused by the fall in cocoa prices.

The military government known as the National Liberation Council (NLC) promised to put Ghana back on its feet again and then return it to civilian rule. They were not successful in solving its economic problems: the debts were too large and cocoa prices remained low. There was also a great deal of rivalry in the NLC, some of it personal, some ethnic. Corruption was not eliminated. However the NLC did keep its promise to return Ghana to civilian rule. After a new constitution had been drawn up, elections were held and Dr Kofi Busia, a long-standing opponent of Nkrumah's, became Prime Minister in late 1969. His Progress Alliance won 105 seats to its opponents 35. Busia faced a continuing economic crisis, and in the face of opposition displayed some of the same authoritarian tendencies

as Nkrumah. Where Nkrumah had been an ardent Pan-Africanist and supporter of African freedom fighters, Busia supported dialogue with South Africa. Busia's Government was also tainted by the same corruption as its predecessors and was overthrown in 1972 by Colonel (now General) Acheampong. The new Military Government known as the National Redemption Council, inherited a depressed economy from Busia and it remains to be seen whether they can solve the considerable economic problems inherited from the Nkrumah regime. They have, however, rehabilitated Nkrumah, as the man who, despite the extravagance and oppression of the last years' of his regime, led Ghana to independence and gave Ghanaians and Africans generally the vision of a free Africa. He did not live to see the near realisation of his dream with the liberation of the Portuguese Colonies. He died of cancer in Bucharest in 1970.

5 Guinea: The struggle to survive

Guinea, as we have seen, became independent in 1957 as a result of its vote of 'No' to de Gaulle's referendum (see page 186). The consequences of voting 'No' were the immediate withdrawal of all French officials and technicians and the cessation of all French aid. The departing French destroyed vital files and even ripped out telephones. Guinea then had to face independence without the assistance that all other states in West Africa received from their former colonial rulers.

Guinea was able to survive the difficulties created by the French for a number of reasons. Most important was the dynamic leadership of its President, Ahmad Sekou Toure. He was a brilliant organiser and brought most of the country under the control of his Parti Démocratique de la Guinée (PDG). He had destroyed the remaining power of the chiefs. This was particularly important as far as the main area of opposition to his rule, the Futa Djallon, was concerned. Deprived of the leadership of their conservative pro-French chiefs, the Fula of Futa Djallon agreed to cease opposition to Sekou Toure in the interest of national unity. He gave places to Fula in his government of national unity. A second important factor in Guinea's survival was its rich mineral and agricultural resources. At first the Russians were brought in to help develop these, but because of their interference in the internal affairs of Guinea, they were expelled in 1961. Since then the USA has been the main source of technical assistance and aid. This has not meant that Sekou Toure has deviated from his socialist vision of Guinea's future. Indeed in 1967 in order to rally the masses behind his government he launched a 'cultural revolution' similar to that of the Chinese. But Sekou Toure, a devout Muslim, is no Communist. He does however believe, like any good socialist, that the wealth of Guinea should be shared by all its citizens and has been prepared to bring in capitalists from the USA to help him achieve this end.

In his efforts to set Guinea economically on its own two feet Sekou Toure has banned all opposition and many opponents of his regime have left to work in neighbouring countries. Many others have sought work elsewhere because of the still depressed state of the economy. Others have sought actively to overthrow him. In November 1970 dissident Guineans allied with the colonial government of Portuguese Guinea which resented the support given by Sekou Toure to Amilcar Cabral and invaded Conakry. They were repulsed but not before destroying the Conakry offices of Cabral's PAIGC and releasing opponents of Sekou Toure from prison. Ninety-one people in Guinea were sentenced to death as a result. The Government has announced two other plots against it since. Sekou Toure has justified his policies in terms of the extraordinary circumstances in which his country achieved independence. However harsh his rule may have been, he proved to the French, with whom he is once again entering into good relations, that Guinea could stand on its feet without them. Indeed Guinea is the only independent African Country that has not had to depend economically on its former colonial master.

6 Senegal: Over-dependence on France and groundnuts

The history of Senegal since independence presents a dramatic contrast with that of Guinea. While Senghor and Dia, the leaders of the governing party of Senegal, considered voting 'No' in de Gaulle's referendum and thus taking independence 'with all its consequences' like Guinea, they finally decided to vote 'Yes'. This was because the consequences for the economic life of Senegal of a rupture with France would have been disastrous. The great city and port of Dakar was heavily dependent on French aid and technical assistance. Senegal's main crop and principal export, the groundnut, was heavily subsidised by France. Strong conservative elements in the country – old soldiers, and powerful Muslim leaders – were opposed to any break with France. So in 1958 Senegal voted against immediate independence. However its leaders demonstrated their independence of France by joining with French Soudan in the Mali Federation to which as we have seen France was bitterly opposed. While France did eventually recognise the independence of Senegal and French Soudan as the Mali Federation in July 1960, the Federation lasted as an independent unit for only two months. Fear on the part of the Senegalese of Soudanese domination and the strong differences in outlook between Senghor of Senegal and Modibo Keita of Soudan led to its break-up in August 1960.

Senghor then became President of an independent Senegal with Mamadou Dia as his Prime Minister. Together they devoted their efforts to developing the rural economy and diversifying the crops grown to lessen the country's dependence on the groundnut crop and therefore French aid. Even so their policy was generally pro-French and French investments and aid continued to be vital to the Senegalese economy. This continued dependence on the French was heavily criticised by Senghor's opponents.

Unlike Guinea, Senghor did not create a one-party state, though after an abortive coup in December 1962, in which Mamadou Dia was arrested and imprisoned for his alleged part in it, the governing party became so powerful that to all intents and purposes Senegal operated as a one-party state.

In a national referendum in 1963 Senghor strengthened his constitutional powers. In the elections to the National Assembly his party gained nearly all the seats. Since then Senghor has been the uncontested leader of Senegal. His party absorbed opposing parties or outlawed them. In 1966 the last of the legally recognised parties joined the governing party and in the 1968 elections to the National Assembly Senghor's party gained 99 percent of the vote.

The main problems of Senegal since independence have been economic: overdependence on the groundnut crop for foreign earnings, and on one country, France, for aid. In 1967 France dropped its subsidies to the groundnut crop, but it still remains Senegal's chief source of aid.

Like Sekou Toure, Senghor has remained in power since independence. But by contrast, he has been a moderate force in African politics. While he operates an effective one-party state, he has been much more tolerant of opposition. There have been no political executions in Senegal. Having chosen to remain friendly with France, he never suffered the traumatic rupture Guinea did; but then Senegal, unlike Guinea, is still unable to stand independently, economically, without the assistance of France.

7 Nigeria: A decade of troubles: 1960–1970

After independence, Nigeria was governed by a coalition of the NPC and the NCNC which controlled the Northern and Southern Regions respectively. The Action Group, which controlled the Western Region, formed the opposition in the Federal House of Representatives. Chief Obafemi Awolowo, head of the Action Group, gave up the post of Premier of the Western Region to become Leader of the Opposition in the Federal House. His deputy, Chief S. L. Akintola, succeeded him as Premier of the Western Region.

This experiment in Westminster-style constitutional democracy did not last long. The Federal Government did all it could to break Chief Awolowo's power. It played on the divisions in the Action Group between those led by Chief Akintola who wanted to join the Federal Government and those led by Chief Awolowo who wanted to continue in opposition in the hopes of winning the next Federal elections. When fights between the two

factions broke out in the Western House of Assembly in May 1962 over the question of an Awolowo loyalist replacing Akintola as Premier, the Federal Government declared a state of Emergency in the Western Region. For six months the Federal Government administered the Region and at the end of it Chief Akintola, who broke with the Action Group, returned to power as Premier, leading a new party.

In the meantime Chief Awolowo and many other Action Group Leaders had been arrested on charges of treasonable felony. Chief Awolowo was eventually jailed.

The Western Region was divided into two with the non-Yoruba area being created a separate region known as the Mid-West. The Action Group objected to this not because it did not agree with the creation of new states. It was in fact an active supporter of the creation of more states in Nigeria. It objected to the fact that only the Western Region had been broken up and not the Eastern and Northern Regions where there were equally strong demands by minorities for new states.

With the Action Group reduced to a shadow of its former self the partners in the Federal Government, the NPC and NCNC, began to turn on each other. The main cause of this was the national census which showed that the Northern Region had more people than the rest of Nigeria combined. Since Parliamentary seats were allocated on the basis of the number of people, the NCNC saw the North forever dominating the South. The Eastern Region Government as well as the new NCNC Government of the Mid-West rejected the census, but the North with the West, led by its new ally Akintola, accepted it.

By the time of the December 1964 elections to the Federal House of Representatives, Nigeria was in a very disturbed state. Workers had been on strike for higher wages. Political violence was becoming the order of the day. The NCNC and Action Group allied to fight the election but accused the NPC and its allies, especially Akintola, of rigging the election. A crisis was only averted when it was agreed to form a government of national unity. Nine months later with the elections to the Western Region House of Assembly the nation was on the brink of disaster. And in January 1966 a group of young majors staged a coup in which the Prime Minister, Sir Abubakar Tafawa Balewa, the Federal Minister of Finance, the Premiers of the Northern and Western Regions were killed along with nine senior army officers. Government was eventually taken over from these majors by the head of the Nigerian Army, Major General J. T. Aguyi-Ironsi.

At first the coup was welcomed as an end to the chaos, violence and corruption that had characterised the civilian regime. But soon fears began to grow that the Igbos were taking advantage of the fact that one of their own people was now head of government to make gains at the expense of others in the Federation. People reflected that no Igbo political leader was assassinated, and that the northerners had lost most of their senior army officers. Their fears seemed to be confirmed by the declaration of Nigeria as a unitary state in which the old regions were abolished and anyone from any part of the country could work anywhere. The northerners who had comparatively few educated men to compete with the more advanced southerners were particularly fearful of domination by the Igbo, who already held many important posts in trade and commerce in their region. Riots flared up against Igbos in northern cities and Major General Aguyi-Ironsi was assassinated. Igbos and other southerners began to pour south.

The army chose Lt. Colonel Yakubu Gowon as the new Head of State, but he was not recognised by the military governor of the Eastern Region Lt. Colonel Odumegwu Ojukwu. Despite protracted negotiations to settle their differences, Lt. Colonel Ojukwu decided to secede from the Federation playing on the fears of his people as a result of the massacres in the north, and believing that the Federation would not be united enough to fight him. What is more, the vast oil reserves to be found mainly in the non-Igbo areas of his region would sustain an independent Biafra as he called his proposed country.

On the eve of the civil war Gowon declared that the Federation would now be split into twelve states. The Eastern Region would be split into three, two of which, the Rivers and South East State, represented its non-Igbo areas. The north was broken up into six states, allaying to a great extent southern fears of domination by a single northern bloc.

Ojukwu declared the secession of Biafra on 29th May and on 1st June Federal forces began the first of their operations in a long war, hard-fought on both sides. The Biafrans gained considerable aid from outside but since the rest of the Federation, including the majority of the people in the minority areas of Biafra, supported Gowon, it was only a matter of time before Biafra would collapse.

The Igbos who formed the hard-core of the Biafran cause fought bravely and when in January 1970 Biafra finally surrendered the Federal government far from carrying out the genocide which propagandists accused them of doing, made an honourable peace with the rebels. Not one was executed; a few rebel army officers were imprisoned; and a few civilians were detained. Apart from this the former Biafrans were allowed to go about their business and many were re-absorbed into the Federal Government in their old posts. Thus ended a troubled decade in Nigeria's independence unity. Though many problems remained to be solved, it seemed clear that Nigeria would now remain a united country.

8 Cultural developments

During the period just before independence, and in the years since, West African states have been almost as concerned with gaining their cultural independence from their former colonial masters as their economic and political independence. Leaders like Kwame Nkrumah and Léopold Sédar Senghor laid great emphasis on the need to revive and preserve Africa's own cultural heritage, which during the colonial period had seemed in danger of being overwhelmed, if not destroyed by that of the colonial masters. Such leaders not only encouraged interest in the pre-colonial cultures of their peoples through research into and presentation of their music and dance, but also encouraged the activities of contemporary artists and writers. Some countries, like Guinea and Sierra Leone, formed their own national dance troupes which presented the traditional dances, music and song of their peoples both at home and overseas.

In April 1966, Senegal hosted the First World Festival of Negro Art and Culture in Dakar, with Nigeria as the 'star' country. There the cultural heritage of the Black Peoples of the world was displayed to an international audience. Nigeria planned to host an even more ambitious follow-up Festival in 1975 but because of delays in preparations it was postponed twice to 1977. The important point was, however, that not only West African, but all African governments, and countries outside Africa with sizeable Black populations, felt that their cultural heritage was so important that they should take part in this Festival. For this Festival would encourage pride in the culture of the Black peoples, and explore and assert the cultural identity of the African.

In the past two decades in West Africa official encouragement of, and interest in, cultural activities has gone hand in hand with a contemporary cultural revival. With the imposition of colonial rule and the spread of Christian missionary activity, as we have seen, more and more people turned away from their traditional religions and cultures to those of the Christian West and the Muslim world. Since much of the sculpture, dance, song and poetry of West African peoples was associated with the traditional religions, these forms of artistic expression inevitably declined. The new educated elites tended at first to look on their traditional forms of artistic expression almost with contempt. From 1900 to 1950 very little creative writing, music or art emerged from West Africa. Many of the old forms were dying: new forms had not come to replace them. But in the 1950s, and perhaps significantly with the approach of independence and freedom from the colonial masters, West Africans began to assert their cultural identity. In the past twenty-five years there has been a cultural renaissance in West Africa with poets like David Diop of Senegal and Christopher Okigbo of Nigeria, achieving international recognition. The novels of Chinua Achebe and Cyprian Ekwensi of Nigeria, Cheicken

Hamidou Kane of Senegal, Camara Laye of Guinea, Ayi Kwei Armah of Ghana and Yambo Oulouguem of Mali have international readership. Wole Soyinka – playwright, poet, novelist, essayist – has a worldwide reputation as a creative writer. Sculptors like Vincent Kofi of Ghana, artists like the Oshogbo artists, Jimoh Buraimoh and Twins Seven Seven, or the western-trained Yusuf Grillo and Obiora Udechukwu have started to define new traditions in African art.

A civilisation is as much remembered for its cultural as for its political and economic achievements. Indeed some civilisations are remembered more for their art than anything else. We know very little about the economic and political history of ancient Ife or Igbo-Ukwu, but we know that their people were superb artists in bronze and that their works of art can rank alongside those of any other civilisation.

Today, West African peoples are once again re-asserting their cultural identity and it is possible that their new artists and writers may be remembered long after memories of current political leaders have faded.

25.6 *Drama students of Ahmadu Bello University, Zaria, performing* Rakinyo *by Segun Ajibade in the university's newly built studio theatre. Increasingly plays by African writers are performed in place of plays by people like Shakespeare and Goldsmith.*

Questions

Questions on Section I of the WAEC syllabus: West Africa 1000–1800 A.D.

These questions deal with the material in Chapters 1–9.

1 Explain how North African influences affected the Western Sudan during this period.

2 Describe briefly the important peoples of the Western Sudan in about the year AD 1000. (WAEC June '73)

3 Why did the Almoravids attack the Ghana Empire? What results did these attacks have on Ghana?

4 Describe the main factors responsible for the fall of the Ghana Empire in the first half of the thirteenth century. (WAEC June '75)

5 Explain the role of trade in the rise of the Mali Empire.

6 What was the importance of the reign of Mansa Musa in the history of the Mali Empire?

7 Describe the part played by trade in the early history of the Western Sudan and mention the main articles of trade. (WAEC November '73)

8 Describe the extent and system of government of the Songhai Empire during the reign of Askia Mohammed.

9 What were the major causes for the Moroccan invasion of Songhai?

10 How permanent were the results of the Moroccan invasion of Songhai?

11 Describe the main features of the system of government, before 1800, of the Kanem-Borno Empire. (WAEC June '75)

12 What factors encouraged the growth of large empires in the Western Sudan during the medieval period?

13 Discuss the changes brought to the Western Sudan by the introduction of Islam.

14 Assess the contribution made by Mai Idris Alooma to the development of Kanem-Borno.

15 How did the Hausa states originate and how were they organised?

16 What were the chief reasons for the rise of the Asante Empire in the seventeenth century and the eighteenth century down to the death of Osei Tutu in 1717? (WAEC June '73)

17 Describe the system of government of a) Asante under Osei Tutu and b) Dahomey under Agaja.

18 Account for the strength and extent of the Oyo Empire before 1800. (WAEC November '73)

19 Explain the role of the Alafin, the Oyo Mesi and the Ogboni in the government of the Oyo Empire.

20 How was Dahomey able to expand into a strong state during the eighteenth century?

21 Explain how Igbo society was organised during the period before 1800.

22 In what ways did Ewuare the Great strengthen the Kingdom of Benin?

23 How did the beginnings of European trade with West Africa in the sixteenth century affect West Africa?

24 Account for the growth of the trans-Atlantic slave trade and explain how it was organised.

25 Describe the growth and political organisation of any two of the following states:
   a) Mossi-Dagomba states.
   b) Denkyira.
   c) Wollof Empire.
   d) Bambara states.

Questions on Section 2 of the WAEC syllabus: 1800–1918
These questions deal with the material in Chapters 10–18

1 What conditions in the Western Sudan in the early nineteenth century encouraged the growth of Islamic reforming movements?

2 How important were political and tribal factors in the jihad of Usman dan Fodio?

3 Why were the Fulani able to gain control of most of Hausaland in the early years of the nineteenth century?

4 Discuss the contribution made by Mohammed Bello to the organisation of the Sokoto Caliphate.

5 Explain the importance of the career of El-Kanemi in the history of Borno.

6 Describe the long-term and immediate causes for the decline and fall of the Oyo Empire.

7 Give an account of the principal causes and the main effects of the Yoruba wars in the nineteenth century. (WAEC June '74)

8 What were the main sources of strength of the Kingdom of Dahomey in the nineteenth century?

9 How was Dahomey able to continue as a strong, stable state even after the suppression of the slave trade?

10 Why did the trans-Saharan trade decline in importance during the nineteenth century?

11 How was the Atlantic slave trade stopped on the Guinea coast following its abolition by the British Government in 1807? (WAEC June '75)

12 In what ways were the Niger Delta city states affected by the suppression of the trans-Atlantic slave trade?

13 Explain the importance of any three of the following:
    a) The Temne-Mende war of 1898
    b) The Poro Society.
    c) The Arochuku oracle.
    d) The Ekpe Society.
    e) The House System.

14 In what ways was the reign of Osei Bonsu important to the history of the Asante Empire?

15 Describe the factors that were responsible for the hostility between the Asante and the British during this period. (WAEC November '73)

16 Explain the main features of the system of government of Asante in the nineteenth century and how these contributed to the empire's downfall.

17 Outline the history of the foundation of Liberia from 1822–48. (WAEC November '73)

18 Why and in what ways were the Creoles of Sierra Leone so important in the history of West Africa during the second half of the nineteenth century?

19 Explain the importance of Christian missionary activities in the history of one of the following countries:
    a) The Gambia
    b) Ghana
    c) Nigeria
    d) Sierra Leone (WAEC November '73)

20 What were the causes and results of the jihad of Seku Ahmadu in Macina?

21 Describe the jihad of Al-Hajj Umar and outline its main results.

22 What role did economic considerations play in bringing about the partition of West Africa?

23 How were the European powers able to conquer most of West Africa so rapidly at the end of the nineteenth century?

24 Describe the political and military organisation of Samori Toure.

25 What methods were used by Samori Toure to resist French conquest for so long?

Questions on Section 3 of the WAEC syllabus: Since 1918

These questions deal with the material in Chapters 19–25

1 In what ways were French and British methods of colonial administration similar and in what ways were they different?

2 Compare the working of indirect rule in northern and eastern Nigeria.

3 What is meant by *assimilation*? Explain why the French found it impossible to introduce the policy on a large scale.

4 What methods were used by the British in ruling either the Gold Coast or Sierra Leone in the period up to 1945?

5 How did the First World War influence the development of West Africa?

6 Explain the importance to the history of West Africa of any two of the following:
    a) Guggisberg,
    b) Blaise Diagne,
    c) Herbert Macaulay,
    d) J. B. Danquah.

7 Describe the development and the general effects of pre-university education in any one West African country since 1925. (WAEC June '75)

8 Using any one West African country as an example, explain the changes brought about by the building of railways.

9 What were the main features of colonial economic policy in the period before the Second World War?

10 Describe the efforts made to develop the production of cash crops in any one West African country during the colonial period.

11 What were the main causes for the growth of nationalism in West Africa in the period 1918–39?

12 In what ways was the Second World War an important turning point in the growth of African nationalism?

13 Why was nationalism slower to develop in French West Africa than in British West Africa?

14 Write an account from 1945 of the stages by which either,
    a) Sierra Leone, or,
    b) The Gambia, attained independence.
                      (WAEC June '74)

15 Why was Ghana the first West African country to free itself from colonial rule?

16 Write an account of the public career of one of the following West African leaders:

a) Sir Abubakar Tafawa Balewa,
b) Sir Milton Margai,
c) Sir Dauda Jawara.
d) Ahmed Sekou Toure,
e) Dr Kofi Busia. (WAEC June '75)

17 Discuss the contribution made by the RDA to the achievement of independence in French West Africa.

18 What have been the major achievements of any one West African country in the field of either,
   a) industrial developments, or,
   b) health services, since the country's attainment of independence. (WAEC June '74)

19 Account for the instability of many West African countries since independence.

20 Describe the main educational developments in any one West African country since independence.

21 What have been the major problems facing Ghana since independence?

22 Outline the causes and events leading to the military take-over of government in 1966 in either Nigeria or Ghana. (WAEC June '73)

23 Give an account of the efforts made since independence by any one West African country to develop its manufacturing industries.

24 How has the increase in petroleum production affected the development of Nigeria?

25 What policies have been adopted by any one West African country since independence to develop agriculture and with what results.

Bibliography

Many useful books are now available to help students of West African history. To improve their interest and abilities in history, students are strongly advised to read as widely as possible. Here is a short list of books suitable for use by students in the higher classes of secondary schools and teacher training colleges.

AJAYI, J. F. A. and ESPIE, I., *A Thousand Years of West African History*, IUP & Nelson, 1966.
This includes some good chapters on most of the major topics in the syllabus.

AKINTOYE, S. A., *Emergent African States, Topics in Twentieth Century African History*, Longman, 1976.
This book deals mostly with the history of post independent Africa.

ANENE, J. C. and BROWN, G. N., *Africa in the 19th and 20th Centuries*, IUP & Nelson, 1966.
This book deals with the whole of Africa. Several chapters contain good, general coverage of West African developments.

ASIWAJU, A. I. and CROWDER, M. (Eds.), *Tarikh*, Longman, twice yearly.
A journal containing many useful articles.

BOAHEN, A. A., *Topics in West African History*, Longman, 1966.
A short, very well-written book which many students find extremely useful. It does not attempt to cover the entire syllabus, but treats many of the major topics clearly and concisely.

CROWDER, M., *Nigeria: A Modern History for Schools*, OUP, new ed. 1976.

DAVIDSON, B., *Growth of African Civilisation: A History of West Africa 1000–1800*, Longman, rev. ed. 1977.
This gives a full coverage of Section I of the WAEC syllabus. A completely revised edition has recently been published.

FAGE, J. D., *A History of West Africa*, CUP, rev. ed. 1969.
A well established, recently revised introduction suitable for the more advanced student.

FYFE, C., *A Short History of Sierra Leone*, Longman, 1962.

FYNN, J. K., *A Junior History of Ghana*, Longman, 1975.

GAILEY, H. R., *A History of the Gambia*, Routledge, 1964.

HATCH, J., *A History of Post-War Africa*, Deutsch, 1965.
Includes some detailed material on the second half of Section 3 of the syllabus.

OGINI, F. G., *An Outline History of West Africa 1000–1800*, Macmillan, 1973.
A simple, well-organised book dealing adequately with Section 1 of the syllabus.

OLIVER, R. and FAGE, J. D., *A Short History of Africa*, Penguin, rev. ed. 1970.
A good, brief history of the whole of Africa, which helps to put West African history into a wider perspective.

STRIDE, G. T. and IFEKA, C., *Peoples and Empires of West Africa: West Africa in History 1000–1800*, Nelson, 1971.
Provides detailed coverage of Section 1 of the syllabus.

THATCHER, P. F., *Longman Certificate Notes: West African History*, Longman, 1974.
Short revision notes on the main topics in the syllabus with some notes on essay writing.

WEBSTER, J. B. and BOAHEN, A. A., *Growth of African Civilisation: The Revolutionary Years: West Africa since 1800*, Longman, 1967.
This gives a detailed and well-illustrated account of most topics in Sections 2 and 3 of the WAEC syllabus.

More advanced books useful for teachers and for reference purposes.

AJAYI, J. F. A. and CROWDER, M., *A History of West Africa* Vol 1 and Vol 2, Longman, 1974.

ARMSTRONG, R. G., *The Study of West African Languages*, IUP, 1964.

BOAHEN, A. A., *Ghana in the 19th and 20th Centuries*, Longman, 1975.

BOVILL, E. W., *The Golden Trade of the Moors*, OUP rev. ed. 1970.

CHAMBERLAIN, M. E., *The Scramble for Africa*, Longman, 1974.

CROWDER, M., *The Story of Nigeria*, Faber, 1962.

CROWDER, M., *West Africa under Colonial Rule*, Hutcheson, 1968.

FAGE, J. D., *Ghana: An Historical Interpretation*, 1959.

FORDE, C. D. and KABERRY, P. M. (Eds.), *West African Kingdoms in the 19th Century*, OUP, 1967.

GRAY, J. M., *A History of the Gambia*, Cass, 1966.

HARGREAVES, J. D., *West Africa: the Former French States*, Prentice-Hall, 1967.

HODGKIN, T., *Nigerian Perspectives*, Oxford, 1960

HOPKINS, A. G., *An Economic History of West Africa*, Longman, 1973.

IKIME, O. (Ed.), *Leadership in 19th century Africa*, Longman, 1974.

POST, K., *The New States of West Africa*, Penguin, 1962.

TRIMINGHAM, J. S., *A History of Islam in West Africa*, OUP rev. ed. 1970.

WOLFSON, F., *Pageant of Ghana*, OUP, 1959.

All the volumes in the Ibadan History Series; General Ed. AJAYI, J. F. A., Longman.

Index